UNDERSTA...
MILITARY CAPABILITY

From Strategy to Decision

Andrew R. Curtis

BRISTOL
UNIVERSITY
PRESS

First published in Great Britain in 2024 by

Bristol University Press
University of Bristol
1-9 Old Park Hill
Bristol
BS2 8BB
UK
t: +44 (0)117 374 6645
e: bup-info@bristol.ac.uk

Details of international sales and distribution partners are available at bristoluniversitypress.co.uk

© Bristol University Press 2024

British Library Cataloguing in Publication Data
A catalogue record for this book is available from the British Library

ISBN 978-1-5292-2989-9 hardcover
ISBN 978-1-5292-2990-5 paperback
ISBN 978-1-5292-2991-2 ePub
ISBN 978-1-5292-2992-9 ePdf

Cover design: Andrew Corbett
Front cover image: Alamy / Navy Photo

Contents

List of Figures and Tables

Figures

Tables

List of Abbreviations

CADMID	Concept, Assessment, Development, Manufacture, In Service, Disposal
CASD	Continuous at Sea Deterrent
CDM	Chief of Defence Materiel
CDS	Chief of the Defence Staff
CSR	Comprehensive Spending Review
DBS	Defence Business Services
DCAR	Defence Capability Assessment Register
DCDC	Development, Concepts and Doctrine Centre
DCP	Defence Command Paper
DE&S	Defence Equipment and Support
DG Fin	Director General Finance
DIO	Defence Infrastructure Organisation
DLO	Defence Logistics Organisation
DLOD	Defence Lines of Development
DOM	Defence Operating Model
DPA	Defence Procurement Agency
DRP	Defence Reform Programme
DSG	Defence Strategy Group
DSTL	Defence Science and Technology Laboratory
ECC	Equipment Capability Customer
EU	European Union
FCO	Foreign and Commonwealth Office
FF20	Future Force 2020
FY	Financial Year
GDP	Gross Domestic Product
HC PAC	House of Commons Public Accounts Committee
HC PACAC	House of Commons Public Administration and Constitutional Affairs Committee
HCDC	House of Commons Defence Committee
HM	His/Her Majesty's
ICBH	Institute for Contemporary British History
IF30	Integrated Force 2030

IOpC	Integrated Operating Concept 2025
IPT	Integrated Project Team
IR	Integrated Review of Security, Defence, Development and Foreign Policy
JCNSS	Joint Committee on the National Security Strategy
JF25	Joint Force 2025
JFC	Joint Forces Command
JSF	Joint Security Fund
MDP	Modernising Defence Programme
Min	Ministers
MoD	Ministry of Defence
NAA	North Atlantic Alliance
NAO	National Audit Office
NATO	North Atlantic Treaty Organization
NED	Non-Executive Director
NRA	National Risk Assessment
NRR	National Risk Register
NSA	National Security Advisor
NSC	National Security Council
NSCR	National Security Capability Review
NSRA	National Security Risk Assessment
NSS	National Security Strategy
PE	Procurement Executive
PUS	Permanent Under Secretary of State
PwC	PricewaterhouseCoopers
RAF	Royal Air Force
RN	Royal Navy
RUSI	Royal United Services Institute
SDR	Strategic Defence Review
SDSR	Strategic Defence and Security Review
SIPRI	Stockholm International Peace Research Institute
SofS	Secretary of State
SPI	Smart Procurement Initiative
SRO	Senior Responsible Owner
TLB	Top Level Budget
TLCM	Through Life Capability Management
VCDS	Vice Chief of the Defence Staff
UK	United Kingdom
UN	United Nations
US	United States

Preface

The first spark of an idea for this book was generated well over 30 years ago when I was still an extremely young pilot officer. It was the summer of 1986, a year after my graduation from the Royal Air Force College at Cranwell, and I was commanding a small supply flight at RAF Coltishall in Norfolk. Coltishall was home to a wing of Jaguar aircraft and my office overlooked the airfield's single metalled runway, allowing me regularly to watch the Anglo-French ground attack aircraft take to the air on their seemingly never-ending training sorties. The Cold War was still the RAF's main effort, and all three squadrons based at Coltishall were earmarked to deploy forward to mainland Europe in the event of hostilities breaking out with the Soviet Union.

The forward deployment of the Jaguars would leave the station free to be used by North American based United States Air Force or Air National Guard aircraft whose war role was to reinforce Western Europe. This concept of co-located operating bases was regularly practised, and that summer was no exception. Numbers 6 and 54(F) squadrons had been deployed to the Royal Danish Air Force Base at Tirstrup, leaving room at Coltishall for a USAF F-16 Fighting Falcon wing to exercise its reinforcement plans. As my war role was with the third Jaguar squadron – 41 Squadron – which was assigned to a photo-reconnaissance role in northern Norway, I had remained at Coltishall.

I still remember vividly the morning after the Fighting Falcons arrived. It was hot and sunny, not a cloud in the sky. The first wave of Jaguars from 41 Squadron had just taken off – a pair of two ships labouring down the runway, struggling to unstick before reaching the piano keys in the far distance. Nothing new there. Then, a couple of minutes later, a single F-16 taxied out onto the runway. The roar from its single Pratt and Whitney F110 turbofan jet engine grew louder and louder as the pilot opened the throttle wide, the aircraft tyres straining against their brakes. Then, when it seemed the noise couldn't possibly get any louder, the pilot released his brakes. The aircraft leapt forward and hammered down the runway. It got little further than halfway before it was airborne. In an instant, the pilot retracted the undercarriage and sat the aircraft on its tail. With afterburner full on, it spiralled vertically upwards and within a few seconds it was no more than a spec in the sky, visible only because of the bright orange flame still shooting from its jet pipe. At that moment, I found myself wondering why my service was making do with the ponderous Jaguar aircraft, while our American cousins were punching holes in the sky with the super-cool F-16. Without even realizing, I was asking the question, why does the UK have the military capability that it has?

Fast forward 25 years, and I had just returned from a second operational tour in Afghanistan to take over as the assistant head for logistics capability at the Ministry of Defence's head office in Whitehall. Although my career was mainly operationally focused, with tours in the Balkans, Iraq, Haiti and North Africa, in addition to my time in Afghanistan, I had also undertaken two appointments in acquisition and support. From 1995 to 1999, as a squadron leader, I had helped to bring into service a contractor logistics support system for the Royal Navy's new Merlin helicopter. Then, from 2001 to 2003, as a wing commander, I held the post of logistics manager in the Hercules integrated project team, responsible for all aspects of traditional and contractor supplied logistics support for the RAF's combined fleet of over 50 Hercules C-130K and C-130J aircraft. Both appointments had taught me much about the 'what' and the 'how' of military capability management, but very little about the 'why'.

However, as the group captain responsible for the oversight of all joint logistics capability, that was surely about to change. For two years, I worked in Whitehall, where I provided the joint logistics input to no end of capability planning committees and working groups. I supported numerous force development events that considered the broadest range of global scenarios and sought to identify appropriate UK military responses to them. At the same time, with staff officers up and down the country, I helped to implement the post-2010 Strategic Defence and Security Review defence reform measures, recommended by Lord Levene in June 2011. As my time in post ended, I realized my knowledge now included the MoD's contribution to the what and how of capability management, but I was no further forward in uncovering the overall why. Moreover, I was coming to the conclusion that understanding why the UK military has the capability that it has would require much more than the passing interest I had been prepared to invest to date.

Four months on the higher command and staff course at the beginning of 2014 rekindled my enthusiasm for academia, and, when I was posted to an uninspiring job in the Defence Equipment and Support organization the following year, the ideal opportunity presented itself. I could use the spare time I now had to unearth a credible answer to the question that had nagged at me on and off for my entire career. After seeking advice from academics at the Joint Services Command and Staff College at Shrivenham, it became clear my best option was to commit to doctoral-level research on the subject. I prepared a research proposal, which was subsequently accepted by the Defence Studies Department at King's College London, and became a part-time PhD student in September 2015.

From the outset, it was obvious that, as a general research question, studying the totality of why the UK has the military capability that it has was way too broad. Because doctoral research is very deep, it must also be very focused. I needed to refine my research question. After several months of background reading, it became obvious that very little had been written about how decisions around military capability are made. Furthermore, all the secondary literature was concentrated on decision making at the political level. Because of this, I decided to focus my research on decision making one level down, specifically the role played by senior military officers and civil servants in the MoD and the armed forces. Having identified what my research would cover, I now had to work out the best way to get to the data. After over 30 years' service, I knew many of the admirals, generals and air marshals who were the current decision makers in Defence. Moreover, I was confident most would be willing to be interviewed as part of my research. And so it proved. Together with an analysis of the relevant government policy documents, elite interviews became the bedrock of my data collection.

This book draws on my doctoral research to unearth the reasons why the UK has the military capability that it has. It describes the relationship between the politicians who provide the strategic direction and the military officers who translate it into armed forces, trained and equipped for the challenges of today and tomorrow. It also exposes the myriad factors that influence this relationship, from fluctuating geopolitical tensions and the economic health of the nation to the criticality of defence reviews and the often unseen interrelations between the single services. In doing so, I have tried to explain why making the right military capability choices is so challenging.

Writing this book has been an immensely rewarding experience and one I could never have achieved on my own. I am truly grateful to all the people who have helped me with my research. In particular, I must thank my two doctoral supervisors, Professor Matthew Uttley and Professor Andrew Dorman. Without them I would never have completed my thesis, and I'm convinced they still know more about my subject than I do! I am also hugely indebted to the 32 senior officers and civil servants who agreed to be interviewed as part of my research. Although they must remain anonymous, their forthright views and wisdom are the foundations on which this book is written. I must also thank Stephen Wenham and Zoe Forbes at Bristol University Press for their encouragement, advice and expertise. Along with the rest of the editorial team, they helped turn my academically rigid drafts into a much more polished and readable manuscript. Of course, any errors that remain are solely my own.

Finally, special thanks must go to my daughter Joanna; I don't believe she has any idea how useful our discussions about both my research and hers were to me. But the biggest thank you is reserved for my wife Laura, without whose unwavering belief and support this book would never have been written.

Dr Andrew R. Curtis
February 2022
mail@andrewrcurtis.co.uk

1

Introduction

In the ten-year period from 2020 to 2030, the United Kingdom (UK) government will spend over £190 billion on military capability (NAO, 2021, p 5). Most of that money will support programmes in the traditional maritime, land and air environments. There will be significant new investment in warships, for example Type 26 and Type 31 Frigates (MoD, 2020a, p 31), armoured fighting vehicles and mechanized infantry vehicles, such as Ajax and Boxer (MoD, 2020a, p 34), and F-35 Lightning II fast jets (MoD, 2020a, pp 37–8). However, over time and in accordance with the nation's new approach to the utility of armed force – the Integrated Operating Concept (IOpC) 2025 – more money will find its way to support operations in the new domains of space and cyberspace (MoD, 2020c, p 1). But who decides what military capability should be procured and, more importantly, why? How much responsibility lies with elected politicians, who generally know little about the practical application of military force, but are accountable to the taxpayers whose money makes up the defence budget? Conversely, how much responsibility defaults to senior military officers and civil servants, who claim to hold the professional knowledge fundamental to the necessary decision making, but cannot be voted out of office?

This book is an investigation of why UK Defence has the military capability that it has. To define Defence, I have borrowed the following definition from the 2015 version of the Ministry of Defence's (MoD) operating model:

> Defence covers all those matters that are the responsibility of the Secretary of State for Defence. In practice, this means the business of the Secretary of State and his fellow ministers, of the MoD as the department of state that supports them, and of the armed forces as constituted by an Act of Parliament. (MoD, 2015b, p 6)

Figure 1.1: Defence decision makers

- Chief of the Defence Staff
- Vice Chief of the Defence Staff
- First Sea Lord
- Chief of the General Staff
- Chief of the Air Staff
- Commander Strategic Command
- Deputy Chief of the Defence Staff (Military Strategy and Operations)
- Deputy Chief of the Defence Staff (Financial and Military Capability)

- Chief of Defence People
- Permanent Secretary
- Second Permanent Secretary
- Chief Operating Officer
- Chief Information Officer
- Chief Scientific Advisor
- Director General Finance
- Director General Security Policy
- Director General Strategy and International

Specifically, it is an investigation of the interrelation between strategic direction, provided by politicians, and the subsequent military capability decisions made within Defence (hereafter referred to as the translation of strategic direction into military capability). At the highest level, the decision making within Defence is undertaken by an exclusive group of military officers and civil servants appointed to the most senior positions in the MoD and the armed forces. Within the book, I refer to them as defence decision makers; the actual appointments concerned are listed in Figure 1.1.[1]

This book concentrates on decisions made at the highest level of Defence to uncover the methodology behind the translation of strategic direction into military capability within the UK. Its analysis draws on historical trends reaching back to the formation of the MoD in 1946 (HM Government, 1946, p 6), together with insights gathered from interviews with today's senior defence officials. The starting point for the research period was chosen because to reach back any further would incorporate a period when UK government policy was consumed by a war of national survival, which skewed most, if not all, decision making. The evidence uncovered during the research has generated a comprehensive catalogue of insights or reasons why the UK has the military capability that it has. It is the substantiation of these insights that provides the understanding this book seeks.

Background and context

Evidence from a range of countries suggests that the successful translation of strategic direction into military capability in the form of equipment, trained personnel and in-service support, which actually meet the requirements of that direction, is not easily achieved (see, for example, Baylis, 1986a, pp 27–32; Sapolsky et al, 2017, pp 140–57; and Louth and Taylor, 2019, pp 40–63). Perhaps the most regularly cited reason for the strategy-to-capability gap is an inability by successive governments to procure equipment to agreed performance time and cost parameters. In the UK, for example, the estimated cost of developing the TSR-2,[2] between 1960 and 1964, rose by 180 per cent (Peden, 2007, p 290). More recently, Bernard Gray (2009, p 7) identified that 'across a large range of [defence acquisition] programmes, the average programme overruns by 80% or c.5 years from the time specified at initial approval through to in service dates. The average increase in cost of these programmes is 40% or c.£300m.' As the National Audit Office (NAO) regularly confirms, this issue remains prevalent today (see, for example, NAO, 2017; NAO, 2018a; and NAO, 2018b). Another reason regularly quoted is untimely changes to government policy, for example, the cancellation of the Nimrod MRA4 programme in the 2010 Strategic Defence and Security Review (SDSR), followed at the very next review by the reintroduction of a maritime patrol capability through the purchase of P-8A Poseidon aircraft. Other commentators identify the costs of modifying existing equipment to meet new operational scenarios as a factor (see Hartley, 2016; and Bangert et al, 2017). Finally, contemporaneous events are often put forward, for example, the Falklands Conflict in 1982 forced the government to reverse several decisions made in the defence review of the preceding year (Dorman, 2001d, p 119). These mismatches between strategic direction and military capability are hardly surprising. For politicians, accurately identifying, and then succinctly articulating, potential future threats and risks to the nation, from which strategic direction is derived, is inherently challenging. For defence decision makers, gaining a thorough understanding of that direction, and then selecting and acquiring new military capability able successfully to counter predicted threats and mitigate those risks, is no simpler.

The view that it is a government's inherent responsibility to protect the citizens of the state – first articulated as long ago as 1651 by Thomas Hobbes – has been, and remains, an entrenched norm in UK politics and society. By way of example, all three UK National Security Strategies (NSS) published as standalone documents between 2008 and 2010 opened with sentences along the lines of: 'Providing security for the nation and its citizens remains the most important responsibility of government' (see HM Government, 2008a, p 3; HM Government, 2009, p 5; and HM Government, 2010c, p 3). To discharge this responsibility, nation states recognize the fundamental requirement to maintain and equip armed forces. In the case of the UK, even in the face of the largest estimated contraction of the economy for more than 300 years, because of the COVID-19 pandemic (Hansard, 2020c), the government committed to spending 2.2 per cent as a proportion of gross domestic product (GDP) in 2024–25 on Defence in 2020 (HM Treasury, 2020b). This equated to a total Departmental Expenditure Limit[3] of £46 billion in the financial year (FY) 2020–21, which will elevate the UK to the top of the European military spending charts, and make it the fifth highest defence spender in the world behind the United States, China, India and Russia (SIPRI, 2021).

In a symposium held at the UK Defence Academy in March 2016, an army three-star general suggested that the role of the nation's armed forces was 'to do harm to the Queen's enemies and blow up their stuff!' Although this definition may have been offered somewhat tongue-in-cheek, it is a good start point for understanding the long-standing political consensus in the UK concerning the maintenance of appropriately equipped armed forces to meet defence and security policy goals. Put in another – and slightly more politically correct – way, the 2015 NSS included the vision: 'a secure and prosperous United Kingdom, with global reach and influence.' Heading the list of activities required to achieve this was to 'strengthen our Armed Forces so that they remain world-leading … [to] project power globally … to deter and defeat our adversaries' (HM Government, 2015, p 9).

A review of the main political parties' manifestos prior to the 2019 general election revealed they all recognized a requirement for the nation's armed forces, although, unsurprisingly, their positions on its size, scope and employment did not accord (see The Conservative and Unionist Party, 2019, p 53; The Labour Party, 2019, pp 100–2; and The Liberal Democrat Party, 2019, p 91). Public endorsement of the armed forces remains equally as important as political support. In a survey undertaken in 2017 by PricewaterhouseCoopers (PwC, 2017, p 11) 70 per cent of those polled trusted the UK armed forces and 73 per cent described their feelings towards the UK armed forces as positive or strongly positive. Furthermore, 89 per cent believed the purpose of the UK armed forces was to protect and defend UK territory and its citizens. To that end, it is a reasonable assumption that all major political parties, and most of the electorate, acknowledge the requirement for the UK to maintain armed forces and equip them with military capability, at least at some level.

The problem space

The way in which strategic direction is translated into military capability can be broken down into a simple, four-step model. First, the government of the day decides on the defence policy it wishes to pursue. Then it allocates resource to achieve it. In the third step, defence decision makers determine the military capability required to meet the policy aims. Finally, resource is spent to acquire and/or maintain that capability. If this simple model is followed, the outcome should be a military force structure able to implement the government of the day's defence policy: in short, armed forces that are fit for purpose. However, the activities within this model are not a simple series of steps undertaken sequentially to achieve an end state. This is because, within reason, the government can elect to amend its defence policy or change the allocated resources at any point during its time in office (Cornish and Dorman, 2010, p 410). In addition, when reacting to strategic direction, defence decision makers generally have the discretion to introduce new, or retire obsolete, capability. Furthermore, the model does not have an easily identifiable end state; it remains ongoing as politicians regularly revisit strategic direction, for example during a defence review. To that end, the model can be more accurately described as an open-ended collection of interacting activities carried out by the government and defence decision makers that translates strategic direction into military capability. In stylized terms, this can be represented in the basic model shown in Figure 1.2.

These interacting activities are also affected by legacy decisions. For example, the UK has fielded military capability for as long as it has existed. In 1661, William Penn and Samuel Pepys established the Naval Discipline Act, which included the articles of war and founded the Royal Navy (RN) by statute (National Museum of the Royal Navy, 2014). This occurred 46 years before the 1707 Act of Union that brought about the political union of England and Scotland, forming Great Britain. The point here is that the interpretation of strategic direction and subsequent resource allocation decisions always take place against a baseline of military capability already in use at that point in time, as a result of previous decisions. Furthermore, there is always military capability making its way through the acquisition cycle[4] to reach the in-service, or in-use, phase, again, as a result of previous decisions. All this capability must be considered whenever strategic direction is interpreted and resources are allocated. This is a considerable constraint on decision making, as in-service military capability may not be the most appropriate to support the aims and objectives of new policy, but there is insufficient resource available to fund its replacement. Furthermore, the time between the decision to procure a capability and its entry into service is usually measured in years, and sometime decades.[5] This too is constraining, as a long procurement lead time may span a change of policy that makes the capability being procured unrequired at the point it enters service. Cancellation before that generally results in the loss of often considerable sunk costs.

The constantly changing capability baseline is an ever-present factor to be considered by defence decision makers; however, there are myriad other factors that also affect the model. It is, for example, regularly disrupted by external events, which require either the government, defence decision makers, or both, to revisit and potentially revise earlier actions. In the context of the model, an event could be defined as an occurrence that has sufficient impact on the actions of the government or defence decision makers to effect a change in any, or all, defence policy, resource allocation or military capability. By this definition, events are extremely wide-ranging. Examples

Figure 1.2: Translation of strategic direction into military capability model

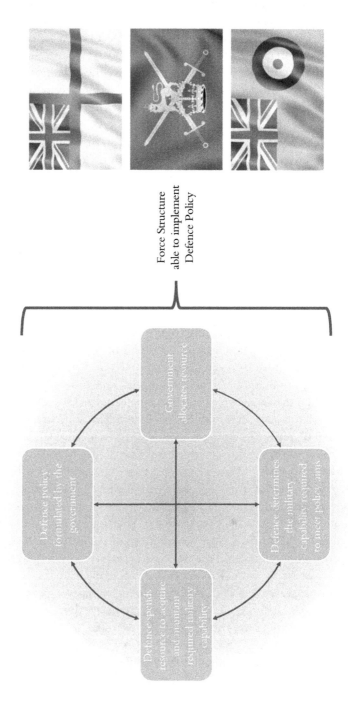

Force Structure able to implement Defence Policy

Government allocates resource

Defence policy formulated by the government

Defence determines the military capability required to meet policy aims

Defence spend resource to acquire and maintain required military capability

could be a strategic shock, such as the aftermath of the Suez Crisis in 1956; a significant deviation in the UK's economic fortunes, such as the 2008 global financial crisis; or an increase in the perceived national threat, such as the impact of Russia's annexation of the Crimea in 2014. Although they have an impact, events are not likely to result in the complete abandonment of actions previously taken by the government or defence decision makers. This is because (at least since the end of the Second World War) no event, or combination of events, has prompted a complete revision of defence policy. As an example, the end of the Cold War led to a significant decrease in the resource allocated to Defence, which, in turn, caused a major reduction in conventional forces across all three services (MoD, 1991, Annexes A–D). Nevertheless, the strategic deterrent was unaffected, and the core associated military capability, that is the Polaris submarine fleet, continued to be fielded as before, even though other supporting elements of the Cold War nuclear arsenal were withdrawn from service.

In addition to the impact of events, the actions of the government and defence decision makers are also affected by less tangible factors. Usually prevalent at the model's decision-making points, they can be grouped together under the title of 'influence'. Some influences occur only once and affect only one action; others are ever present and disrupt every decision. Within the model, an influence could be defined as a structural factor that impacts one or more of the decision-points within the model. As with events, influences are extremely wide ranging, and their interpretation provides scope for agency[6] by stakeholders within the activity. Examples of agency manifesting itself could be through any of the following: personalities, that is the egos and ambitions of politicians, senior military officers and MoD civil servants; process, the way in which policy is formulated or defence reviews are undertaken; and lobbying, generally by external pressure groups (allies, the defence industry and the media) seeking to influence a particular policy or capability decision to their advantage.

There are any number events and influences that impact on, and add complexity to, the translation of strategic direction into military capability model. Moreover, these events and influences are often both disruptive and uncontrollable. It is against this backdrop that decisions regarding military capability are made. As a result, a comprehensive appreciation of the events and influences that impact on the translation of strategic direction into military capability model offers the best chance of understanding why the UK has the military capability that it has.

Research methodology

The evidence that underpins this book was the product of research undertaken as part of my doctoral thesis. The research methods used were a combination of qualitative content analysis of relevant government policy documents and semi-structured elite interviews. Defence review command papers are a primary source for understanding how strategic direction is communicated, and doctrine publications and associated policy documents are the traditional repositories for information that shapes the development and maintenance of military capability. Interpreting and understanding this primary literature is best achieved through qualitative content analysis, an approach to the analysis of documents and texts that seeks to analyse content in terms of predetermined categories and in a systemic and replicable manner (Bryman, 2012, pp 304–6). To that end, a qualitative content analysis was undertaken on all the post-Second World War defence review command papers,[7] as well as appropriate joint doctrine publications (see, for example, MoD, 2014a; and MoD, 2014b) and other noteworthy primary literature (see, for example, MoD, 2020b; and Chilcot et al, 2016). This was supplemented with additional analysis of relevant secondary literature from the defence academic commentariat, which was principally used to confirm the significant factors that impact the translation of strategic direction into military capability, identified in the first instance through the qualitative content analysis.

Potential research participants were identified as those military officers and civil servants who were able to provide an in-depth and first-hand opinion of the translation of strategic direction into military capability. This focus on senior practitioners indicated that the principal data collection mechanism should be elite interviews, as elite interviewees can be classified as 'highly skilled, professionally competent, and class specific' (McDowell, 1998, p 2135). Semi-structured interviews using mainly open-ended questions are generally considered the best method for interviewing elites (Aberbach and Rockman, 2002, p 674). Data from 32 elite interviews were transcribed, and anonymized in accordance with the MoD's ethical guidelines (GOV. UK, 2019a).

The research methodology selected was constructivist grounded theory. In grounded theory, the researcher uses thematic analysis to derive a general, abstract theory of a process, action or interaction grounded in the views of the participants. It involves multiple stages of data collection and the refinement and interrelationship of categories of information (Glaser and Strauss, 1967, pp 1–18). However, the original creators of grounded theory, Anselm L. Strauss and Barney G. Glaser, developed it along different paths over time (see Glaser, 1978; Strauss, 1987; Strauss and Corbin, 1990; and Glaser, 1992). The result of this divergence of views is that there are now myriad approaches to grounded theory, all with subtle differences in the way they are applied. One of these approaches is constructivist grounded theory, the principal architect of which is Kathy Charmaz. Starting with the assumption that social reality is multiple, processual and constructed, Charmaz (2014, p 27) argues that the researcher's position, privileges, perspective and interactions must be considered as an inherent part of the research reality. Aligned to this, a constructivist approach to grounded theory requires 'the creation of a sense of reciprocity between participants and the researcher in the co-construction of meaning and, ultimately, a theory that is grounded in the participants' and researcher's experiences' (Mills et al, 2006, p 9). Given my own professional knowledge and experience of the subject area, attained through a 35-year military career, an approach that embraced these as positive contributors to the theory development was a logical fit.

As my analysis unfolded, it became clear that the secondary literature concerning strategic direction provided by politicians to defence decision makers tended to focus on the immediate outcomes of a particular defence review (see, for example, Greenwood, 1975; McInnes, 1998; and Taylor, 2010b). There have, of course, been books and journal articles published that consider defence policy in the round (see, for example, Bartlett, 1972; Darby, 1973; and Carver, 1992). However, the defence landscape has changed considerably since the end of the Cold War, and the older works are of their time. Accordingly, they are only of limited use when comparing all strategic direction, from the beginning of the Cold War to the present day. Contemporary analysis does exist that considers linkages between all the defence reviews undertaken since the end of the Second World War (see Blackburn, 2015; Cornish and Dorman, 2015; and Thomson and Blagden, 2018), though it is not as plentiful as was the case a generation ago. This point is recognized by Paul Cornish and Andrew Dorman (2009a, p 253) who attribute the paucity of up-to-date scrutiny around defence policy to a 'post-Cold War shift in British academia away from traditional strategic studies towards the rather broader, and arguably more diffuse, subject of security studies'.

From the first defence review of the research period, up to and including the most recent – the 2021 Integrated Review of Security, Defence, Development and Foreign Policy (2021 IR) – there is no shortage of rigorous analysis on specific defence reviews. However, most of the associated analysis is focused on policy formulation at the government level. Very little of the secondary literature has considered the impact of associated actions one level down; specifically, the role played by defence decision makers in the interpretation of policy and allocation of resource. A rare exception to this was Timothy Garden's (1999) exploration of the consequences of the 1998 Strategic Defence Review (SDR) for the power and influence of the service chiefs. Therefore, in concentrating below the political level, on decision making that underpins the development of UK military capability, this work fills a significant gap in the academic literature.

Literature review

The cumulative body of academic literature about UK defence reviews prior to the introduction of the quinquennial review process in 2010 is limited in scale and scope. In a recent quantitative bibliometric study, Andrew Dorman and Matthew Uttley (2015) highlighted the paucity of relevant journal articles published during this time. For example, over their 1950 to 2014 survey period, *International Affairs* was the largest publisher of peer reviewed articles on UK defence policy (accounting for 16 per cent of all articles published), yet it included only two articles on the subject during the time of Duncan Sandys' review (1957), just one article over the period of Denis Healey's reviews (1966 to 1968), and no articles at all during the time of Roy Mason's review (1975). In all, only 20 (or 36 per cent) of the relevant articles were published between 1950 and 2000, with the remaining 36 (or 64 per cent) all published in the 14 years to 2014. This shortage of contemporaneous journal articles before 2000 necessitates a reliance on more recently published historical treatments when studying defence reviews from the twentieth century.[8] By comparison, similar searches that I undertook to generate material for my thesis's literature review uncovered over 50 journal articles produced in the last decade concerning the 2010 and 2015 SDSRs.

In addition to journal articles, there are also a modest number of defence review monographs, published over this period, that include aspects of the decision making behind the procurement and maintenance of UK military capability. The first such works appeared in the early 1970s, their publication peaked around the end of the Cold War, and output has tapered to no more than a trickle since the turn of the twenty-first century. The monographs that have emerged can be broadly divided into two categories: those that concentrate specifically on defence policy formulation and implementation, and a smaller group that covers related aspects of UK defence policy, including the employment of Britain's armed forces on operations, but use the history and context of defence reviews as a handrail to do so. All relevant titles are included in the bibliography at the end of this book.

Book structure

An examination of the events and influences that impact on the translation of strategic direction into military capability model reveals that they can be loosely grouped into several general categories. These include the geopolitical landscape and the UK government's associated grand strategy; the way in which defence reviews are undertaken; what the government and the nation expect from Defence; the affordability of Defence; and the roles played by the MoD and the armed forces. These categories form the backbone of the book, with a chapter committed to each. It is the analysis within these chapters that exposes the insights or reasons why the UK has the military capability that it has. Unsurprisingly, some of the insights do not fit neatly into a single category; instead, they straddle at least two, and, in some cases, more. However, to simplify the book's structure, each insight has been consigned to a single chapter, with a consideration of the overlapping aspects of the insights included as part of a final, concluding chapter. Prior to the analysis of the events and influences, I have included a context chapter that explains what is meant by strategic direction and military capability. As already mentioned, the book's research period spans 75 years, from the formation of the MoD in 1946 to the publication of the 2021 IR. To provide a manageable architecture, the research period has been divided into three distinct epochs. The first is the Cold War, which lasted from 1946 until 1990. The second is the Early Expeditionary period, from 1991 to 2009. The third is the Quinquennial Review period, which began in 2010 and lasts to the present.

2

Strategic Direction and Military Capability

At the highest level, strategic direction is provided by senior figures within the UK government. Speeches and interviews given, as well as newspaper and journal articles written by prime ministers, chancellors of the exchequer, foreign and defence secretaries, provide insight and guidance on how the incumbent government is approaching its defence obligations. More recently, with the convergence of defence and security through the articulation of a strategy for national security, this list has grown to include other ministers, for example the home secretary and the Cabinet secretary. In addition, there are a number of non-elected officials who also write and speak on defence and security matters in an official capacity, the most notable being the National Security Advisor (NSA), the Chief of the Defence Staff (CDS) and the service chiefs, as well as the permanent secretaries to the ministries served by the politicians listed above.[1] What flows from this verbal and written direction is defence and security policy, which, in simple terms, is what the government chooses to do, or not do, about a particular defence- and/or security-related issue or problem. The government has a generic approach to the formulation of policy; however, there are peculiarities specific to departments, including those responsible for defence and security. An obvious example of this is the defence review process.

Military capability is a term that has only recently been added to the UK defence lexicon. In 1997, the newly elected Labour government introduced the Smart Procurement Initiative (SPI) intended to deliver equipment 'faster, cheaper and better' (Taylor, 2003, p 7). This initiative was a significant theme in the 1998 SDR and was subsequently re-launched as 'smart acquisition' in October 2000. The currency of smart acquisition was military capability, defined as 'an operational outcome or effect that users of equipment need to achieve' (MoD, 2002, p 51). Since then, the process for the acquisition of military capability has developed significantly and is now cohered through a formal list of Defence Lines of Development (DLOD),[2] which were endorsed by the defence management board in 2005 (MoD, 2005b, p 1). The 2015 version of the MoD's operating model defined military capability as 'the combination of equipment, trained personnel and support that gives the armed forces the capacity to achieve the tasks they are given' (MoD, 2015b, p 8).[3] This definition of military capability was not updated in the 2020 version, and is, therefore, the one that I have chosen to use in this book.

Prior to the formation of the MoD Procurement Executive (PE) in 1971, the separate branches of the armed forces were responsible for bringing their own weapon systems into service. Furthermore, before the SPI was adopted, their focus was firmly on the supply of equipment, rather than a consideration of military capability in the round (see Bell, 2000; and Kirkpatrick, 2003). While the years since the adoption of smart acquisition have not been without further reform, the central tenet of Defence's approach to acquisition remains management at the capability level, underpinned by the DLOD structure. The most significant developments with regard to the management of military capability have been: the restructuring of the organizations within the MoD responsible for the procurement of new equipment and its through-life support; the seemingly constant drumbeat of transformation initiatives aimed at improving processes and procedures; and the department-wide financial realignment that occurred as part of the Defence Reform Programme (DRP) introduced after the 2010 SDSR (MoD, 2011a, pp 36–44).

This chapter provides the context for the analysis chapters that follow. It opens with an examination of what strategic direction has been given by politicians to defence decision makers since the end of the Second World War. It then moves on to discuss defence policy, outlining what is contains, how it is decided upon and how is it promulgated. This, in turn, leads to a consideration of defence reviews, which seeks to identity exactly what a defence review entails and why they have occurred when they have during the research period. The second half of the chapter focuses on military capability. It begins with an explanation of the genesis of military capability as part of the SPI, and moves on to identify how Defence's approach to military capability has changed as a result of the 2011–2015 DRP.

Strategic direction

During the Cold War, the cornerstone of UK grand strategy was prevention of war with the Soviet Union through deterrence. This was first publicly acknowledged by prime minister Winston Churchill in the House of Commons in 1955 (Hansard, 1955). However, it was another Churchill speech almost ten years earlier, on 5 March 1946 in Fulton, Missouri, that introduced still-in-use phrases such as the special relationship and the Iron Curtain, and is generally recognized to be the date of the beginning of the

Cold War (International Churchill Society, 2017). Often referred to as 'The Sinews of Peace' speech, it provided the strategic direction that would shape UK defence policy until the collapse of the Soviet Union in 1991.

Even though the UK was adapting its force structure to provide the 'flexibility and mobility to respond to new circumstances' (MoD, 1991, p 6), no explicit new strategic direction was forthcoming at the national level during the period of the Conservative government from the end of the Cold War until 1997. It was not until two years after the Labour Party won the 1997 general election that prime minister Tony Blair unveiled his doctrine of the international community in a speech to the Chicago Economic Club (The National Archives, 2003a). The doctrine outlined the circumstances that, in Blair's opinion, warranted the international community to intervene in the affairs of other nations, and built upon the 'force for good' approach that underpinned the UK military's pivot to an expeditionary posture in the 1998 SDR (Robertson, 1997). This new strategic direction resulted in the increased use of UK military capability in intervention operations during the Blair administration, most notably in Kosovo (1999), Sierra Leone (2000), Afghanistan (from 2001) and Iraq (from 2003).

After 2010, the Conservative/Liberal Democrat coalition government's strategic direction continued to be based on an expeditionary approach, although it shifted from an 'over-relian[ce] on military intervention to a higher priority for conflict prevention' (Hansard, 2010). This subtle but significant change of direction was announced by prime minister David Cameron during a parliamentary debate on the 2010 SDSR. In the decade that followed, senior members of government reinforced this position, through carefully selected speaking opportunities, although these may have been less about providing strategic direction, and more about reassuring an international audience of how the UK saw its place in the world once it had left the European Union (EU) (see, for example, Johnson, 2016; and GOV.UK, 2018a).

Since 2018, the Conservative government's strategic direction has coalesced around its vision for Global Britain, which it argues is about 'reinvesting in our relationships, championing the rules-based international order and demonstrating that the UK is open, outward-looking and confident on the world stage' (GOV.UK, 2018b). This policy has been regularly confirmed by senior members of the present government (Hansard, 2020a), and was the cornerstone of its 2021 IR. Specifically, the government's approach to national security and international policy was described as:

> [S]ustaining the UK's openness as a society and economy underpinned by a shift towards a more robust position on security and deterrence. This runs alongside a renewed commitment to the UK as a force for good in the world – defending openness, democracy and human

rights – and an increased determination to seek multilateral solutions to challenges like climate change and global health crises. (HM Government, 2021b, p 14)

Senior non-elected officials also influence strategic direction through speeches and in writing, although an examination of their contribution suggests it is usually either in support of an already-stated government position or is intended to highlight a specific issue or concern that is quite tactical in nature. For example, in a 2017 lecture, the then CDS, Air Chief Marshal Stuart Peach, warned of the vulnerability of communication lines under the sea and the resultant need to match and understand Russian fleet modernization (Royal United Services Institute [RUSI], 2017). A year later, during his first public speaking engagement since taking over as the permanent secretary at the MoD, Stephen Lovegrove reinforced the government's position on the Modernising Defence Programme (MDP) (RUSI, 2018).

Set-piece oral and written input, from both senior government and non-elected officials, have played their part in the articulation of strategic direction from the end of the Second World War to the present day. Their role has varied widely, from the introduction of an enduring defence policy or a minor change in policy direction, to the reinforcement of an existing course of action or explanation of a specific, and normally tactical, situation. Moreover, the choice of messenger or the place and time of transmission are also relevant. Unsurprisingly, senior politicians like to reserve major policy announcements for themselves and leave the more tactical announcements to their non-elected officials. Furthermore, when Blair chose the Economic Club in Chicago in 1999, he was clearly seeking to maximize the global exposure that the occasion offered. Similarly, Theresa May outlined her prime ministerial vision for security co-operation with Europe in a post-Brexit world at a security conference in Munich in 2018. Big ideas demand a big stage. That said, having decided to undertake a National Security Capability Review (NSCR) after the 2017 general election (GOV.UK, 2017b), the government's study was beset by negative media attention concerning anticipated reductions in military capability (see, for example, Urban, 2017; and Press Association, 2017). Possibly because of this, notification of the publication of the NSCR's final report was limited to no more than a written statement by the prime minister, released a day before the start of the 2018 Easter holiday (UK Parliament, 2018). The political landscape and the anticipated reaction to any given defence- or security-related policy, at the time of its conception, undoubtedly have a bearing on how that policy is announced. It should not be a surprise that political spin impacts the articulation of strategic direction.

During my research, a regular question that I asked senior officials was *how good are politicians at giving strategic direction?* From those who answered directly, the response was generally lukewarm. Comments ranged from 'we received very little' and 'they are not' to 'quite good and getting better'. The middle ground was occupied with statements like 'pretty poor, although I don't think it's for the want of trying', 'not as bad as one might imagine', and 'as far as it goes, not bad'. In exploring why so few positive responses were received, one two-star officer suggested that 'pressures relating to the media, international events, allies, [and] party politics can all make it difficult to give clear policy direction'. A few senior officials considered the question from the politicians' perspective. One three-star general said that 'the responsibility is incumbent on us [the military] to more clearly articulate the trade-offs and the choices that a range of potential options represent, and also be clearer as to the risks and the resources that are necessary to either implement or otherwise any of their [the politicians'] decisions'. This view was supported by another three-star general who considered 'what we're very bad at from within Defence is understanding how politicians perceive Defence'. He went on to observe that 'to understand why we behave as we do, you've almost got to walk in their shoes, and I think that's quite hard for us'. Aside from these comments, there was little recognition from the senior officials interviewed that both the givers and receivers of strategic direction have a role to play in improving the process.

One four-star officer suggested that 'one of the reasons strategic direction has been absent is ... [a] lack of education and training, the particular experience of recent events, and a simple judgement [by the government] that it wasn't helpful to them'. This observation also highlights concern about just how qualified and well-prepared today's politicians are to give strategic direction. Although the number of military veterans in UK politics is on the increase (Parker and Pickard, 2015), none achieved one-star rank before entering Westminster;[4] indeed, most left their respective service at a rank no higher than junior field officer or equivalent.[5] As one two-star army officer noted 'you've got people in parliament who have commanded companies in Afghanistan, but I don't think they would claim to be experts on the higher management of defence'. One senior airman also pointed out that government ministers are regularly trained in the tactical decision-making process potentially to shoot down a highjacked civilian airliner, in a 9/11-type scenario (Morris, 2017); however, there is no equivalent war-gaming, requested or offered, for decision making at the strategic level. He asked:

> 'Why would you not want to walk yourself through the sorts of process, the sorts of thinking, the sorts of risk assessments of what it would mean to put ... two squadrons of Tornados at Minhad? Well, I know what would have happened. We'd have been schwacked within five minutes if Iran was playing nasty. Now, if you put that to a minister who insists on "Something must be done, and my Abu Dhabi friends

need my help", OK, well these are the threats then, these are the risks. You now know (a) what the risks are and (b) what you need to do to fix them. We've never done that. We've never taken them to that level of understanding, of what it means in terms of politics, in terms of military risks and ultimately casualties, as to what those decisions ultimately translate into. We do it at the tactical level.'

A government's strategic direction should be aligned to its defence policy. It is, therefore, helpful to confirm an understanding of what is meant by defence policy. In doing so, my research joins with George Dillon in borrowing Hugh Heclo's and Aaron Wildavsky's definition of policy as 'a series of ongoing understandings built up by political administrators over time, understandings left to run where practicable, repaired where necessary, and overturned where they are desperate' (Helco and Wildavsky, 1974, p 346). Dillon (1988, p 11) went on to assert that 'in defence [these understandings] happen to be concerned primarily with the provision and use of armed forces to protect the state from external attack and internal subversion, as well as to advance what those in power consider to be the country's international interests'.

In a recent study of British defence in the twenty-first century, John Louth and Trevor Taylor recognized there were several identifiable objectives and purposes for defence policy. They wrote that: 'In principle, a country's defence policy may be neither in the public domain or ever written down. It can take the form of a series of implicit assumptions and beliefs that form a significant element of the culture of a government's defence sector' (Louth and Taylor, 2019, p 29). Of course, if this were applied literally by the UK government, it would have not been possible to research and write this book. Louth and Taylor go on to confirm that a publicly available written policy can serve four valuable purposes, namely to: shape the development of the armed forces; promote the civilian and political direction of defence; inform national stakeholders and publics; and so, send messages to international audiences. The first two of these purposes can be considered strategic direction that has an influence of the development of military capability.

This definition and amplification of defence policy aligns with my observations from Chapter 1 regarding military capability. In the same way that the UK has always had military capability, it has always had defence policy. Correspondingly, policy made in the past influences policy being made in the present, which will, in turn, influence policy made in the future. This point is reinforced by the adage 'the policy-maker's difficulty is not to decide where to go, but where to go from here' (Dillon, 1977, pp 209–10). To this end, politicians are like actors in a long-running West End stage production. As today's stars of the show, they are simply the custodians of the series of ongoing understandings at a given point in time. During their time in the spotlight, it is incumbent upon them to maintain those understandings – repairing and overturning where necessary – and then hand them over to their successors, when their time comes to leave the stage.

Heclo's and Wildavsky's definition of policy could conjure an image of steady-state serenity, suggesting the role of a policy administrator is not an arduous one; however, regarding the maintenance of defence policy, this could not be further from the truth. Although commentators on defence policy may disagree on many things, they are almost unanimous in confirming the complexity of the task (see, for example, Owen, 1972; Carver, 1992; and Gray, 2014). Jeremy Black aptly described the challenges facing defence planners:

> Defence policy unites several key problems facing Britain. It stands at the juncture of foreign and fiscal policy, external goals and domestic security. Defence policy has to respond to rapidly changing circumstances; at the same time, an able execution of its unpredictable tasks requires adequate preparation in the shape of appropriate doctrine, training and weaponry. (Black, 2006, p 67)

In considering the formulation of defence policy, many academics defer to the work of two leading social scientists, David Braybrooke and Charles Lindblom. Braybrooke and Lindblom (1964) discuss two methods of policy decision making: the cost-benefit analysis approach and serial disjointed incrementalism. As the name suggests, in the first approach all the costs and benefits associated with a specific course of action are assembled so policy makers can compare benefits to costs, to decide if a policy is worthwhile, or, given a choice, which policy is the more or most worthwhile. The second approach involves making policy through a series of small decisions, which, as they are taken in steps, can be reversed, or at least amended, if they subsequently prove to have been a mistake. Clearly, the idea of keeping options open is central to this approach. John Baylis (1989, p 203) believed the latter approach, more popularly known simply as incrementalism or 'muddling through', has been the dominant method of formulating defence policy since the end of the Second World War. This point of view was endorsed by Michael Dillon (1977, p 209) who wrote 'it is accepted that the defence policy process, like any other, is incremental', and, more recently, by Paul Cornish and Andrew Dorman (2012, p 220), who introduced the concept of 'smart muddling through' in their investigation into the longer-term implications of the 2010 SDSR. Considering the merits of a cost-benefit analysis versus an incrementalistic approach to the formulation of defence policy is beyond the scope of this book. To progress with the analysis of historical UK defence policy, and the identification of trends that may be relevant to current and future behaviours, it is sufficient simply to recognize the primacy of incrementalism in the post-Second World War formulation of defence policy (Uttley et al, 2019).

The methods by which defence policy has been promulgated have, unsurprisingly, evolved since the end of the Second World War. This is as much to do with improvements in methods of communication available to the government (for example, increased use of the internet), as it is with changes to the organizational structure of the MoD and the armed forces. In the immediate post-Second World War period, the minister of defence presented an annual statement on defence to parliament. By way of example, the 1949 Statement of Defence ran to 16 pages, and included a strategic context introduction, as well as sections on developments in the last year, finance, manpower and equipment (MoD, 1949). By the mid-1960s, this report had become known as the statement on the defence estimates, and had grown into a wide-ranging document that set out a comprehensive overview of policy, as well as detailing the annual activities of the armed forces, and listing plans for the provision of manpower, equipment and budgets (Walker and Mills, 2015, p 4). Following the establishment of the unified MoD in 1964 (MoD, 1963), the report increased in size, but kept to a standardized form. However, as Dillon (1988, p 15) notes, from 1979 onwards, when Defence became a major political issue, the annual statements became 'big and glossy affairs accompanied by detailed statistical appendices'. By the late 1980s, the document had grown to between 40,000 and 50,000 words long, plus illustrations and graphics. The last formal statement on the defence estimates was published in the final full year of John Major's Conservative government in 1996, and ran to 154 pages (MoD, 1996). The Labour government produced a single defence white paper in 1999, which was a statement on the defence estimates in all but name (MoD, 1999). Thereafter, the practice ceased, because the new government considered that defence policy was relatively stable and an annual restatement was no longer required (HCDC, 2001).

In 2008, the MoD published its first defence plan, an unclassified command paper that 'set out the defence objectives for the current, and next three, financial years' (MoD, 2008a, p 2). Although it included sections on strategic context and expenditure, it was considerably more management orientated than its predecessors, with over half of the document – some 36 pages – devoted to a defence balanced scorecard. Today, the MoD maintains an outcome delivery plan. It is no longer a stand-alone document; instead, it is hosted on the government's website (GOV.UK, 2021d). Its aims are to detail how the department will deliver its priority outcomes, how it will measure success, and how it will ensure continuous improvement. In addition to the web-based plan, the MoD also presents an annual report to parliament, which includes sections on performance, accountability and annual accounts (MoD, 2020d). Both productions are readily obtainable and form the basis of the UK's publicly available written defence policy. However, the MoD also maintains an internal annual defence plan, classified Secret UK Eyes Only. It is designed to allow organizations across the department to formulate and finalize all subordinate planning documents. This is the part of defence policy not in the public domain; therefore, its implications have not been included in my analysis.

The MoD's outcome delivery plan and annual report reflect a balanced view of all three services' contributions to defence output; as a result, they are relatively uncontentious. However, the same cannot be said for its predecessors. According to Dillon (1988, p 17), statements on the defence estimates were 'a powerful statement about defence plans that locked defence programmes into place in political terms'. He also asserted that: 'The Defence White Paper is an annual statement about where we are at! Little surprise, therefore, that different groups in the MoD should want It to define their current positions as accurately or favourably as possible' (1988, p 18). For a long time, the process for promulgating defence policy was adversarial, encouraged self-serving behaviour and perpetuated inter-service rivalry. Although that may not be entirely the case today, all three services have a long corporate memory and are unlikely to have forgotten both the successes they have enjoyed, and the failures they have endured, in past figurative battles they have fought amongst themselves over securing favourable policy decisions. These experiences cannot be overlooked when considering how each of the single services approaches the translation of strategic direction into military capability.

Cornish and Dorman (2010, p 396) recognized that, 'as well as being a difficult process, the term defence review is contested'. They determined that it is appropriate 'where there has been an overt reference to a defence review, or a significant change to overall defence policy, which may have led to a new policy document being produced, or a major change to the defence equipment programme' (2010, p 398). Thus, their emphasis is on the level of adjustment or change, rather than titles of documents. Caterina P. Thomson and David Blagden (2018, p 583) developed this thinking by considering the overall aims of an SDSR. They suggested that it seeks to 'procure and assign forces/capabilities to address such risks [assessed within the NSS]' and is therefore intended to 'conduct comprehensive cross-departmental analysis of national security/defence needs, in line with the NSS, before setting/ allocating resources via capability choices'.

The reason Cornish and Dorman, and Thomson and Blagden, had to undertake their analysis is because there is no UK government-endorsed definition for a defence review, and, therefore, no conclusive list of the number of reviews that have taken place during the period between the end of the Second World War and the present day. For example, Claire Taylor (2010a, p 3) pointed out that 'many analysts consider the first major, wholesale strategic defence review conducted after the Second World War to be the Sandys review as it represented the first proper forward-looking assessment of Britain's strategic interests and requisite military requirements'. Conversely, Robert Self (2010, p 163) believed the Sandys white paper, published in April 1957, to be 'the seventh review of defence policy undertaken in the eleven years since the end of the [Second World] war'. A House of Commons briefing paper of previous British defence reviews, published immediately prior to the 2015 SDSR, suggested that there have been only eight defence reviews between 1945 and 2004, although the document fails at any point to explain specifically what is meant by the term (Walker and Mills, 2015, pp 3–5). To add a further complication, part one of the 1966 statement on the defence estimates is titled *The Defence Review* (MoD, 1966), but additional major changes to defence policy were also published by the Labour government as supplementary statements in the following two years (MoD, 1967; and MoD 1968). This led William Jackson and Edwin Bramall (1992, p 360) to observe that Denis Healey's review was, in fact, a 'rolling programme of studies with three major revisions'. There is, therefore, no defined period for a defence review either.

In 1981, defence secretary John Nott was adamant that his command paper, *The UK Defence Programme: The Way Forward*, was not a defence review, but simply a 'realignment of forces to meet the financial situation of the time' (Institute for Contemporary British History [ICBH], 2001, p 27). This view was supported by Dorman (2001, p 19) who claimed, 'the Nott Review was never formally a review but instead a re-alignment of forces to meet the financial situation of the time'. In a similar vein, according to Lawrence Freedman (1999, p 96), the Options for Change exercise of the early 1990s was never described by the then defence secretary Tom King as a defence review. That said, Tom Dodd (1993, p 13) argued that 'Options bears all the hallmarks of a defence review'. Options for Change was also the first occasion when the incumbent secretary of state, perhaps learning a lesson from the 1981 Nott review, did not lend their name to the output of the review – a trait that has continued to this day. Perhaps this is because the latest generation of politicians are more attuned to the public's perception of them, and do not want to be associated with the negative connotations of military and civil service redundancies, or cuts in capability.

An examination of the purpose of the reviews, as identified by their authors, is also revealing. In the introduction to his defence review in 1957, Duncan Sandys wrote that 'the time has now come to revise not merely the size, but the whole character of the defence plan' (MoD, 1957, p 1). His only stated reasoning for this approach was that, although the threat from communism remained extant, its nature had changed. That said, the nature of this change was not specified in the command paper. This explanation may seem a little scant, considering, in Sandys' opinion, it drove 'the biggest changes in military policy ever made in normal times' (1957, p 9). Nine years later, Denis Healey asserted that the Labour government's 'far-reaching examination of the nation's defence needs' had two objectives: 'to relax the strain imposed on the British economy by defence programmes which it had inherited, and to shape a new defence posture for the 1970s' (MoD, 1966, p 1). The first objective, which is expanded considerably in the paper's opening paragraphs, is a thinly disguised attempt to assign the blame for future cuts onto the previous Conservative government. This is an early example of political manoeuvring that is present in most defence review documents, particularly those that have been undertaken immediately after the return to government of a political party following a general election.

The same tactic was used by Roy Mason, author of the next defence review, which was published in 1975. In an early paragraph, he wrote 'when the Government came into office in March 1974, it inherited a defence programme of world-wide political and military commitments, and military forces stretched to meet those commitments' (MoD, 1975, p 1). Significantly, Mason's review was driven directly from a manifesto pledge to 'progressively reduce the burden of Britain's defence spending to bring costs into line with those carried out by our main European allies' (The Labour Party, 1974, p 11). To that end, the explicit aim of the review was to 'achieve savings on defence expenditure of several hundred million pounds per annum over a period' albeit 'while maintaining a modern and effective defence system' (MoD, 1975, p 1).

By contrast, in 1981, John Nott avoided completely any notion that the outcome of his 'fresh and radical look at the defence programme' would be cuts or reductions (MoD, 1981, p 4). Instead, he stated the appraisal 'in no way rests on a desire to cut our defence effort. On the contrary, it reflects a firm resolve to establish how best to exploit a substantial increase, which will enable us to enhance our front-line capability in very many areas' (1981, p 3). The protection of the Conservative Party's reputation is very much in evidence here. As Michael Dockrill (1989, p 112) explained, during the 1979 general election campaign, the Conservatives had promised to make greater efforts than the Labour government in improving Britain's defences. Regardless of the adverse effect of the world depression on the British economy at that time, and prime minister Margaret Thatcher's insistence of the imposition of rigid monetary control on public expenditure, Nott could hardly present a defence review that appeared to be constructed around a decrease in military capability. To that end, his command paper was very carefully written, especially the maritime tasks section. Enhancements to maritime patrol and attack submarine capability were introduced early and explained in detail, before the surface fleet reductions were exposed (MoD, 1981, pp 8–10).

The end of the Cold War changed the landscape for defence reviews. In the statement of the defence estimates that followed the 1990–1 Options for

Changes exercise, Tom King recognized that, because of 'total changes in eastern Europe … we can make some reductions in defence' (MoD, 1991, pp 5–6). However, not forgetting the importance of preserving his party's reputation for being strong on defence (Harrois, 2015), he concluded his introduction to the command paper with the words: 'our determination is to produce forces which, while smaller, are well equipped, properly trained and housed, and well-motivated' (MoD, 1991, p 6). Three years later, Malcolm Rifkind published *Front Line First: The Defence Costs Study*. The study was also never called a defence review, nor was it presented to parliament as a command paper. However, under the heading *Why a Defence Costs Study Was Needed* it confirmed 'there was good reason to believe that even greater savings could be achieved, without damaging operational capability, by taking a much more radical look at the way in which we did business across the whole range of support activities' (MoD, 1994, p 6). The final, explicitly stated, defence review of the Early Expeditionary period was the 1998 SDR. In his command paper, George Robertson was extremely clear about the purpose of the review: 'The publication of this White Paper fulfils the Government's manifesto commitment to conduct a foreign policy-led strategic defence review to reassess Britain's security interests and defence needs and consider how the roles, missions and capabilities of our Armed Forces should be adjusted to meet the new strategic realities' (MoD, 1998a, p 5).

Although there are obvious similarities in the purpose of the reviews undertaken during the Cold War and Early Expeditionary period, as stated by their authors, there are also differences. It is, therefore, unsurprising that no government during the period sought formally to codify what a defence review did, or did not, consist of. Flexibility, or ambiguity, was more useful to them. Moreover, few scholars who have studied defence reviews from the end of the Second World War onwards have offered a definition either. Even Cornish and Dorman's analysis detailed above, while helpful, falls short of specifically defining a defence review. One exception is Freedman (1987) who defined a defence review as an examination of 'the whole range of defence commitments to see if existing priorities are correct, whether resources are being used most efficiently, and, if cuts are necessary, where they should be made'. Although a good start point, this definition pre-dates the recent encompassing of security issues (discussed further in the next chapter). It also does not offer an opinion on who should be doing the examining. For example, many commentators appropriately point to the significance of the service chiefs' 1952 global strategy paper with regard to UK defence policy in general, and its influence on Sandys' 1957 defence review in particular (see, for example, Darby, 1973, pp 46–8; and Dorman, 2001a, pp 10–12). However, even though its findings were subsequently adopted in part by the government, it was a report submitted for 'consideration by the Defence Committee' (Chiefs of Staff, 1952, p 2) and not, on its own standing, government policy. Moreover, it was also classified Top Secret, and not available in the public domain until 2003, over 50 years after it was produced. A defence review must be led, and hence endorsed, by the government of the day; to that end, the definition of a defence review used in this book is: an examination, by the UK government, of its defence and security commitments and associated resources to ascertain whether they are still appropriate and, if necessary, initiate corrective action. As a result, notwithstanding the influence it had on shaping policy, which is identifiable in several of the Cold War defence reviews, the 1952 global strategy paper cannot be considered a defence review.

In line with my definition, and regardless of assertions made in some cases to the contrary by their authors, the command papers listed in Table 2.1 are considered to be defence reviews undertaken during the Cold War and Early Expeditionary period.

In trying to ascertain why the defence reviews between 1945 and 2010 were undertaken when they were, a simple examination of the left-hand column in Table 2.1 confirms that they were not initiated against any regular timetable. However, ignoring the immediate post-Second World War election, each time the Labour Party returned to government during this period, in 1964, 1974 and 1997, it initiated a defence review. Furthermore, on all three occasions, it did so as it was beholden to pre-election pledges,

Table 2.1: Defence reviews undertaken between 1945 and 2009

Year	Command paper
1957	*Defence: Outline of Future Policy*, Cmnd 124 (Sandys' Review).
1966–1968	*Statement on the Defence Estimates 1966: Part 1 – The Defence Review*, Cmnd 2901 (Healey's Review), supported by: • *Supplementary Statement on Defence Policy 1967*, Cmnd 3357. • *Supplementary Statement on Defence Policy 1968*, Cmnd 3701.
1975	*Statement on the Defence Estimates 1975: Chapter 1 – The Defence Review*, Cmnd 5976 (Mason's Review).
1981	*The United Kingdom Defence Programme: The Way Forward*, Cmnd 8288 (The Nott Review).
1991–1994	*Statement on the Defence Estimates 1991: Volume 1 – Britain's Defence for the 90s*, Cm 1559-I (Options for Change), supported by: • *Front Line First: The Defence Costs Study 1994*.
1998–2004	*The Strategic Defence Review 1998 – Modern Forces for the Modern World*, Cm 3999 supported by: • *The Strategic Defence Review: A New Chapter 2002 Volume I*, Cm 5566-I. • *Delivering Security in a Changing World 2003 Volume I*, Cm 6041-I. • *Delivering Security in a Changing World – Future Capabilities*, Cm 6269.

which were not necessarily defence related. George Younger (1976), for example, suggested that Mason's review was an undisguised mechanism to generate the financial headroom to fund the government's higher political priorities. Without making judgements on Labour Party priorities, non-defence related political ambition certainly appear to have been a factor in its decision making around the commissioning of defence reviews.

At first glance, the same does not appear to be the case for the Conservative Party's defence reviews of the period. In 1981, the newly appointed defence secretary, John Nott, was faced with an ongoing and increasing MoD overspend (Dorman, 2001b, p 99), and, ten years later, Tom King had to contend with the aftermath of the fall of the Berlin Wall. Neither of these factors can be linked to pre-election pledges, and, therefore, were not underpinned solely by wider political ambition. However, the situation in 1957 was much less clear. The strategic shock of the Suez Crisis is often identified as the reason why a defence review was undertaken in 1957 (Dodd, 1993, p 4). Specifically, Dorman (2001a, p 12) suggested 'the failure of the Anglo-French expedition [in Suez in 1956] served as a trigger for a major reconsideration of British defence policy'. However, Richard Powell, who was deputy secretary at the MoD in 1957, offered a differing view:

> The aftermath of Suez to me was not the most important element in this situation. Suez was certainly the proximate cause of the White Paper, in the sense that it led to a change of Prime Minister and Minister of Defence. If these things had not happened, the White Paper would not have happened in the form that it did. (ICBH, 1988, p 2)

Jackson and Bramall (1992, p 314) also recognized the significance of Harold Macmillan becoming prime minister in January 1957, suggesting his political aspirations were the real reason behind the defence review later in the year. They identified that he had three years in which to establish himself, before the next general election was due, and his aspirations were underpinned by radical changes in defence policy: 'improving standards of living demanded swingeing cuts in defence spending to release skilled manpower into the economy ... and an imaginative defence policy, which was perceived as providing adequate security at much lower cost, could help his Party's electoral image.' This conclusion supports the view that political ambition was often a significant factor in the decision to undertake defence reviews during this period. In the main, however, governments allowed defence policy to run over time, until it required revision or, in certain circumstances, overturning. Minor revisions to defence policy were undertaken through the annual statement on the defence estimates process, whereas significant change required a more comprehensive response. Thus, defence reviews occurred when the government decided that its policy required either some revision, which could not be undertaken through the statement on the defence estimates process, or its policy needed to be changed.

As part of the 2010 SDSR, the Conservative/Liberal Democrat coalition government introduced a quinquennial defence and security review process (HM Government, 2010c, p 35). Following this, identifying recent defence reviews should have become a simple task. Five years later, in November 2015, the Conservative government duly completed another SDSR, the report for which also included a revised NSS (HM Government, 2015). However, as I pointed out in a 2019 article for *The RUSI Journal*, for a seventeen-month period between July 2017 and December 2018, and completely outside the quinquennial cycle, the government was in an almost constant state of review – initially through the Cabinet Office-led NSCR, and then by the MoD co-ordinated MDP.

The House of Commons and House of Lords Joint Committee on the National Security Strategy (JCNSS) (2018, p 23) identified that the NSCR had 'inadvertently become an uncomfortable "hallway-house" between a refresh [of capabilities] and a full review', while the House of Commons Defence Committee (HCDC) (2018a, p 3) considered the MDP to be a 'defence policy review'. Nonetheless, neither resulted in a significant change to overall defence policy, nor did they generate a major change to the defence equipment programme. Moreover, neither activity was an examination of the whole range of defence commitments, nor did they take a view on priorities or the efficient use of resources. On balance, therefore, it is difficult to consider either the NSCR or the MDP to be a defence review.

Following the 2019 general election, prime minister Boris Johnson announced that his new government would undertake a review 'to define the government's ambition for the UK's role in the world and the long-term strategic aims for our national security and foreign policy' (GOV.UK, 2020c). From the outset, it was billed as a more wide-ranging version of the SDSRs held in 2010 and 2015, and, although it was considerably delayed as a result of the COVID-19 pandemic, the Integrated Review of Security, Defence, Development and Foreign Policy was finally published in March 2021 (HM Government, 2021b). The review was supported by a Defence Command Paper (DCP), released one week later, with the mission 'to seek out and to understand future threats, and to invest in the capabilities to defeat them' (MoD, 2021b, p 1). The 2021 IR and its supporting DCP were clearly both underpinned by an examination of defence commitments and associated resources; furthermore, the command paper included a substantial re-balancing of military capability. To that end, the 2021 IR certainly fits the defence review definition. Given this analysis, the command papers listed in Table 2.2 are recognized as the defence reviews of the Quinquennial Review period.

Table 2.2: Defence reviews undertaken between 2010 and 2021

Year	Command paper
2010	*The Strategic Defence and Security Review 2010 – Securing Britain in an Age of Uncertainty*, Cm 7948, supported by: • *The National Security Strategy 2010 – A Strong Britain in an Age of Uncertainty*, Cm 7953.
2015	*National Security Strategy and Strategic Defence and Security Review 2015 – A Secure and Prosperous United Kingdom*, Cm 9161, supported by: • *National Security Capability Review*. • *Modernising Defence Programme*.
2021	*Global Britain in a Competitive Age – the Integrated Review of Security, Defence, Development and Foreign Policy*, CP 403, supported by: • *Defence in a Competitive Age*, CP 411.

Military capability

As a concept, military capability has grown appreciably in prominence since its introduction as part of the SPI. Indeed, it is now recognized as one of Defence's three high-level outputs (MoD, 2020b, p 5). Nevertheless, although it remains the central tenet of the MoD's approach to acquisition, it has been the subject of considerable scrutiny and upheaval over the last two decades. The breakdown of MoD expenditure for the previous four financial years (FY) is detailed in Table 2.3 (see MoD, 2017f, p 14; MoD, 2018c, p 16; MoD, 2019, p 15; and MoD, 2020d, p 13). Apart from operations and peacekeeping, war pensions and other costs benefits, all remaining expenditure contributes to the generation and maintenance of military capability.[6] The two primary cost drivers are equipment[7] and personnel.

Policy makers are naturally drawn to the major areas of expenditure when considering improvements in effectiveness or efficiency savings in the generation and maintenance of military capability. Nevertheless, although changes to terms and conditions of service can reduce spending, the main cost driver for personnel is the actual number of service and civilian manpower being paid for by the MoD. The size of the armed forces and supporting civil service workforce is a very emotive subject, and decisions concerning headcount revisions, which have consistently been downward revisions, are invariably the preserve of politicians. Moreover, they are generally made as part of a wider examination of policy, for example during a defence review. Here they can be included within a package of change that also contains positive announcements, including, for example, the purchase of new weapon systems or enhancements to existing capability. That is not the case for equipment. The management of defence equipment can broadly be divided into its initial purchase – procurement – and its through-life

Table 2.3: Breakdown of MoD expenditure between financial years 2016–17 and 2019–20

Area of expenditure	2016–17 (£ bn)	2017–18 (£ bn)	2018–19 (£ bn)	2019–20 (£ bn)	Average percentage
Capital expenditure	8.80	9.43	10.29	10.29	26
Service personnel	8.90	8.97	9.09	9.95	24.5
Equipment support	6.40	6.55	6.79	6.98	18
Infrastructure	4.10	4.06	4.26	4.64	11
Administration	1.50	1.47	1.68	1.91	4.5
Civilian personnel	1.30	1.36	1.38	1.54	3.5
Inventory	1.20	1.19	1.17	1.27	3
Defence Equipment and Support	1.00	1.11	0.98	1.10	3
Cost of operations and peacekeeping	0.40	0.80	0.63	0.48	1.5
Other costs	0.70	0.79	0.88	0.87	2
War pensions benefits	0.80	0.72	0.70	0.68	2
Arm's length bodies	0.20	0.61	0.20	0.29	1
Total	35.30	36.61	38.05	40	

Source: MoD, *Annual Report and Accounts 2016–17*, MoD, *Annual Report and Accounts 2017–18*, MoD, *Annual Report and Accounts 2018–19*, MoD, *Annual Report and Accounts 2019–20*

operation in service – support.[8] Since the introduction of the SPI, there have been several significant organizational changes and major reforms to procurement and support policy and processes, to improve the efficiency and effectiveness of the management of military capability (Spellar, 1998, p 35). The most prominent are shown in Figure 2.1 and explained in more detail in the next sub-section.

In addition to the acquisition reforms imposed since the 1998 SDR, the single, greatest influence on the management of military capability was the DRP, which began in 2011. The two recommendations from the DRP that had the most impact were:

- Make the MoD head office smaller and more strategic, to make high level balance of investment decisions, set strategic direction and a strong corporate framework, and hold to account.
- Focus the service chiefs on running their service and empower them to perform their role effectively, with greater freedom to manage, as part of a much clearer framework of financial accountability and control. (MoD, 2011a, p 4)

Figure 2.1: Major procurement and support reforms between 1998 and 2021

Smart Procurement Initiative
- The aim of smart procurement was to enhance defence capability by acquiring and supporting equipment more effectively in terms of time, cost and performance.

Defence Procurement Agency (DPA)
- The DPA was an Executive Agency of the MOD responsible for the acquisition of materiel, equipment and services for the armed forces.

Defence Logistics Organisation (DLO)
- The DLO amalgamated the single service logistics departments and MOD central logistics agencies to maintain military equipment in service and coordinate its storage and distribution.

Defence Logistics Transformation Programme
- Focused on end-to-end logistics reform to improve effectiveness, efficiency and flexibility of in-service support, storage and distribution.

Through Life Capability Management (TLCM)
- The acquisition and in-service management of military capability in which every aspect of new and existing military capability is planned and managed coherently across all DLODs from cradle to grave.

Defence Equipment and Support (DE&S)
- Formed from the merger of the DPA and DLO to manage the acquisition and support of military capability for the armed forces, Became a bespoke trading entity in 2014.

Gray Report
- An independent review to separate and clarify roles and accountabilities between the MOD Centre and the DE&S and to significantly improve the operation of TLCM.

Defence Support Review
- High-level examination of associated cost trends and previous ideas, and to scope new ones to identify areas where further savings in support could be made across the department.

Defence Support Network Transformation Programme
- A strategy to reform MOD's approach to support, vested in a globally agile network that is strategically prepared, globally responsive and operationally precise.

1998	Strategic Defence Review
1999	Smart Procurement (later Acquisition) Initiative / Defence Procurement Agency formed
2000	Defence Logistics Organisation formed
2001	
2002	Strategic Defence Review – A New Chapter
2003	Delivering Security in a Changing World
2004	Defence Logistics Transformation Programme
2005	
2006	Through Life Capability Management introduced
2007	Defence Equipment and Support formed
2008	
2009	Gray Report published
2010	Strategic Defence and Security Review
2011	Defence Support Review / Defence Reform Programme initiated
2012	
2013	
2014	
2015	Strategic Defence and Security Review
2016	Chilcot Report published
2017	National Security Capability Review
2018	Modernising Defence Programme
2019	Defence Support Network Transformation Programme
2020	
2021	Integrated Review of Security, Defence, Development and Foreign Policy

These recommendations resulted in major changes to SOME of the key features of smart acquisition (for example, the first and second customer concept was discarded), and fundamentally revised financial responsibilities. Within the MoD today, the rules governing the management of military capability are still primarily influenced by the outcomes of the DRP, the implications of which are explored later in this section.

Before the SPI was introduced in 1998, new equipment projects were managed in phases, with funding for each phase only being approved once the work in the previous phase had been completed. This approach followed the acceptance of recommendations from a report[9] produced by a steering group on development cost estimating in 1969, chaired by William Downey (Ministry of Technology, 1969). In addition, for many years after the Second World War, the UK defence industry was seen as an essential component of national security, and the MoD was obliged to maintain a close relationship with it. As David Kirkpatrick (2003, p 5) recognized, at one stage MoD PE had 'specific responsibility for "promoting the welfare" of the defence-related sectors of UK industry'. The most obvious effects of this were limited competition for defence contracts and a preponderance of cost-plus contracts.[10] However, this policy was radically altered by Peter (later Lord) Levene, following his appointment as Chief of Defence Procurement in 1985. He believed that defence equipment acquisition should be more commercially focused, with open competitions wherever possible and fixed price contracts replacing the traditional cost-plus approach. He also favoured a more hands-off approach with projects entrusted to prime contractors to manage (Markowski and Hall, 1998). Notwithstanding these reforms, Kirkpatrick (2003, p 6) noted that many equipment projects still substantially exceeded the predicted values of their procurement cost and timescale, and much of the associated MoD process to manage them remained unduly bureaucratic and cumbersome. It was against this backdrop that the Labour government introduced the SPI as part of the 1998 SDR.

The SPI was launched under the strapline: faster, cheaper, better. Within two years, it had been re-branded as 'smart acquisition', to 'stress the point that the MoD is concerned not only with buying equipment, but with acquiring the means to support it throughout its in-service life' (Taylor, 2003, p 3). That said, the following key features of the SPI were fundamentally unaltered:

- A streamlined process for project management and approvals – the acquisition (or CADMID) cycle – to replace the existing Downey cycle.
- The introduction of a through-life systems approach, embodied in a single integrated project team (IPT) that brought together all the main stakeholders in a project, including industry (except where competition made it impracticable).

- The creation of clearly identifiable customers of the IPTs. An equipment capability customer (ECC) in MoD head office, responsible for requirement setting and acting as lead customer for the equipment until it entered service. A second customer (the service ultimately to receive the equipment, or the majority user) responsible for in-service management.
- A new open and constructive relationship with industry, based on partnering.
- More comprehensive project planning earlier in the procurement cycle with appropriate trade-offs between military requirements, time and costs in an effort to assuage later cost overruns and delays.
- The introduction of new equipment techniques including incremental acquisition, whereby equipment would be initially accepted into service with less ambitious capability and subsequently upgraded in lower-risk steps. (MoD, 2002, pp 2–3)

The SPI was primarily focused on MoD practices and procedure, although it did consider views from industry (Smith, 1998, p 40). It also included three organizational changes within the MoD. The single services' operational requirements teams were amalgamated and expanded into a central defence customer – the ECC – under a newly established three-star deputy chief of the defence staff for equipment capability. MoD PE became an executive agency[11] and was renamed the Defence Procurement Agency (DPA). The third change was not specifically driven by the SPI but was analogous, and certainly improved the conditions for the successful implementation of the SPI. A new, four-star Chief of Defence Logistics post was created to assume overall control of the three single service logistics organizations to maximize the scope for rationalization of logistics functions and processes on a defence-wide basis. The result was the formation of the Defence Logistics Organisation (DLO).

The changes to the acquisition landscape that the SPI introduced have been built upon over the years; however, the whole-life approach has endured and the CADMID cycle is still the framework for equipment projects today. The role of the IPTs remains relatively unchanged, although, as David Moore and Peter Antill (2001, pp 183–4) predicted, there is no longer a requirement for them to transfer from the DPA to the DLO as these organizations merged to form the Defence Equipment and Support (DE&S) in 2007 (MoD, 2008b, p 144). Partnering continues to be one of a variety of methods for engagement between the MoD and industry, as confirmed in the 2021 Defence and Security Industrial Strategy (MoD, 2021a, p 29). The one feature of the SPI that has been completely superseded is the customer roles, which were disestablished under the DRP.

Since the commencement of the SPI, there have been several transformation initiatives within Defence, aimed at improving the effectiveness and efficiency of procurement and support. They have broadly followed two approaches. An internal study, usually supported by external consultants, followed by an implementation period (see, for example, Dowdy, 2003; MoD, 2010b; and Deloitte LLP, 2017), or an independent review of defence practices that is accepted by the MoD or government with its recommendations adopted over time (see, for example, Gray, 2009). These initiatives have had mixed success. Of the internal studies, the Defence Logistics Transformation Programme, which ran from 2004 to 2007, was extremely successful in removing costs from in-service support, particularly in the air domain. For instance, the replacement of four lines of aircraft servicing with a simple forward and depth approach reduced military headcount and increased fleet availability (HCDC, 2006, p 29). It remains the standard model for supporting aircraft from all three services today. By contrast, even though the Defence Support Review suggested a potential value for money savings profile of almost £3 billion over 10 years (MoD, 2010b, p 50), its outline plans to optimize industrial performance and employ support-chain leverage though life were never progressed. The external studies fared somewhat better. After completing his review of acquisition in 2009, Bernard Gray was invited by the Conservative/Liberal Democrat coalition government to implement his recommendations as the Chief of Defence Materiel (CDM) in January 2011 (GOV.UK, 2010a). Gray did preside over some improvements in procurement programmes and project management during his tenure as CDM (NAO, 2014, pp 5–9); however, his flagship proposal, that the DE&S should convert to a government-owned, contractor-operated entity (Gray, 2009, p 8), proved impossible to achieve (NAO, 2015, p 7). Instead, he had to be content with his minimum option for it to become a bespoke trading entity, which it attained in 2014 (Hansard, 2014).

The final transformation initiative, and the one that potentially had the greatest impact on the way military capability is managed today is Through Life Capability Management (TLCM). Through life management had been a key feature of the SPI. In 2003, however, the NAO (2003, p 1) reported that through life management had 'yet to become fully embedded in the Department and to yield widespread benefits in terms of demonstrable improvements in military capability'. This was, in part, due to the continuance of the MoD's traditional narrow focus on equipment. To rectify this, the MoD introduced new ways of working to improve its acquisition management, under the auspices of TLCM (MoD, 2005a, p 17). TLCM required capability to be managed, over time, by a series of creative activities that synthesized a set of fundamental inputs, or components, expressed as lines of development (Yue and Henshaw, 2009, p 55). As already explained in Chapter 1, these lines of development were formalized as the DLODs, which was described by the MoD as 'a checklist to be used by senior responsible owners[12] (SRO), top level budget (TLB) holders[13] and other deliverers of capability to ensure all key factors relevant to the capability have been considered, and that issues for resolution have been identified' (MoD, 2005b, p 1). Yue and Henshaw (2009, p 55) also recognized the interdependent nature and operational focus of the DLODs, confirming that 'a desired capability can only be achieved if the activities within all eight DLODs are at an appropriately matched level of readiness'.

The enduring nature of TLCM was confirmed following an internal MoD study that emphasized the importance of capability planning and strengthened the role of the ECC (MoD, 2006b).[14] TLCM was also reinforced through both the contemporaneous Defence Industrial Strategy (MoD, 2005a), and Defence Technology Strategy (MoD, 2006a). It overlaid a six-stage capability planning process[15] onto the CADMID cycle (MoD, 2007) that survived the DRP, and remains in use by capability managers across the single services today.

As we shall examine further in Chapter 5, the 2010 SDSR was undertaken too swiftly to consider the reform of MoD processes and procedures (Dunn et al, 2011, p 14). Instead, a follow-on piece of work was commissioned, under the chairmanship of Lord Levene. Its remit was to 'conduct a fundamental review of how the MoD is structured and managed, in order to design a model for departmental management which is simpler and more cost-effective, with clear allocation of responsibility, authority and accountability' (MoD, 2011a, p 9). Levene developed a consolidated summary of the core functions that the MoD needed to undertake to meet its basic purpose of defending the UK and its Overseas Territories, citizens and interests:

- **Direct**. Understand the strategic context, make defence policy and strategy, define and resource the necessary military capability and strategically direct operations and Defence diplomacy.
- **Generate and Develop**. Generate force elements to meet current operations and potential military tasks and develop the future force.
- **Acquire**. Procure and support the equipment systems and commodities needed in the short and long term.
- **Enable**. Enable the other functions by performing or commissioning supporting services, such as infrastructure, corporate services and science and technology.
- **Operate**. Use military capability on operations and other military tasks, as directed by government; and,
- **Account**. Manage, control and account for the resources voted by parliament, and report on defence activities to parliament and the public. (MoD, 2011a, p 16)

These functions were grouped into a construct that articulated who was responsible for each function, gave owners the authority and resources to discharge them, and identified how they would relate to each other. The result was the Defence Operating Model (DOM) schematic shown in Figure 2.2.

The Conservative/Liberal Democrat coalition government published Levene's report on 27 June 2011, and defence secretary Liam Fox endorsed its 53 recommendations in a parliamentary statement the same day. He considered it a 'thorough and compelling analysis that deserves close attention'. He also suggested that 'people in defence' would recognize it as a 'constructive critique of a Department in need of reform' and 'relish ... the challenges that it represents' (Hansard, 2011a).

While there is no evidence to confirm whether the people in Defence agreed with their secretary of state, it is clear that the MoD set about implementing the DRP at pace. The Defence Reform Unit, which had supported Levene during the study, was retained to provide assistance to the reforming directorates within MoD head office and, within four months, Fox was able to confirm the establishment of the new Defence Board and major projects review board; the creation of the Defence Infrastructure Organisation and Defence Business Services organization; and the appointment of the first commander of the new Joint Forces Command (JFC), Air Chief Marshal Stuart Peach (Hansard, 2011b). Understandably, the changes necessary to accommodate the single services' new financial delegations for capability management took longer to implement, and it was not until April 2014 that they achieved full operating capability (RAF, 2015b). Following the resizing and refocusing of MoD head office and the empowering of the service chiefs, Taylor (2011, p 4) recognized a shift in the manner in which strategic direction was given, and received, to provide military capability: 'under the new model, the service chiefs would receive clearer strategic direction from the defence board, carry out the detailed military capability planning required across equipment, manpower and training, and then propose how best to deliver that strategic direction through the provision of an annual command plan.' Furthermore, in his 2015 annual review of the DRP, Levene (2015) recognized that the MoD had achieved the great majority of the reform programme he had set for it in 2011. He also confirmed that the one activity on which the department still needed to concentrate to complete the defence reform agenda was changing behaviours. Behaviours across Defence is a major issues that we will return to in Chapter 7.

Over the last decade, the DRP has had time thoroughly to bed in, and the MoD now has a well-documented process for the department-wide management of military capability. At the highest level, the latest version of the DOM – *How Defence Works, Version 6* – includes a broad explanation

Figure 2.2: Original version of the defence operating model schematic

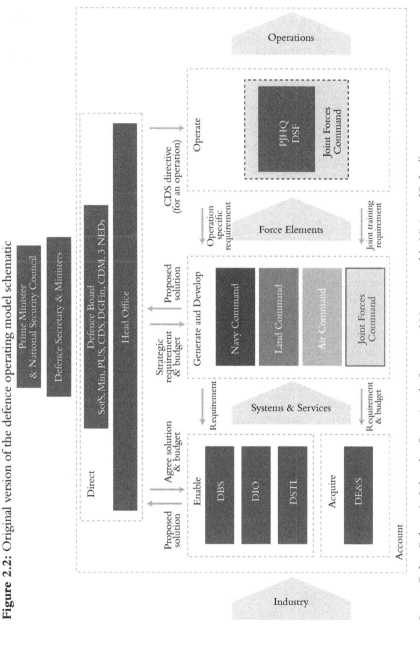

Source: *Defence Reform: An Independent Report into the Structure and Management of the Ministry of Defence*[16]

of the way military capability should be delivered (MoD, 2020b, pp 21–2). Beneath this direction is a layer of overarching functional guidance, which consists primarily of department-wide operating models for finance and military capability (MoD, 2015a) and the acquisition system (MoD, 2017a). The acquisition system operating model is underpinned by the acquisition system handbook (MoD, 2018a), which replaced the acquisition handbook. At the bottom of the governance structure is the internal direction written by the single services for their own capability managers. Unsurprisingly, this direction has taken different forms, with the British Army (2016) including it in its own service-wide operating model, the RN (2015) producing a capability management handbook, and the Royal Air Force (RAF) (2015a) opting for a specific finance and military capability operating model.

Summary

Strategic direction does not have clearly defined boundaries and has evolved considerably over the last 75 years. It is provided through a mix of set-piece events, such as defence reviews, and both verbal and written articulation by senior politicians and their officials. The repository for strategic direction is defence and security policy, which, in its simplest form, is an expression of the government's approach to a particular situation. From the commencement of the Cold War to the present, the principal approach to creating defence policy has been incrementalism. Often described as 'muddling through', this involves taking a series of small decisions about a subject that can be subsequently amended or reversed if required. For much of the last 75 years, defence policy was promulgated via an annual statement of the defence estimates; however, today it is expressed through the combination of a web-based outcome delivery plan and yearly report to parliament, both in the public domain, plus an internal, classified annual plan. During the Cold War and Early Expeditionary period, major changes to defence policy were considered during defence reviews, which can be defined as an examination, by the UK government, of its defence and security commitments and associated resources to ascertain whether they are still appropriate and, if necessary, initiate corrective action. In 2010, the government introduced a quinquennial review cycle that conducted a comprehensive cross-department analysis of defence and security needs, followed by the allocation of resource via capability choices.

The management of military capability has evolved since its introduction as a concept in 1998 but remains the central tenet of the MoD's approach to acquisition. It is defined as the combination of equipment, trained personnel and support that gives the armed forces the capacity to achieve the tasks they are given. Its two main cost-drivers are personnel and equipment. Due to the contentious nature of manpower numbers, decisions on the size of the armed forces have traditionally been made at the political level during defence reviews. However, since smart acquisition was introduced, there have been a significant number of change initiatives, introduced and managed within the MoD, designed to improve the efficiency and effectiveness of equipment procurement and support. Although not solely focused on military capability, the initiative that has had the greatest impact on it was the DRP, which introduced a new operating model for Defence with clear allocation of responsibility, authority and accountability. The most noteworthy changes delivered through the DRP were to re-focus MoD head office to make high level balance of investment decisions and set strategic direction, while providing service chiefs with greater freedom to manage their service as part of a much clearer framework of financial accountability and control. At the macro level, the processes and procedures used by Defence today remain those introduced by the DRP.

3

The UK's Approach to Strategy

Hew Strachan (2005, p 48) wrote that strategy is not just a matter for historians – it concerns us all. As discussed in the previous chapter, the UK's grand strategy during the Cold War was framed squarely around the expansionist Soviet military and nuclear threat. According to Julian Richards (2012, p 8), this impelled a strong military conception of security, whereby 'a balance of hard power was the underpinning principle of national security'. This thinking was reflected in the language used throughout annual statements on the defence estimates of the time, and in the defence reviews of Sandys, Healey, Mason and Nott. Moreover, the concept was so obvious and uncontested that it did not require any additional amplification. This does not imply the non-existence of other pressures on national security during the Cold War. Environmental concerns like global warming were clearly an issue long before the fall of the Berlin Wall in 1989 (see, for example, Sawyer, 1972). It was simply that the perceived nature of the Soviet threat was so great that most of the security-related capability and resources were prioritized to counter it. Because of this, once the policy of deterrence had been established, it could be argued that the UK's strategic thinking during the rest of the Cold War became moribund.

After the Cold War, the discourse around strategy at the national level, by both commentators and practitioners, increased considerably. The demise of the Soviet Union allowed the security focus to be re-directed, and other pressures could be considered and prioritized, with resources to mitigate them now accessible (Richards, 2012, pp 8–9). Unsurprisingly, in the environment of strategic uncertainty that existed during the 1990s, academic opinion on what was now important was divided. On the one hand, it was argued that a wide range of defence capabilities should be retained to ensure the UK had sufficient flexibility to tackle a diffuse range of potential future global risks and crises (see Quinlan, 1992, p 162; and Sabin, 1993, pp 277–85). Conversely, Michael Asteris (1994, p 43) took a more focused approach, suggesting that, once the homeland security had been established, the nature of the UK's military provision beyond that should have become much more a matter of national choice. As analysis in Chapter 6 will expose, even though the geopolitical landscape was far from clear, the defence reviews of this time were overwhelmingly focused on the affordability of defence and, in particular, the need to realize savings from the defence budget. These turbulent times were summed up neatly by Andrew Dorman (2001a, p 22) who wrote: 'the end of the Cold War had transformed the state of world affairs, but nobody was quite sure how.'

In 2008, for the first time, the Labour government published an NSS, which was designed to address and manage the diverse but interconnected post-Cold War era of threats and risks facing the country (HM Government, 2008a, p 3). A year later, prime minister Gordon Brown updated the NSS (HM Government, 2009), with further iterations published following the 2010 (HM Government, 2010c) and 2015 (HM Government, 2015) SDSRs. These documents, together with the foreign, defence and security policy decisions made by the government over the last 15 years, have fuelled ever more scrutiny of the UK's approach to making strategy. While the abundance of contemporary secondary literature considers a huge range of issues, two themes attract by far the most attention: appreciating what strategy encompasses, and considering how well it is formulated and enacted (see, for example, Clarke, 2007; Savill, 2011; Freedman, 2013; Strachan, 2013; and Blagden, 2015).

This chapter considers how the UK's approach to grand strategy impacts on military capability decision making. It opens with a brief examination of grand strategy in the round before focusing on how it has been employed by UK governments over the 70 years of the research period. From this, it is clear that politicians and defence decision makers have different perspectives regarding the usefulness of strategy at both the national and the military level. The chapter then moves on to scrutinize the broadening of the UK's approach to developing national strategy. Over four iterations, the basic risk management approach that underpinned the NSS has been refined and improved. Although not perfect, the methodology used in the 2015 SDSR was comparatively mature and, more importantly, well understood across Whitehall. It is, therefore, worrying that the approach was abandoned for the 2021 IR.

The chapter's final section examines whether fielded military capability meets the needs of defence policy. This is achieved by exploring how well it aligns to both the strategic direction provided by the government and the threats articulated in national strategy. The obvious conclusion from this chapter's analysis is that developing national strategy is more challenging today than it was during the Cold War and Early Expeditionary periods. More contentious, perhaps, is the view that today's politicians are less inclined than their predecessors to develop and follow a comprehensive national strategic approach to the UK's place in the world, especially since Brexit.

Furthermore, my analysis suggests that this reduced reliance on making and undertaking strategy is having a detrimental effect on the translation of strategic direction into military capability.

Understanding grand strategy

Edward Luttwak (2009, p 409) observed that 'all states have a grand strategy, whether they know it or not'. This view is supported by Hal Brands (2012, p 3) who defined grand strategy as 'the theory or logic that binds a country's highest interests to its daily interactions with the world'. There is an almost universal acceptance among academics that grand strategy occurs at a national level, and most recognize that it involves the harnessing of 'all a nation's resources to accomplish objectives defined by national policy' (Wedemeyer, cited by Milevski, 2016, p 68). It is also a commonly held view that making grand strategy is both an iterative and integrated process that involves understanding how a nation's actions in the present can deliver its desired end state (see Brands, 2012, p 50; and Layton, 2012, p 58). In other words, grand strategy is 'about how one uses whatever one has to get to wherever it is one wants to go' (Gaddis, cited by Layton, 2012, p 59). Perhaps a final commonly held view is that practising grand strategy is a complex and difficult task, which may account for the regularly offered academic view that it is often undertaken poorly (see, for example, Porter, 2010, pp 6–7; and Edmunds, 2014, pp 526–7). Brands suggests the reason why is that the challenge of grand strategy flows directly from its meaning:

> Grand strategy is an inherently difficult endeavour that will tax the abilities of even the most capacious leader. ... [it] is not simply a struggle against one enemy or another; it is a fight against the complexity, disorder, and distraction that inevitably clutter the global scene. It is bound to be an exacting task, one full of potential pitfalls. (Brands, 2012, pp 10–11)

There are myriad definitions of grand strategy offered by academics. Tellingly, however, the latest draft of the UK's capstone doctrine publication – Joint Doctrine Publication 0-01 (MoD, 2021c)[1] – does not include the term anywhere in its 35 pages. Instead, it refers to the highest level of strategy making as national strategy. In its words, strategy directs the coordinated use of the four instruments of national power: diplomatic, information, military and economic to achieve the desired attitude and behaviours in target audiences (2021c, p 9). National strategy is defined as the '[coordination of] the instruments of national power in pursuit of national policy aims to secure our national interest' (2021c, p 10). The reason for no longer using the term 'grand strategy' may be traceable to a 2010 investigation into the

UK's national strategy by the House of Commons Public Administration Committee. It began its work by examining whether the concept of grand strategy was still of value, and concluded that 'the historical connotations of grand strategy could prove to be a hindrance because the term is associated with Empire and in some quarters is seen as hubristic' (2010, p 9). In a similar vein, Lucas Milevski (2016, p 98) suggested that 'despite its return to academic popularity, [grand strategy] may simply no longer be politically correct'. Whatever the reason, contemporary strategic direction is now seen by UK governments as national, rather than grand, strategy.

Is this fixation with terminology relevant? The *Oxford English Dictionary* (2018) defines strategy as 'a plan or a scheme' ahead of 'the art or practice of planning or directing the larger movements or long-term objectives of a battle, military campaign, etc'. Regardless of how accurate the latter definition may be, the fact that it is listed behind the former is significant – in today's world the military definition no longer has primacy. Debating the appropriateness of using the word strategy outside a military context is irrelevant; it is now widely used in many everyday environments, particularly business and sport. Richard Knighton (2009, p 3) points out that strategy and strategic level have become shorthand for big and long-term. In other words, as Strachan (2005, p 34) claims, 'the word strategy has acquired a universality which has robbed it of its meaning and left it only with banalities'. In the context of understanding why the UK has the military capability that it has, excessive, non-military use of the word is problematic because it introduces confusion when it *is* used in a military context (see Newton et al, 2010, p 49; and Porter, 2010, pp 7–8). As Colin Gray pointed out, this is significant because the importance of a shared understanding of the lexicon that supports civil–military relations cannot be over-stated:

> When we fail to define our terms, and neglect to use the key terms with a consistent meaning, it is not possible to hold an intelligent debate or make rational decisions. Moreover, if the misuse and general abuse of strategic conceptual language reflects not simply intellectual idleness, but rather a substantive misunderstanding, then we really are in trouble. (Gray, 2008, pp 13–14)

The confusion created when political and military leaders have a different interpretation of the framework within which strategic direction is imparted is well recognized by senior officials within the MoD. In simple terms, the problem is how can both sides know the message has been accurately heard and understood? As an RAF two-star officer observed, the general expectation for those receiving strategic direction is for 'a high-level position, which frames and guides the activities that we partake in'. However, a typical view on the reality of the situation was summed up by an army major general as follows: 'it doesn't feel like it's knitted into a coherent whole. We are too focused on attending "events, dear boy, events" rather than setting out a broad framework.' Some officials suggested a strategic plan was needed around where Defence should be at specific points in the future, while others believed that an ill-considered approach to prioritization was a key problem. This manifested itself in two specific ways. In the first instance, too many risks articulated in the NSS made everything seem like a priority, and, as an army two-star officer suggested, the need for Defence to be able to respond to any eventuality 'mean[t] no guidance, [just] the illusion of prioritization'. Furthermore, due to over-prioritization, there was a reluctance to disinvest in capability, or cancel programmes. As a former senior civil servant, now in a senior defence industry role, offered, 'what the MoD really should be doing is stopping some stuff'. He went on to confirm, '[in industry] I can do it without fear; in fact actually it's applauded. I sometimes talk of strategy being the art of deciding what not to do.' In the resource-constrained environment occupied by defence decision makers, thinking of strategy as being as much about deciding what not to do, as about deciding what to do, is a sound approach.

One four-star army officer theorized about the disconnect between the positions of the political givers and military receivers of strategic direction. He suggested that the demands placed on the government to deliver defence and security policy would always outstrip the resource it was prepared to allocate to the relevant departments. In his view, 'it fundamentally is about the drivers of politics generating a situation in which we cannot afford to do all we want to do, and that's true of every government under the sun'. Moreover, he considered that governments were all too aware of the problem, but aimed for the unachievable nevertheless:

'[The government] prefers to set a level of ambition that it sort of knows is undeliverable, and then send everybody charging off trying to deliver that level of ambition, and fail in certain parts of the machine. That is a preferable thing to actually accepting failure at the start.'

A more conciliatory view of recent governments' approach to strategy was advanced by those officers who had experience of operating outside the MoD. An air marshal, who had worked in the Cabinet Office, posited that the present-day politician's view of strategy was basically not the same as that learned by generations of military officers. In his opinion, politicians advocated a far simpler approach. For example, in the early stages of the 2015 SDSR, he suggested that the prime minister's strategy could be explained simply as 'making Britain prosperous', arguing 'What more do you need? The key way of doing that is economic and defence security. [They] are two sides of the same coin. That's the grand strategy.' Although using just three words to articulate the nation's strategy may seem meagre, on becoming prime minister in 1940, Winston Churchill's grand strategy for winning the war with Hitler's Germany – argued by Lawrence Freedman (2013, p 141) as to 'drag the United States in' – is only two words more.

A former civil servant, with a diplomatic rather than defence background, also offered an alternative view. To him, strategy was 'a slippery word that generates difficult discussions across the defence and security community'. He suggested the military's request for strategic direction normally meant 'give me some clarity on what my objectives are, so I can get on with it'; unfortunately, in his view 'it's never as simple as that'. Furthermore, he considered grand strategic choices to be generally of a former time and, although he conceded that 'post-Brexit, there will be grand strategic choices to be made about Britain's role in the world', he also believed 'that's a very occasional moment'.

There is a widely held view among senior officials that politicians and the military occupy very dissimilar worlds, often with different priorities, different aims and objectives, and different ways of doing business. As a result, although there are occasions when they are aligned, there are also times when they are not, and then the gearing between the two becomes severely strained. An example of positive alignment, cited by one four-star officer, was the decision in the 2015 SDSR to purchase nine Boeing P-8A Poseidon aircraft to alleviate the RAF's maritime patrol capability shortfall. In his view, this was a 'good military decision based within the logic of the overall [SDSR] package, and it was also a good political decision'. However, others suggested that the reason there was a maritime patrol capability shortfall in the first place was politically driven, and an example of misalignment between politicians and the military. One former three-star civil servant, who had been closely involved with the 2010 SDSR, believed that the then defence secretary Liam Fox brought politically motivated, pre-conceived ideas into the review, suggesting 'he had his axe out for Nimrod when he came in … he wanted to set an example to industry because he'd come in with a prejudice that the defence industry in this country was taking us for a ride'. This view was supported by an air marshal who undertook a review of maritime patrol capability during the latter stages of the SDSR, after the initial decision to cancel the Nimrod MRA4 programme had already been made. He reported that 'you couldn't afford to cancel the MPA [maritime patrol aircraft] but with four weeks to go it's too late – you can't put a £9 billion slug back into the programme, because its already constructed'. His conclusion was 'What it [a defence review] has to accept is politically driven inserts and therefore it completely skews the outcome'.

Although many of those interviewed were quick to blame politicians for misalignment problems – more than one commented that politicians confuse the urgent with the important – there were also some pragmatic observations about the relationship between politicians and the military. For example, a former civil servant recognized that 'for the politician, there's no good news in defence and security'. It was recognized by most senior officials that ultimately the decisions made in defence reviews are political and politicians will be held to account for those decisions; to that end, the defence review report is their document. One air marshal concluded, 'It's not our place to make decisions. Politicians make decisions. Ministers make decisions.' It was also recognized that planning horizons for politicians and the military are often unaligned. Several senior officials noted the pressures between Defence's longer-term focus and the government's attention on the shorter-term electoral cycle. The prevailing view was summed up by an RAF four-star officer, who noted, 'in that debate between the two, generally the political thing will win out for obvious reasons'.

For whatever reason, be it the lack of a common language or conflicting views as to the importance of the process, this misalignment of politicians and the military is seen by many defence decision makers as a major problem in the UK's present-day approach to strategy. Although the view that politicians tend to be motivated by tomorrow's headlines was prevalent, many officials also recognized that both sides needed to up their game. For example, a two-star army officer accepted that 'we need to be able to adapt and be much more agile in our strategic planning'. Another, in recognizing the complexity of the situation, perhaps more pragmatically offered: 'I can't remember the words, but I think it was Michael Howard who talked about "the idea is not to be so wrong that you can't adapt". That's the key. That's one of the wisest things anyone has ever said.'[2]

Practitioners involved in the translation of strategic direction into military capability often have markedly different views about grand strategy, particularly its relevance in today's fast-moving geopolitical environment and how it should be used to direct, or constrain, political and military activity. In the main, defence decision makers favour detailed planning, underpinned by high-level direction that is both considered and attributable. Politicians, on the other hand, tend to leave decision making to the last safe moment, and prefer to be as vague as possible about its provenance. The academic consensus that making strategy is difficult is also relevant. The current Quinquennial Review period has been considerably more turbulent than most of the Cold War; getting strategy right in the twenty-first century is not easy. Perhaps because of this, it has fallen out of favour amongst the current crop of British politicians, who are increasingly consumed by the short-term issues that tend to drive the news cycle. This is a problem for defence decision makers, as the direction they seek can either be skewed by the here and now or is sometimes not forthcoming at all. Poor and inconsistent strategic direction only increases the complexity around military capability choices.

Introducing a national security strategy

It should come as no surprise that the government's Hobbesian responsibility has been its default start point when making and undertaking strategy. Over the years, views of exactly what must be protected, and exactly what they must be protected from, have understandably changed because of shifting geopolitical risks. For example, in the 1950s, the government recognized that the world was 'poised between the hope of total peace and the fear of total war' (MoD, 1958, p 1). Moreover, it fully expected that total war would be a major interstate conflict involving the use of nuclear weapons. As a result, in the 1957 defence review, the government's strategic direction was clear that 'the overriding consideration in all military planning must be to prevent war rather than to prepare for it' (MoD, 1957, p 3). In 2021, the government still considered protecting the British people against threats to be at the heart of its defence and security policy. In the 2021 IR, its commitment to security and resilience started 'at home, by defending our people, territory, critical national infrastructure, democratic institutions and way of life – and by reducing our vulnerability to the threat from states, terrorism and serious and organized crime' (HM Government, 2021b, p 11).

UK grand strategy during the Cold War and Early Expeditionary period was primarily defence orientated. However, in the first decade of the twenty-first century, the single Cold War threat to the UK had been replaced by new threats, such as international terrorism, weapons of mass destruction, conflicts and failed states, pandemics and transnational crime. A wider understanding of the problem set and a more joined up response was considered necessary. To that end, in his first year as prime minister, Gordon Brown opted to develop a strategy for national security. The first document of its kind – *The National Security Strategy of the United Kingdom: Security in an Independent World* – was published in March 2008 (HM Government, 2008a). Richards (2012, p 14) recognized that security is 'a constructed concept for any given state at any given time', and considerations such as political realities and media interest play a major part in determining which issues are securitized. Accordingly, he argued that it was as much these factors, as it was the removal of the priority to counter the existential Soviet threat, that led to the broadening of securitized issues beyond hard power concerns and into civil and environmental dimensions. This was reflected from the outset in the UK's inaugural NSS as, following the obligatory confirmation to provide security for the nation and its citizens, the opening paragraphs confirmed that the nation now faced a 'diverse but interconnected set of threats and risks' brought about by a 'more complex and unpredictable set of [international] relationships' (HM Government, 2008a, p 3). Only 15 months after the publication of the 2008 NSS, the UK government produced an update, titled *Security for the Next Generation* (HM Government, 2009). This document ran to 112 pages (over 50 more than its predecessor), and included a foreword by the prime minister, suggesting an increasing level of attention at the very top of government.

In his study *The Risk Society at War*, Mikkel Vedby Rasmussen (2006, p 1) argues that the standards by which we measure our security have changed since the end of the Cold War. In his view, a threat[3] could be understood in a means–ends rational framework – it was measurable and finite – therefore, it could be defeated to achieve security. However, he also contends that 'today's strategic agenda is about "risks" rather than threats', and, furthermore, 'from a risk perspective a danger is much less computable than from a threat perspective' (2006, p 2). As a result, a risk scenario demands a policy proposal that details the prevention of the scenario's occurrence. Rasmussen concludes that such a policy proposal cannot achieve perfect security because, although good policy can treat, tolerate, transfer, terminate or take the opportunity of a risk (MoD, 2017e, p 13), new risks will always arise as an effect of defeating the original risk. There is no clear evidence as to whether Rasmussen's opinions influenced UK government thinking. Sandra Bell (2007, p 21), for example, suggested that the commencement of national risk management was a response to vulnerabilities brought about by our interconnected society, reinforced by the nationwide crisis triggered by the fuel price protests of 2000. However, it is known that the government had been developing a risk-based approach to emergency management since 2005, when it undertook its first National Risk Assessment (NRA) – a classified assessment of the risks facing the UK. Furthermore, the 2008 NSS was accompanied by another first – the National Risk Register (NRR) (HM Government, 2008b). What is clear, therefore, is that the UK government opted for a risk management methodology to underpin its first strategy for national security.

The final chapter of the 2008 NSS explains its risk assessment process. In short, the NRA balanced historical and scientific data with the professional judgements of experts to analyse the risks to the UK. Analysis was carried out in three stages: identification of risks; assessment of the likelihood of the risks occurring and their impact if they do; and comparison of the risks. The NRR then summarized the risks into three categories: accidents; natural events (collectively known as hazards); and malicious attacks (known as threats). In this way, the NRR set out the government's assessment of 'the likelihood and potential impact of a range of different risks that may directly affect the UK' (2008, p 3). This allowed the authors of the NSS to attempt to determine how the government would 'address and mange this diverse though interconnected set of security challenges and underlying drivers, both immediately and in the longer term, to safeguard the nation, its citizens, our prosperity and our way of life' (2008, p 3).

The basic risk management process used to underpin early NRAs and NRRs aligns reasonably well with both national and international direction on the subject (see Institute of Risk Management, 2010; and International Organisation for Standardisation, 2018). That said, the focus of the risks considered – in duration, location and type – all present problems when applied to a strategy that drives military capability decision making. Impacts and likelihoods of risks were assessed over a five-year period, which, given the planning capacity of most of the register's target audience (for example, other government departments, local government and authorities, emergency services), is a logical timeframe. However, defence decision making is informed by analysis that projects significantly further into the future, for example the MoD's Global Strategic Trends document describes a strategic concept for defence and security looking out to the middle of the twenty-first century (MoD, 2018b, p 8). A five-year risk analysis period is, therefore, not complementary. It cannot be relied upon to provide sufficient detail to inform procurement decisions, especially for military capability that may remain in service for decades.

In addition, the 2008 NRR was 'intended to capture the range of emergencies that might have a major impact on all, or significant parts of, the UK' (HM Government, 2008b, p 3). As a result, overseas concerns were specifically excluded. This is in direct contrast to the government's direction for Defence at the time – *Delivering Security in a Changing World* – which included eight assumptions around expeditionary operations, and only one concerning the safety and security of the UK (MoD, 2004, p 14). The major risk groupings within the NRR (natural events, major incidents and malicious attacks) covered only a small part of the military tasks against which defence planners were making capability-based decisions at the time. Without knowing the actual output of the NRA that influenced the 2008 NRR (the report remains classified), a complete assessment of the government's first attempt at applying risk management principles to the formulation of national strategy cannot be made. That said, simply because of its limited timeframe and UK homeland focus, the output from this approach did not provide sufficient detail to underpin a comprehensive strategy for national security.

The very first sentence of the 2008 NSS re-affirmed the commitment that 'providing security for the nation and for its citizens remains the most important responsibility of government' (HM Government, 2008a, p 3). It went on to assert that, in the post-Cold War era, the UK faced a diverse but interconnected set of threats and risks. It also confirmed the aim of the NSS was to address and manage them. The introductory chapter concluded with the acknowledgement of a single, overarching national security objective, that of 'protecting the United Kingdom and its interests, enabling its people to go about their daily lives freely and with confidence, in a more secure, stable, just and prosperous world' (2008a, p 5).

The executive summary of the 2009 NSS justified its publication by recognizing that 'the fast-changing nature of the security challenges …

required an ongoing evaluation and adaption of our approach [to national security]' (HM Government, 2009, p 5). It also fulfilled a previous commitment to present regular updates of the strategy to parliament and the public. It re-affirmed the single national security objective from the 2008 NSS, but also re-prioritized the extant risks and introduced new ones: for example, maritime security and cyber security. In addition, it underpinned the government's approach to national security through a new national strategic framework, which focused UK actions on threat drivers (the why), threat actors (the who and the what), and threat domains (the how) (2009, p 31).

The simplicity of a single objective for national security is appealing, although there is always the danger of constructing it in such a broad manner that it becomes meaningless. The attempt in the 2008 NSS did provide a recognizable goal, albeit the subjective nature of the language used made it a very wide goal that would be difficult to miss. In addition, the loose language around the aim of the strategy is unhelpful: simply detailing the threats and risks facing a nation does not constitute a national strategy. However, as Gray (2010, p 167) points out, strategy links ends, ways and means. Although not obviously signposted, the document did have an end,[4] and, in its chapters on guiding principles and the UK's response, it did attempt to articulate ways and means.[5] In addition, through the medium of security challenges, that is the threats and risks, it attempted to join them all up. Notwithstanding this, it made no attempt to prioritize, even though the most cursory analysis of the risks identified would suggest a dearth of resources to underpin the means. It is difficult to align either the construct or the contents of the document with any of the definitions of strategy considered earlier in this chapter, but that does not necessarily make it unfit for purpose. The 2008 NSS explicitly stated that the government's view of national security had expanded beyond protection from attacks by other states; furthermore, it saw the need to bring together objectives and plans from all departments, agencies and forces to protect it. Accordingly, the consequence of this new approach could only be less focus on the roles and responsibilities of the armed forces and their military capability.

The 2009 NSS did not benefit from an update of the NRR. It clearly recognized, however, that the world had changed in the 15 months since its predecessor had been released. For example, it devoted two complete pages to an assessment of the implications of the 2008 global economic downturn. This swift acknowledgement of change that affected national security justified, in part, the requirement to create and regularly update the strategy. Moreover, the focus of the strategy was expanded to consider a 20-year horizon, and the new national strategic framework provided a mechanism for government thinking on national security to keep pace with the rapidly evolving geopolitical situation. That said, it did not address the prioritization concerns from the 2008 document and the need for an executive summary suggests that it was too large and unwieldy to be regularly referred to by either decision makers or defence planners.

Sharon Caudle and Stephan De Spiegeleire (2010, p 19) considered the strategies produced by the Labour government in 2008 and 2009 to be 'a step in the right direction in addressing the strategic environment of contemporary times'. As a first attempt at tackling national security through the medium of risk management, the 2008 NSS was a reasonable attempt, despite its limited timeline, inward-looking focus and lack of prioritization. The 2009 NSS resolved the limited timeline issue and offered a greater global focus, although it too overlooked the need to prioritize. However, by expanding into accidents and natural events, both documents offered less direction on military matters than the MoD might have hoped. Furthermore, evidence suggests that, probably as a result, it was not considered to be a significant influence on defence planning. Specifically, the MoD's unclassified defence plan for 2008–2012, completed in June 2008, did not contain a single reference to the NSS, published only three months earlier. Instead, it drew upon requirements detailed in a classified document, *Defence Strategic Guidance*, and included over 20 references to the 2007 Comprehensive Spending Review (CSR) (MoD, 2008a). The most significant influence on defence decision makers appears to have been their department's financial settlement, rather than a macro-level, broadly targeted and cross-government strategy document. To that end, while the government's attempt to articulate a more holistic strategy for national security to meet the growing post-Cold War security challenges was clearly a step in the right direction, its early efforts had little impact on military capability decision making.

The 2010 SDSR was the first defence review to take place in conjunction with the development of an NSS. Like the 2008 and 2009 strategies, the 2010 NSS was constructed around a risk management methodology. However, there were some noticeable differences. The NSSs published under the Labour government were both aligned to the 2008 NRR and its underpinning NRA; however, the new government chose to undertake a separate National *Security* Risk Assessment [italics added] (NSRA) to prioritize 'all major disruptive risks to our national interest, which are of sufficient scale or impact so as to require action from government and/ or which have an ideological, international or political dimension' (HM Government, 2010c, p 37). Cornish and Dorman (2012, p 214) believed that the 2010 NSS's risk management approach was a considerable improvement on what had gone before, in that it was able to identify and prioritize threats and challenges to the UK and its interests, and then use the outcome as the basis for government decision making and response. The JCNSS (2012a, p 11) also reinforced the point that risk management would not always predict the next big problem; therefore, continual horizon-scanning remained essential, with resources available to deal with unpredicted risks as they emerge.

Commissioning the NSRA also allowed the 2010 NSS to be de-coupled from the NRR, which remained focused on short-term (within five years) risks internal to the UK. The new edition of the NRR was also re-titled *The National Risk Register of Civil Emergencies* (HM Government, 2010b). While this change may seem innocuous, it allowed the strategy to encompass all aspects of national security, and enabled a prioritization system for the risks identified. Furthermore, by doing so, it also introduced a mechanism to allow choices to be made, which aligns with Strachan's (2008, p 8) assertion that 'strategy is an exercise in choice and often an exercise in making hard choices'. In managing an equipment programme that is always resource constrained, prioritization at the political level is essential to ensure that senior officers within Defence have sufficient direction to make the right military capability decisions one level down.

The 2010 NSS was a considerably slimmer document than its immediate predecessor, running to 37 pages versus 112. It concentrated on the strategic context and risks to UK security. In its own words, it identified the ends against which the 2010 SDSR would articulate the ways and means. It defined the UK's strategy for national security in a single sentence: 'to use all of our national capabilities to build Britain's prosperity, extend our nation's influence in the world and strengthen our security' (HM Government, 2010b, p 9). This assertion was supported by two complementary strategic objectives: 'ensuring a secure and resilient UK' and 'shaping a stable world' (2010b, p 22). The 2010 NSS also recognized that UK defence and security capability decision making should be driven by a reappraisal of foreign policy, the identification of risks faced and a judgement of the role the country should play in the world. This was followed up with the assertion that the National Security Council (NSC) had reached the clear conclusion that 'Britain's national interest requires us to reject any notion of the shrinkage of our influence' (2010b, p 11). However, that statement was considered wholly unrealistic by both the JCNSS and the HCDC. The JCNSS suggested that the UK needed to plan for a changing and more partnership-dependent role in the world, particularly when considered with the NSS's recognition of 'the rise of new global powers, shifts in the centres of economic activity, and reduced resources in the UK' (JCNSS, 2012a, p 13). HCDC members simply did not believe the UK could maintain its influence while reducing departmental budgets at the MoD and the Foreign and Commonwealth Office (FCO) (HCDC, 2011a, p 33). This view from Westminster was strongly backed up by former Royal Marine lieutenant general Robert Fry (2014, p 28), who observed that 'The NSS ... observed a policy of no strategic shrinkage. The authors of the strategy may have kept a straight face when it was written in 2010, but the subsequent evisceration of the British military's capability now makes such assertions risible.'

Overall, the document addressed its immediate predecessor's shortfalls around limited timeline, inward-looking focus and lack of prioritization. Moreover, by linking itself to the SDSR through the medium of ends, ways and means, it ensured its relevance to defence decision makers. Finally, its commitment to review the NSRA every two years (HM Government, 2010b, p 37), and produce a new NSS and SDSR every five years (2010b, p 11), went some way to addressing many of the recurring criticisms of the unstructured and inconsistent way UK defence reviews have traditionally been carried out (see, for example, Clarke, 2008; Dorman, 2010; and Cornish and Dorman, 2010).

Although the analysis above suggests that the 2010 NSS was a considerable improvement on its predecessors and had a positive impact on the SDSR, it did not entirely escape criticism in the secondary literature. Mark Phillips (2012, p 32) believed that no real consideration was given as to how non-traditional departments and agencies could have contributed to the strategy, specifically the Ministry of Justice and the Department for Education. Of more relevance, he also questioned the sequencing of the NSS, in relation to the SDSR, and posited that an NSS should be published in advance of an SDSR to provide the necessary guidance for the staff involved in drafting the latter. Furthermore, he suggested that the tribalism and inter-service rivalry seen during the development of the SDSR was caused because the service chiefs were waiting for the following, broad direction that an early NSS should have provided:

[An NSS] clearly defines and prioritises the UK's non-discretionary national interests for security and prosperity, and the risks to them, clarifies non-discretionary tasks that are a political priority, and sets a doctrine or concept that breaks down barriers and integrates the defence and security departments, focusing on what the government wants to achieve and designing solutions for this. (Phillips, 2012, p 32)

The JCNSS also expressed a view over timings for the NSS, although it was more concerned with the relationship with the government's CSR. It considered the order in which the NSS, SDSR and CSR were undertaken not to be particularly significant; instead, what it believed crucial was that all three must be able to influence each other (JCNSS, 2012a, p 8).

While the 2010 NSS was, in many ways, an improvement on the two previous iterations of a strategy for national security, its authors could not resist using it as a platform to score political points over the previous Labour administration. In the four pages of the *Forward* section alone, the new prime minister and deputy prime minister included no fewer than six detrimental references to their political opponents. Phrases such as 'Nowhere has the legacy we inherited been more challenging than in the state of the defence budget our predecessors left behind' (HM Government, 2010b, p 5) and 'The Strategic Defence and Security Review will set out how we intend to sort out the mess we inherited' (2010b, p 6) add nothing to the strategy. They do, however, provide a clear touchstone to the political manoeuvring that regularly appears as a significant factor in the formulation of defence reviews and often skews the articulation of strategic direction to defence decision makers.

The decision to amalgamate the 2015 NSS and SDSR in a single command paper was logical in some respects, although it does make a comparison of the 2015 and 2010 version of the NSS more challenging. As a positive, there was a degree of repetition in the 2010 NSS and SDSR command papers, particularly regarding the high-level direction and guidance that was solved through merging. However, by consigning outcomes of the SDSR to one of three chapters that covered each of the national security objectives in turn, the document gave the impression that specific ways and means aligned with only one of the strategy's ends, whereas the reality in any strategy is that the linkage between ends, ways and means is a many-to-many relationship. As part of his evidence to the JCNSS in January 2014, prime minister David Cameron conceded that the NSS needed a refresh but stopped short of advocating a complete overhaul. This view was not shared by the committee. It believed that 'The rapidly changing world demonstrates the need for a thorough revisit of the NSS even if fundamental assumptions remain the same' (JCNSS, 2015, pp 10–11). Cameron's view prevailed and the new NSS was unsurprisingly close in content to its predecessor.

At the highest-level, the 2015 NSS adopted a vision, values and approach construct, which, although a departure from its immediate predecessor, did borrow methodologies used in previous iterations. For example, the 2009 NSS had a vision (HM Government, 2009, p 9), and the 2008 version underpinned its approach in a set of core values (HM Government, 2008a, p 6). A cynical commentator might suggest that, although episodically produced government documents need to have a fresh look and feel, there are only a finite number of frameworks that can be used, and what goes around inevitably comes around. The 2015 vision for a 'secure and prosperous United Kingdom, with global reach and influence' (HM Government, 2015, p 9) was not a great departure from the 2010 NSS's single sentence strategy 'to use all of our national capabilities to build Britain's prosperity, extend our nations influence in the world and strengthen our security' (HM Government, 2010b, p 9). Supporting the 2015 vision were three, high-level, enduring and mutually supporting national security objectives, which were built around the straplines: protect our people; project our global influence;

and promote our prosperity (HM Government, 2015, pp 11–12). The first two objectives aligned very closely with the two security objectives from 2010 (HM Government, 2010b, p 22), whereas the third recognized the government's more overt policy of supporting UK industry. This was further reinforced two years later in a refresh of its defence industrial policy (MoD, 2017d) and the publication of an international defence engagement strategy (MoD and FCO, 2017).

The 2015 NSS retained the same risk-based approach as its predecessor, underpinned by an updated NSRA, which followed the original assessment in 2010 and a refresh in 2012 (HM Government, 2015, p 85). Predictably there were many overlaps between the 2010 and 2015 risks, although the number of tier one and two risks had both increased in 2015. Finally, as part of a single document, the 2015 NSS was leaner than the 2010 version. As Jon Lunn and Eleanor Scarnell (2015, p 13) noted, it contained less explanation of the methodology used and omitted completely the detail of the eight cross-cutting national security tasks and their associated detailed planning guidelines. One consequence of the publication of a single report in 2015 was a dearth of academic scrutiny of the NSS element of the review. Lunn and Scarnell (2015, p 13) suggested that, despite better integration between the overarching strategy and specific policy- and capability-related actions than there was in 2010, 'discussion of the 2015 document … has been conducted almost entirely in terms of policies and capabilities (the SDSR element)'.

An examination of the secondary literature confirms that the amalgamation of the NSS and SDSR resulted in a noticeable reduction in the scrutiny of the review's underpinning strategy when compared with the aftermath of the review process in 2010. This may be partly because of the similarities between the new strategy and its predecessor, so little new commentary was considered necessary. It may also be that the EU referendum, the 2017 general election and subsequent NSCR simply diverted attention elsewhere. Lunn and Scarnell (2015, p 13) considered the 2015 document 'more convincingly a "whole-of-government" document than were its two 2010 predecessors'; however, the single document approach certainly did not solve Phillips' sequencing problem highlighted earlier. The JCNSS questioned whether the merger was the product of a joined-up process where strategy was combined with decisions on investments and capabilities. It also suggested that the 2015 SDSR did not meet its primary goal of setting out what the UK wants to achieve, and how it intends to achieve it. Overall, the JCNSS was critical of many aspects of the 2015 SDSR. By contrast, however, many defence decision makers, especially those in single service appointments, considered its outcomes to be very positive. This highlights a question that will require further consideration in Chapter 5, namely what outcomes are sought from a defence review, and by whom?

In a 2016 JCNSS evidence session, the then NSA, Mark Lyall Grant, stated that it would be taken as a sign of success if the 2015 NSS and SDSR did not have to be updated before 2020 (JCNSS, 2016b, pp 16–17). However, he also confirmed that reviewing both was an option if 'something absolutely fundamental changes' (JCNSS, 2016a, p 8). On 20 February 2016, David Cameron announced that a referendum on membership of the EU would be held in the UK on 23 June 2016 (BBC, 2016). The subsequent decision of the UK electorate to leave the EU certainly qualified as Grant's fundamental change. In the immediate aftermath of the referendum, academic commentary on how Brexit would affect defence and security was pessimistic (see, for example, Street and Reeve, 2016, p 6; and Young, 2016, pp 7–8). The two most significant factors initially identified were the potential financial consequences, which are covered in Chapter 6, and the effect on the UK's place in the world.

The impact of the EU referendum result on UK's international standing are likely to be felt long into the future. When the result was announced, the government moved quickly to confirm the UK would not be withdrawing from the world stage (GOV.UK, 2016). However, although the initial academic consensus was that leaving the EU would have no direct effect on the UK's permanent membership of the United Nations (UN) Security Council (Lang, 2016, p 2), subsequent concerns were raised that its influence was waning (Gifkin et al, 2018). In addition, Malcolm Chalmers suggested that exit from the EU would 'diminish UK influence in NATO [North Atlantic Treaty Organization] as one of the things it has brought to NATO is its ability to bring along other European member states' (Chalmers, cited by Borger, 2016).

In a pre-EU referendum briefing paper, Chalmers (2016c, p 2) also posited that a UK decision to leave the EU would be as significant a shift in national strategy as the country's decision to withdraw from bases East of Suez in the late 1960s. He believed that, in these circumstances, current plans for defence spending over the next decade might have to be revisited (2016c, p 7). Furthermore, it would be appropriate for the government to conduct another SDSR, notwithstanding the fact that the 2015 SDSR had only been completed eight months previously (2016c, p 11). Although not advocating the same, Trevor Taylor (2016a) conceded that the referendum result had left the 2015 SDSR in disarray. As we know, another SDSR was not forthcoming, even though the government did embark on two further examinations of its defence and security policy following the 2017 general election (the NSCR and the MDP, both of which took place during 2017 and 2018). Neither the NSCR nor the MDP introduced any major changes to defence policy, but they both generated significant upheaval within Whitehall, and especially within MoD head office. When reviews of this kind are taking place, much of the routine decision making around the development of military capability is put on hold pending their outcome. This can have a major impact on the front line, with delays or sometimes even cancellations to new delivery or capability upgrades. That said, the effect of long periods of policy review on military capability decision making is seldom part of the political calculus.

On the positive side, the NSCR did introduce a new national security doctrine – the Fusion Doctrine. It stated that Fusion Doctrine would be used 'to improve our collective approach to national security' and stated its principle as 'to deploy security, economic and influence capabilities to promote and protect our national security economic and influence goals' (HM Government, 2018, p 3). It also confirmed the NSC would take decisions about strategic prioritization to inform departmental business plans. The key explanatory paragraph is reproduced in full here:

> For each of its priorities, the NSC will consider UK interests and objectives, the situation we face and the outlook, and then the wider national or international strategy to decide how to make a catalytic contribution, considering our full range of capabilities. The NSC's ambition must match the resources committed so that we pursue realistic objectives and prioritize scarce resources where they can make the most difference as part of our collective approach. Rigorous implementation is also essential. (HM Government, 2018, p 3)

What is clear over the last three years is that the government has doubled down on its Global Britain vision (see, for example, GOV.UK, 2019b; and GOV.UK, 2020d). Even though the aspirations of Global Britain are questioned more and more (see, for example, Kellner, 2021; McGuire, 2021; and Shapiro and Witney, 2021), Boris Johnson clearly still saw it as the cornerstone of a new chapter in the nation's history and fundamental to making the UK and 'open and democratic societ[y] … [that is] match-fit for a more competitive world' (HM Government, 2021b, p 3). What remains unclear is how this vision of Global Britain will affect military capability choices.

The most recent update to UK national strategy is provided in the 2021 IR. From the outset, the Integrated Review was promoted by the government as being a far more wide-ranging exercise than the previous two SDSRs of the Quinquennial Review period. It was designed to re-examine the UK's foreign policy, defence, security and international development priorities and objectives, and encompass all aspects of the UK's place in the world (GOV.UK, 2020c). In his critique of the 2021 IR, Paul Cornish suggested that the following main themes of the Integrated Review linked directly to the government's Global Britain idea:

- The UK's commitment to European security is 'unequivocal', not least through NATO and various bilateral defence arrangements.
- The rules-based international system (the mechanism of international politics formerly known as order) is 'no longer sufficient' and will require the UK and others to 'reinforce' its 'architecture'.
- Liberal democracies should become more robust, resilient and self-confident, demonstrating the 'benefits of openness' to the rest of the world. But they can only do so if they first put 'the interests and values' of their own populace 'at the heart of everything we do'.
- The most important interests of the British people are sovereignty, security and prosperity. (Cornish, 2021, pp 6–7)

Cornish also argues that the politics of security and defence are becoming less and less straightforward, and, as a result, the design and articulation of national strategy is not a simple undertaking. Nevertheless, he believes the review 'gives the impression of having been written inside an echo chamber, where the premises of an argument are not recognised as such but as self-evident "facts" which then go unchallenged'. He concludes that the resultant national strategy is incoherent (2021, p 16).

In July 2021, the Centre for Defence Studies at King's College London published a series of essays that considered the question: *The Integrated Review in Context: A Strategy Fit for the 2020s?* (Devanny and Gearson, 2021a). Unsurprisingly, the views offered by its authors were mixed. John Sawyers (2021, p 23) described the review as 'a credible effort to chart a way forward for the UK in the new, more contested geopolitical environment'. He also believed it put 'some intellectual structure around the bumper sticker of Global Britain'. Similarly positive, Alexander Downer (2021, p 53) recognized that a characteristic of good governments is they have a strategic plan and manage events within it. In that vein, he applauded the 2021 IR for developing a medium-term plan for the UK's international engagement, as well as identifying international trends, spelling out where the UK has specific strengths and leading capacity and outlining a plan for implementing a strategy for the future. Conversely, the former NSA and coordinator of the 2010 NSS, Peter Ricketts (2021b, pp 13–14), asked some serious questions of the 2021 IR. While he recognized it has many strengths, he questioned whether the review succeeds in turning the Global Britain slogan into a new national strategy. In answering his own question, he applies John Lewis Gaddis's definition of strategy: 'the alignment of potentially unlimited aspirations with necessarily limited capabilities' (Gaddis, cited by Rickets, 2021b, p 13). Measured against that yardstick, Ricketts posits that the Integrated Review marks an important first step but falls well short of a fully rounded strategy for post-Brexit Britain. Specifically, he takes issue with the review's total lack of prioritization and its inability to make choices. The 2021 IR completely abandoned the risk assessment approach that underpinned both the 2010 and 2015 SDSRs. More significantly it was not replaced by any other priority setting methodology. Ricketts argues that the review sets out bold aspirations for Britain to play a leadership role in almost every area of international cooperation but fails to recognize that the nation's resources – 'whether of people, budgets or ministerial energies' – are limited. He rightly argues that, in the end, good strategy comes down to making choices, but none are contained within the 2021 IR report. His conclusion, therefore, is the Integrated Review does not provide a useful guide to resource allocation.

Although its evidence and engagement annex refers to a strategy development process (HM Government, 2021b, p 106) the 2021 IR does not include the basic components of a strategy. According to Gray (2013, p 2), at its simplest, strategy can be defined as 'the direction and use made of means by chosen ways in order to achieve desired ends'. The 2021 IR details the following four objectives within its strategic framework: sustaining strategic advantage through science and technology; shaping the international order in the future; strengthening security and defence at home and overseas; and building resilience at home and overseas (HM Government, 2021b, p 21). These objectives could be interpreted as the Integrated Review's ends. There are, however, no strategic concepts or courses of action in the document to explain how these ends are to be accomplished. In other words, there are no ways. In addition, there is no explanation of what specific resources are to be used in applying the strategic concepts to meet the objectives. There are no means either. Finally, there is no explanation of the gap between what is to be achieved and the concepts and resources available to achieve the objectives, so no recognition of risk. To that end, the 2021 IR is not a coherent national strategy. It does, however, point to significant amounts of strategic jam tomorrow. For instance, before the end of 2021, it promised a new cyber strategy (HM Government, 2021b, p 41), a new national space strategy (2021b, p 58), and a new national resilience strategy (2021b, p 88). At the time of writing, only the national space strategy had been released (HM Government, 2021c). A new international development strategy is promised in 2022 (HM Government, 2021b, p 46), and there are numerous references to other, standalone strategies (for example, a national data strategy, a defence AI strategy, and a UK border strategy). What is missing from this list is a strategy for national security. Indeed, the only reference included in the 2021 IR simply confirms the NSC remains 'the key formal mechanism through which ministers collectively set National Security Strategy and policy, and oversee implementation' (2021b, p 97). It could be concluded that the current government now longer sees the need to recognize and maintain a publicly accessible national strategy. It may still be somewhat premature to take the 2021 IR to task, after all, it has generated a reasonable degree of positive comment within the defence academic community. That said, and as my analysis in the next two chapters will make clear, when considering the translation of strategic direction into military capability, the 2021 IR and its supporting DCP both fall short in several areas.

Aligning strategy and capability

An understanding of how national strategy is developed provides good context for the four-step translation of strategic direction into military capability model introduced in Chapter 1. It is, however, equally important to examine if, and how well, the military capability acquired and maintained by the armed forces meets the needs of defence policy. In other words, are the military capabilities chosen by defence decision makers aligned to both the strategic direction provided by the government and the threats articulated in national strategy?

Most senior officials interviewed during my research offered an opinion on whether extant military capability was suitably aligned to the strategic direction that defence decision makers received from the government. Not unexpectedly, a range of views were expressed. In broad terms, those responsible for the procurement of capability, either the deciders within the single services or the providers in defence's delivery agents,[6] were generally positive, with those elsewhere less so. The following view from an RN four-star officer was typical of the deciders: 'There is a gap [in the alignment of capability to strategic direction]. It's not perfect [but] I don't think the gap is any bigger at the moment than it's been.' By contrast, an army general, working in MoD head office at the time of his interview, was unequivocal: 'Do we actually have our current and planned capability aligned to the strategic direction that's coming down? The answer to that is no.' He went on to confirm that in many respects UK military capability was world-beating but within quite narrowly defined parameters. Moreover, in pursuing ground-breaking capabilities across the traditional domains of maritime, land and air, he argued that Defence was not investing sufficiently in novel technologies in the new domains of space and cyberspace, where he considered the UK was strategically vulnerable.

Accepted capability gaps, unrealistic political ambition, finite resources and the limited opportunity to veer and haul within the department's budget were all reasons given for the disparity between strategic direction and the extant force structure. Another four-star navy officer suggested that the reality of operations drives capability usage, which is regularly at odds with the original strategic direction for what kind of armed forces a government thought it wanted. He also considered that, in the current geopolitical climate, the pace of these revised requirements would invariably outstrip the reaction time of the procurement pipeline, against which the new capability was being delivered. Furthermore, the MoD simply did not have the almost limitless funding and programming headroom required regularly to change multi-billion and multi-year procurement programmes. He suggested the solution was to develop a constant ability to adjust existing and near-future capability to map onto changed strategic environments and concepts for the use of military power, whilst, at the same time, trying to draw the lessons from that for future capability. He also suggested this should be deliverable by creating the capacity to reset capability rapidly in all future acquisition programmes. However, this approach is not straightforward. In some instances, the ability of defence decision makers to influence capability development is limited, for example in a multi-national programme like the F-35 Lighting II aircraft. In others, national industrial capacity may simply be unable to react in the timescales required.

The views stated above were all from military officers or MoD civil servants. However, one former civil servant, whose 40-year career was spent entirely as a member of the diplomatic service, had a different opinion. He questioned the fundamental proposition that strategy drives capability, arguing instead that capability was the result of ad hoc decisions taken over 20 or 30 years, accreted together, and which are continuing to be taken. His example to support this assertion was the carrier strike group, the UK's newly acquired maritime power projection capability built around the RN's two Queen Elizabeth Class aircraft carriers (RN, 2019b), which undertook its maiden operational deployment in 2021 (GOV.UK, 2021a):

> [Carrier strike] was a capability "dans tous les azimuts" as the French would say – you know, capable of going in any direction – rather than a response to a strategic need. I guess it's always been thus and will always be thus. In war time, you have operational requirements and so on. In peace time, it's incremental adjustments to your stock of capability – not strategy. So, it's muddle through.

Given the nation's acceptance of the UN principle 'to refrain ... from the threat or use of force against the territorial integrity or political independence of any state' (UN, 1945, p 3), focusing on external threats and aligning military capability to them is a logical, macro-level approach for the UK to take to defence planning. To that end, a key focus of my research involved the recognition of current and future threats and the matching of capability choices to them.

Of the senior officials who expressed an opinion about the UK's ability to recognise current and future threats, most were positive. That said, there was a general acceptance that the present-day threat environment was both complex and subject to rapid change. One two-star officer offered a different view, suggesting 'we've probably not articulated well enough the threat the nation faces'. However, for various reasons, none of the interviewees were comfortable with how adequately UK military capability was aligned to those recognized current and future threats.

At one end of the scale was the view, offered by a three-star general, that aligning capability to threats was 'about getting it as least wrong as possible', or as another senior officer even more pessimistically put it, 'We're trying to do an impossible task, to predict the future and structure ourselves against [it]'. An air marshal with considerable procurement experience offered a pragmatic view:

> '[B]ecause of the fluidity of the business that we're in, the potentially unforeseen nature of threats changing and expanding, we're never going to get to the point where our capability is fully aligned [to the current and future threats we face]. It's a case of getting it to an acceptable level and veering and hauling from there.'

Another concern raised was the inconsistent application of threat-related assumptions when making capability choices. One three-star officer applauded the decision to procure the F-35 Lighting II aircraft, suggesting it was based on a recognition that every future environment would be contested and that necessitated the best survivability Defence could afford. However, he went on to point out that the same approach to survivability had not influenced other procurement decisions, questioning 'the assumptions around that contested environment have not played out across the rest of Defence. How can that be?'

The flexibility to adjust existing and near-future capability, explored earlier in this section, was seen by some of the more operationally experienced interviewees as the best way to counter the fluidity of the contemporary threat-based environment. Although that was often recognized as a difficult ask, especially in collaborative programmes where the UK was not the dominant partner, several success stories were highlighted. For example, one RAF four-star officer offered the following:

> 'The Tornado force [has been] continuously committed to operations for 27 years now. Has done those operations against the massed Iraqi forces of 1991. Done it in a more limited way in support of UN resolutions through the '90s, in almost a rerun in 2003. Then counter insurgency there and in Afghanistan. Then in Libya something different again. Kosovo something different again. Now, in Iraq and Syria something different again. This is essentially a capability in a force structure, which was designed in the '70s, implemented in the '80s and has delivered for 27 years from 1990–91 onwards. It's done alright.

Something must not be too bad in our processes. It is absolutely the case that the Tornado, if you use that as an example, was designed for something different but it had the flexibility in the platform, in the people and the conceptual thinking to evolve.'

How has the UK's approach to national strategy affected military capability decisions?

The enduring theme of UK defence policy during the Cold War was prevention of war with the Soviet Union through deterrence. Viewed through a strategic lens, this was the nation's desired end. What the armed forces needed to accomplish prior to 1990 was readily identifiable, agreed by successive governments throughout the period, and did not change. However, although this objective was static, how it should best be achieved – the ways – and the specific resources to be used – the means – were not. Moreover, the decisions made as to how to achieve this end, and with what resources, were subject to external factors, these being the events and influences discussed in the problem space section in Chapter 1. To summarize, throughout the Cold War, in the 'ends equals ways plus means' trinomial, the ends were fixed but the ways and means were variable. This presented a complex, but manageable, challenge for defence decision makers.

To use a modern vernacular, the fall of the Berlin Wall in 1989 was a game-changer. Within a few short years, as Robert Self (2010, p 171) observed, 'The bipolar tensions of the Cold War which had so decisively shaped British policy objectives for over 40 years were now a thing of the past'. What the armed forces needed to accomplish during the Early Expeditionary period was no longer easily identifiable. They were also subject to change over time: change that was driven not only by persistent geopolitical churn, but also by the views and aspirations of successive governments. This meant the UK's strategic end was no longer fixed and, crucially, strategic decision making was now subject to external factors that had only impacted on ways and means during the Cold War. This significantly altered the Early Expeditionary period's 'ends equals ways plus means' trinomial. The introduction of variables to the left-hand side of the equation greatly increased the complexity on the right-hand side. The possibility of more than one end increased the number of ways and means that had to be considered, as well as the interaction between then, to balance the equation. The resultant calculation that faced defence decision makers had become substantially more complex, to the point of being potentially unsolvable.

Many commentators agree that the geopolitical backdrop of the Quinquennial Review period has become ever more complex (see, for example Jessett et al, 2020, pp 7–8; and Allen, 2020, p 15). In its first annual report on the 2015 NSS and SDSR, the government confirmed:

We are witnessing the resurgence of state-based threats – as displayed most obviously by Russia's actions in Syria and Ukraine; terrorism and extremism threaten our security; cyber-attacks are on the increase from both state and non-state actors, and we face renewed challenges to the rules-based international order that provides the bedrock of our security. (HM Government, 2016, p 3)

This intensification was recognized by the JCNSS (2018, p 19) who confirmed there had been 'major changes to the wider security environment' between the publication of the SDSR report, in November 2015, and the commissioning of the NSCR, in July 2017. Amid the COVID-19 pandemic, the then CDS, General Nick Carter, offered the following thoughts on the strategic context to the HCDC:

[E]ven before COVID-19, I would have described the strategic context as being dynamic, complex and with the defining condition being instability. It has become a much more competitive playing field … We see a more assertive Russian threat, and we see the challenge of China very vividly. Then there are other players, whether Iran or North Korea, who cause us to question what is happening. All of that is overlaid by the threat from terrorism, and radical extremism is not going anywhere; indeed, in places – in parts of the world – it is growing. On top of all that, the political context of nationalism and populism has an effect on whether or not one is able to get together the international contributions you need to be able to do something about it. (HCDC, 2020b, p 2)

The conclusion that can be drawn from this may be obvious but, nevertheless, still requires stating. Developing national strategy is more challenging today than it was during the Cold War and Early Expeditionary period. Moreover, the complexity that surrounds it is likely to endure for the foreseeable future. As a recently retired senior civil servant suggested:

'It's so much easier … to develop a grand strategy when the threat is clear and unitary. But at the moment, the risks and threats are seen to be so multifaceted, whether it's resurgent Russia, whether it's "so called" ISIS, whether it's migration, whether it's climate change. It's quite difficult.'

Given the differing opinions of exactly what strategy at the national level involves, it is unsurprising that recent judgement of the UK's ability to undertake it is mixed. On the one hand, there is the view that the UK has maintained a grand strategy, on which UK foreign and security policy has been based for the last 70 years. Chalmers (2015a, p 1) argued that, since the formation of NATO in 1949, the UK's strategy at the national level has 'consistently been based on a permanent alliance and economic partnership with fellow democracies in the United States (US) and Western Europe, and on support for the rules-based international order created after 1945'. On the other, there is the blunt view held by Porter (2010, p 6) that 'the UK doesn't do strategy coherently'. This is supported by Newton et al (2010, p 44), who advanced that 'the problem with the UK "debate" on strategy … is that for many observers there does not seem to be one'. These views are shared by the House of Commons Public Accounts Committee (HC PAC). In its 2010 report *Who does UK National Strategy?*, it stated that the overwhelming view from its witnesses 'was that the UK is not good at making National Strategy and there is little sense of national direction or purpose' (2010, pp 27–8).

Prior to the 2021 IR, the UK's approach to strategy during the Quinquennial Review period was to broaden its thinking to include wider security issues, and then tackle those issues through a risk management methodology. This was reflected in the introduction, and subsequent development, of a strategy for national security. In his critique of the 2010 NSS, Michael Clarke was positive in his assessment that this process 'represents a whole of government approach to everything that can be deemed a security threat'. However, he went on to assert:

> The problem with it [NSS 2010], as it presently stands, is that it is not really a strategy as such, but a methodology for a strategy. It does not make hard choices between real things – which is what strategists have to do. It creates all the right boxes and describes how we should fit them together – who should lead in this or that area, who else would be involved, and so on – but it doesn't put anything specific into the boxes. (Clarke, 2010)

This assessment is equally valid for the 2015 NSS and confirms the government's preference for adaptability and flexibility in its decision making regarding the allocation of finite military capability. The NSS became a strategic framework, based on a judgement of extant risk, from which a decision could be generated, when required, in response to a specific situation. This was recognized at the highest political level. For example, when asked by a member of the JCNSS if the NSS could be summed up by saying 'we will do what we can that looks sensible at the time, with rather limited resources', Oliver Letwin, the then minister of state for government policy, responded 'That is not a bad description' (JCNSS, 2012a, p 15). Notwithstanding the differing academic assessments of the UK's post-Cold War record on making and undertaking strategy, recent governments have at least made public their approaches to national strategy. It is also clear, however, that these approaches are at best guidelines and do not necessarily survive contact with emerging geopolitical realities. According to Peter Ricketts, this is not unexpected:

> In democracies, all aspects of national security are permanently contested in the rough and tumble of the political process. Governments have to win public support for their approach, and then defend their policies against all comers. Published strategy papers are above all documents of political advocacy, not of dispassionate analysis. They are often couched at a safe level of generality. (Ricketts, 2021, p 125)

Ultimately, the government of the day sees national strategy as simply another tool in its political toolbox, which can be adjusted to fit the circumstances of the time. While this may be at odds with the scholarly view of strategy, it is the reality of the current political construct within the UK. It could, for example, be argued that the risk methodology process, which underpinned all four previous NSSs, was deliberately omitted from the 2021 IR to make it more difficult to hold the government to account if, and when, a declared risk materializes in the future. Boris Johnson's government was severely criticized over its lack of preparedness when the COVID-19 pandemic struck (BBC, 2021), particularly as a result of inadequate stockpiles of personal protective equipment, because 'a major human health crisis' was one of the five tier one risks it had inherited from the 2015 SDSR (HM Government, 2015, p 87). No risk methodology means no prioritized list of risks, which removes a potential stick to beat the government were it to fall short again in the future. While the current lack of recognition and prioritization of risk could be considered a fundamental gap in strategic planning, it proves that UK governments' approach to strategy is politically orientated, and national strategy is not necessarily considered a long-term or constant undertaking.

Overall, this analysis presents a mixed view of how the UK's approach to grand or national strategy has affected military capability choices. On the one hand, it could be argued that successive governments have recognized the increasing challenge of developing national strategy since the end of the Cold War and responded with a sophisticated risk methodology approach to strategy making, which has been well honed over the last decade. Of course, that argument does not survive contact with the 2021 IR. On the other, Michael Clarke's theory that NSSs are no more than a methodology for a strategy has merit. By their own admission, politicians react late to short-term imperatives and, in the main, are interested in little beyond the five-year parliamentary lifetime. This does not align with the long-term nature of the defence acquisition cycle, particularly the in-service period that can run into decades. The result is often scant and inconsistent strategic direction that puts the onus on defence decision makers to make all but the highest profile, high-level military capability choices. While defence decision makers may like the freedom of manoeuvre of this approach, its lack of both ownership and attention to detail at the political level in no way guarantees that the right capability is chosen to meet the future threats that the UK armed forces may end up having to face.

4

Defence Roles, Missions and Tasks

Most studies into post-Second World War UK defence matters spend at least some time examining comparisons between what the armed forces had and currently have in terms of manpower and equipment. Considering the substantial reductions that have occurred during this period, that is unsurprising. As an example, when Duncan Sandys was deliberating on the contraction of the armed forces in 1957, the combined size of the three services was approximately 690,000 (MoD, 1957, p 7). The start point for the 2021 IR was a full-time trained strength of 135,444 (Dempsey, 2021, p 5). For a statistic closer to home, when I left regular service in 2019, the RAF had an active fast jet fleet of 121 aircraft (GOV.UK, 2020e). When I joined 35 years earlier, it had more fighters and bombers than that just based in Lincolnshire (Mason, 1982, pp 142–3). Of course, no-one is suggesting the English Electric Lightning, which was the RAF's first supersonic jet fighter and entered service in 1960 (1982, p 13), is comparable to its namesake, the RAF's newest and most advanced fast jet the Lockheed Martin Lightning II. Nevertheless, since the 1957 defence review, the UK's armed forces have seen a regular decline in personnel and equipment numbers. From the end of the Cold War percentage reductions in front-line strength have been more substantial. However, as Keith Hartley (2011, p 12) observed, the published data do not allow any assessment of these smaller forces and the impact on aggregate defence capability.

The defence budget is used to procure and maintain military capability through expenditure on each of the MoD's eight DLODs. Clearly some of these, for example equipment, personnel and infrastructure, attract more cost than others, such as doctrine and concepts and organization. The DLODs are the inputs that enable Defence's outputs; however, pinning down exactly what Defence's outputs are is no easy task. Hartley (2011, p 11) suggested that UK defence output is a multi-dimensional concept embracing the protection of the nation's citizens and their assets, its economy and economic infrastructure, its national institutions and its national interests. It could be argued, therefore, that defence output is reflected in deterrence, war fighting capability, military aid to the civil authority, and contributions to peacekeeping, disaster and humanitarian relief. Defence spending can also be considered as an insurance policy, designed to meet a range of known and unknown future threats and contingencies. Ultimately, a judgement must be made on the value of these defence outputs. The government of the day makes that judgement on behalf of the nation, and in line with its manifesto commitments, during its spending review process. It decides on the relative priority of all its policies and financial responsibilities and sets the defence budget accordingly.

In addition to budgetary limitations, the government also directs defence decision makers through the use of output targets. These output targets are a form of strategic direction, usually expressed in the command papers that follow a defence review. Sometimes they are headline-grabbing policy decisions, for instance the ending of national service in the 1957 review (MoD, 1957, p 7). An output target may also be the amplification of policy made between reviews. As an example, in the 1959 command paper that detailed the MoD's progress of the five-year defence plan announced two years earlier by Sandys, it was stated that:

> The aim of British policy is to promote peace and security through the settlement of international differences and comprehensive disarmament. At the same time, Britain, in co-operation with other members of the Commonwealth and with her allies in NATO, SEATO and the Baghdad Pact, must continue to play her part in the collective defence of the free world. (MoD, 1959, p 1)

More recently, the government has also used defence reviews to express output targets in the form of roles, missions and tasks. This is still strategic direction but nested in the broad policy decisions identified above. As these output targets have become more descriptive, there is a danger they may encroach on the responsibilities of defence decision makers. It is a fine line, as not giving enough guidance is also problematic. John Louth and Trevor Taylor (2019, p 29) pointed out that insufficient direction 'simply allow[s] the different sections of the armed forces to build the capabilities that they themselves appreciate'. Unsurprisingly, senior officials also have views on the level of direction they receive in defence reviews. Some see it as a freedom, others as a constraint. One RAF capability management expert believed the lack of detail included in formal defence review documentation was a positive, as it gave both the government and the MoD flexibility to do things differently as and when circumstances changed. However, other officials expressed the view that the loose language in defence review reports was counterproductive, with one RAF three-star officer suggesting it was not 'taut enough to actually describe what's required'. Another senior RAF officer believed the way direction had been given in recent SDSRs meant that the single services could 'easily attribute their aspirations against the strategy and effectively argue for any force structure'. Either way, output targets have become a fundamental part of the strategic direction narrative.

This chapter steps through the three epochs of the research period to understand how Defence's roles, missions and tasks have developed over time, and how well they have contributed to the strategic direction that the government has given to defence decision makers. While the defence roles of the Cold War shrank considerably in the 1960s and 1970s, they were easily identifiable and aligned with government policy and Defence's supporting military strategy. The pivot to expeditionary warfare complicated the situation, and, for most of the 1990s, declaratory policy failed to keep up with actual defence activity. However, as analysis of the Quinquennial Review period reveals, although terminology may have changed, defence missions and tasks have remained relatively stable. That said, recent changes in the character of conflict are likely to affect how the armed forces approach some of their more traditional roles, such as deterrence. The introduction of persistent engagement overseas as a new operating method in the 2021 IR (HM Government, 2021b, p 73) is an obvious example that will impact on the missions and tasks of the armed forces in the coming decade.

Defence roles of the Cold War

The single decision that had the most significant impact on the UK's Cold War defence policy was the adoption of deterrence. John Baylis and Alan Macmillan (1993, pp 206–8) recognized that the service chiefs had been thinking in terms of deterrence as early as 1945. It was included in the overall strategic plan document of 1947, as well as being the cornerstone of their defence policy and global strategy papers of 1950 and 1952. However, the first public acknowledgement of a deterrence policy was made by Winston Churchill in a speech to the House of Commons on 1 March 1955, in which he said:

> Unless a trustworthy and universal agreement upon disarmament, conventional and nuclear alike, can be reached and an effective system of inspection is established and is actually working, there is only one sane policy for the free world in the next few years. That is what we call defence through deterrents. This we have already adopted and proclaimed. These deterrents may at any time become the parents of disarmament, provided that they deter. To make our contribution to the deterrent we must ourselves possess the most up-to-date nuclear weapons, and the means of delivering them. (Hansard, 1955)

The adoption of the policy of deterrence was confirmed in the 1957 defence review (MoD, 1957, pp 2–3) and restated in all the subsequent Cold War reviews (see MoD, 1966, p 5; MoD, 1975, p 10; and MoD, 1981, p 5). The argument was simple. Throughout the Cold War, there was no means of providing adequate protection for the UK against the consequences of an attack with nuclear weapons. Therefore, the only existing safeguard against major aggression was the power to threaten retaliation with nuclear weapons.

As recognized in the previous chapter, the 1957 defence review was carried out under the UK's grand strategic umbrella of defence against, and deterrence of, the Soviet Union. Early in the review's command paper, it was recognized that an effective and economical plan for the nation's defence had to be based on a clear understanding of the military responsibilities to be discharged by the armed forces. To that end, it confirmed that they had to be capable of performing two main tasks. In the first instance, they had to play their part with the forces of allied countries in deterring and resisting aggression. They also had to defend British colonies and protected territories against local attack, and undertake limited operations in overseas emergencies. The aim of defence minister Sandys was to provide well-equipped forces sufficient to carry out these duties, while making no greater demands than were absolutely necessary upon manpower, money and other national resources (MoD, 1957, p 2). These were the government's clear output targets, which shaped the rest of the review.

The 1957 review lent heavily on the service chiefs' global strategy papers of 1950 and 1952. It was the first review to consider the impact of nuclear weapons; indeed, it placed considerable emphasis on Britain's nuclear forces as a means of reducing the financial cost of the nation's defence (Dorman, 2001a, p 13). In that regard, Sandys' plan was to reduce defence expenditure from 10 per cent to 7 per cent of Gross Domestic Product (GDP) by 1962, with the budget falling by £180 million to a total of £1,420 million in FY 1957–58 (Dockrill, 1989, p 68). The 1957 defence review was not the 'biggest change in military policy ever made in normal times' that Sandys claimed it to be (MoD, 1957, p 9). Instead, it confirmed and extended the existing trends in UK defence policy that had begun with the global strategy papers (Darby, 1973, p 95; and Baylis, 1989, p 52). It did, however, make clear the government's aim to 'keep military expenditure and its demands on resources within the limits of the country's economic capacity, while, at the same time ensuring that Britain could continue to play a leading part in upholding freedom and peace' (MoD, 1958, p 13). Although not being as explicit as some of the defence reviews that followed, Sandys' review set the benchmark for expressing output targets for defence decision makers, even if some of those targets had been generated by defence decision makers (through the service chiefs' global strategy papers) in the first place.

The defence reviews undertaken by the Labour government over the period 1966–68 were not only intended to shape a new defence posture for the 1970s, but also 'to relax the strain imposed on the British economy by the defence programme which it had inherited' (MoD, 1966, p 1). That said, prime minister Harold Wilson was determined that Britain should maintain a world military role. Accordingly, the 1966 defence review sought to reduce costs not by changing policy, but through the adoption of more efficient means of implementing it (Dorman, 2001a, p 16). Perhaps because of this, even though the 1966 command paper had a chapter titled 'Britain's Military Role', it did not actually articulate any specific roles, missions or tasks for Defence. The closest defence secretary Denis Healey got was to confirm the Hobbesian assertion that 'the first purpose of our armed forces will be to defend the freedom of the British people' (MoD, 1966, p 5). Notwithstanding this, the reality was that events over the next two years forced change upon change to the government's declaratory defence policy. Most was taken with the utmost reluctance, and, as Malcolm Chalmers (1985, p 87) argued, only as a result of 'severe and repeated financial crises over and above the underlying problems of long-term economic decline'.

The government's clearest output target in the 1966 review was financial. It amounted to an expenditure reduction of £400 million, or 16 per cent, on its predecessor's spending plans by FY 1969–70 (MoD, 1966, p 1). The impact of the economy on the government's strategic direction and defence decision makers maintenance of military capability is considered in Chapter 6. Nevertheless, the worsening of the UK's economic situation through 1966 and beyond is recognized by many as the key driver in additional reductions to UK defence commitments made at this time. In particular, Michael Carver (1992, pp 83–5), Michael Dockrill (1989, pp 93–7) and Michael Chichester and John Wilkinson (1982, pp 20–6) all link reductions to in-year defence spending to the deterioration of the UK economy. Across these reviews, Healey had aimed to make significant savings of money and foreign exchange in return for a comparatively small reduction in military capacity (MoD, 1966, p 15). Nevertheless, the constant changes to output targets during this time made it incredibly difficult for defence decision makers to manage military capability. It was, as advocated by Christopher Mayhew, 'an intense, sustained, sophisticated and barren attempt by large numbers of able people to square a circle' (Mayhew, cited in Chichester and Wilkinson, 1982, p 14).

In a similar vein to the Labour government's defence reviews of the 1960s, the over-riding output target for the 1975 review was financial and, in particular, a planned reduction in defence spending from an estimated 5.8 per cent of GDP to around 4.5 per cent over ten years (Walker and Mills, 2015, p 10). Moreover, in a final move away from Britain's worldwide role, defence secretary Roy Mason also confirmed that the government planned to concentrate its defence effort on NATO, describing the alliance as 'the linchpin of British security' (MoD, 1975, p 7).

Within NATO, the government decided to focus on four areas where it believed it could make the most significant contribution to the nation's, and the alliance's, security. They were: the deployment of land and air forces in West Germany; the protection of supply routes in the Eastern Atlantic and English Channel; the defence of the UK; and the strategic nuclear deterrent (1975, pp 9–10). In defining these four areas, Mason was articulating clear missions for the armed forces, all of which attracted minimum force levels necessary to maintain extant treaty obligations. These missions then shaped the decision making in the remainder of the document. However, the savings generated by withdrawing forces completely from the Five Powers Agreement and the Central Treaty Organization (Baghdad Pact), and dispensing with those forces earmarked for the associated worldwide roles, did not provide the requisite reductions in expenditure the government sought. To that end, as Andrew Dorman (2001a, p 18) noted, more savings were forced upon infrastructure and support services. While the service chiefs may not have liked Mason's overt declaration of shrinking defence roles, they provided clear strategic direction to defence decision makers that helped shape military capability choices for the rest of the Cold War.

In explaining the need for change in the opening pagers of the 1981 defence review command paper, secretary of state John Nott stated that 'The Government's appraisal of the defence programme … in no way rests on a desire to cut our defence effort' (MoD, 1981, p 3). However, the reality was that when Nott succeeded Francis Pym as secretary of state for defence in January 1981, he inherited an overspend from the previous financial year of £200 million and a projected overspend of £400 million (over 3 per cent of the defence budget) for FY 1980–81 (Dorman, 2001a, p 19). The MoD's spending plans over its ten-year programme were simply unrealistic. Even with an additional 3 per cent increase in defence spending already announced, the allocated resources could not fund the existing force structure and all the intended improvement plans. As Nott himself said, 'the aspirations of the defence lobby had outrun the amount of money that was likely to be available' (McIntosh, 1990, p 117). Action was required to re-balance military capability aspirations with financial reality.

Nott confirmed four main defence roles, which broadly aligned to those that had underwritten the 1975 review. An independent element of strategic and theatre nuclear forces committed to NATO; the direct defence of the UK homeland; a major land and air contribution on the European mainland; and a major maritime effort in the Eastern Atlantic and Channel. He also identified what became known as a half role: 'to exploit the flexibility of UK forces beyond the NATO area so far as resources permit, to meet both specific British responsibilities and the growing importance to the West of supporting our friends and contributing to world stability more widely' (MoD, 1981, p 5). As there could be no question of abandoning any of these roles, Nott's output targets had to guide how best to undertake them in future from a resource allocation that fell well short of what extant defence planning called for.

Rather than spread the pain equally over the four defence roles, Nott decided to prioritize them. He confirmed the government's commitment to modernizing the strategic nuclear deterrent through the Trident programme, and pledged not to reduce efforts in direct defence of the UK. Similarly, he stood by the nation's Brussels Treaty commitment of land and air forces in West Germany. That meant significant cuts had to be made in the maritime role. The result was a planned reduction of the RN's share of the defence budget from 29 per cent to 25 per cent by the end of the 1980s. Although some of the proposed cuts were abandoned in the aftermath of the 1982 Falklands Conflict, the general approach adopted in the 1981 defence review remained in place until the fall of the Berlin Wall in 1989 and the end of the Cold War (Mills et al, 2020, p 13).

The defence roles of the Cold War were forcibly narrowed because of successive governments' decisions to reduce defence spending in relation to GDP. Analysis of the impact of the economy and the affordability of defence is included in Chapter 6; for now it is enough to recognize that over the Cold War period, defence roles were reduced further and further, until they eventually reflected the absolute minimum contribution Britain could make to NATO and still fulfil its treaty obligations. Even then, John Nott was forced to prioritize expenditure in 1981, which had serious repercussions on the balanced force structure. That said, although this retrenchment reduced the amount of military capability fielded by the armed forces, all the defence reviews of the Cold War period provided clear strategic direction to defence decision makers. By the end of the Cold War, capability choices were undoubtedly becoming more painful, but they remained relatively straightforward.

Military missions of the Early Expeditionary Period

Throughout the Cold War, the predominant threat to the security of the UK from the Soviet Union, and the deterrence policy that countered it, did not change. However, the fall of the Berlin Wall in 1989, together with the dissolution of the Soviet Union and subsequent disbanding of the Warsaw Pact two years later, completely transformed the landscape on which UK defence policy was constructed. The certainty of the Cold War threat had given way to an uncertainty that defence planners struggled to accommodate. Lawrence Freedman (1999, p 14) observed that: 'without a Soviet threat, ... [the UK] was faced with the awkward question of whether there was anything left that the country really needed to defend against.' Rather than respond to the emerging geopolitical situation with a major change to defence policy, the Early Expeditionary period saw the adoption of a flexible and incrementalistic approach. This was aimed at maintaining force structures with the adaptability to meet the evolving new circumstances.

This response to the removal of the Soviet threat began the transition towards a capability-based, rather than threat-based, defence policy (Dorman, 2001a, p 21). It also acknowledged that choice had been re-introduced into UK defence policy making. As Philip Sabin (1993, p 271) pointed out, 'more demanding missions than protecting British territory have now become much more *discretionary* than hitherto' [italics in original]. The use of the armed forces for discretionary activity was certainly a theme favoured by the Labour government that came to power in 1997. Writing prior to the 1998 SDR, defence secretary George Robertson (1997, pp 3–4) stated: 'we believe there is a consensus for using our military assets to support the United Kingdom's role as a *force for good* in the world' [italics in original]. This approach confirmed the re-emerging expeditionary focus of UK military strategy (Codner, 1998, p 6). By default, it also affirmed the aspiration for the UK to re-establish a global role.

Aside from the COVID-19 pandemic, the fall of the Berlin Wall and subsequent collapse of the Soviet Union was possibly the greatest world-wide strategic shock of the last 75 years. Even though there was a strong argument for a reappraisal of defence commitments during the late 1980s, in light of the steadily increasing financial pressure of the MoD's budget (Dodd, 1993, p 10), it was 'the transformation of the European security scene in 1989–90 [that] provided ample justification for the long-resisted defence review' (Greenwood, 1991, p 63). David Dunn (1992, p 60) wrote that 'only by assessing the strategic roles which it is necessary for Britain to fulfil, and the capabilities and costs which are necessary to fulfil these, can a prudent defence policy be achieved'. Nonetheless, and almost certainly because of the pressing need to deliver savings, the Options for Change exercise was completed in July 1991, five months before the dissolution of the Soviet Union. Given this, it is no surprise that Dorman (2001a, p 21) suggested the work was conducted in a strategic vacuum.

It was clear that the government had attempted to reflect the change in the geopolitical situation in its approach to the Options for Change exercise. At the same time, however, it was also content to exploit the opportunity to reduce considerably its defence spending commitments. Speaking in parliament, secretary of state for defence Tom King confirmed:

> In the options for change studies, we have sought to devise a structure for our regular forces appropriate to the new security situation and meeting our essential peacetime operational needs ... Our proposals

will bring savings and a reduction in the share of GDP taken by defence. We need force levels which we can afford, and which can realistically be manned, given demographic pressures in the 1990s. (Hansard, 1990)

The defence roles of the Cold War clearly did not align with the situation the country found itself in during the Early Expeditionary period. Even so, the 1991 Options for Change command paper made no attempt to change them. Instead, it reaffirmed the four roles from the 1981 review, although it did recognize that the armed forces should 'retain the organisation, skills and military technology to permit the rebuilding of larger military capabilities to meet an increased threat should the need arise' (MoD, 1991, p 40). The first changes to the Cold War defence roles were not made until the following year's statement on the defence estimates, published by the new defence secretary Malcolm Rifkind. They replaced the old roles with the following: ensuring the protection of the UK and dependent territories, even when there is no major external threat; insuring against any major external threat to the UK and allies; and contributing to the UK's wider security interests through the maintenance of international peace and stability (MoD, 1992, p 6). While these new roles may have reinforced the government's strategic aims to make the armed forces more mobile and flexible and less focused upon a single contingency of defence against the former Soviet Union, Sabin (1993, p 269) believed they were vague and lacked real guidance for defence decision makers.

Although not a defence review in its own right, *Front Line First: The Defence Cost Study* did have a significant impact on future output of the armed forces. There was no doubting the focus of this study. The report stated:

Front Line First has succeeded in its fundamental objective. It has identified a coherent package of proposals for achieving savings of some £750 million a year in 1996/97 and more thereafter. This will allow us to accommodate the reduction in defence expenditure announced in the 1993 Budget without reducing our fighting capability. (MoD, 1994, p 8)

The study did not change the 1992 defence roles, nor did it implement any proposals that would have reduced the armed forces fighting capability. Instead, its output targets were reductions in the support and management aspects of defence. However, with the continuing shift away from a threat-based policy focused on Central Europe towards a capability-based policy with much wider horizons, the logistics capabilities most affected by the Defence Costs Study would soon become critical to underpin the armed forces' new world-wide, expeditionary posture. Dorman (2001a, p 22) argued that the pursuit of these output targets 'led to a complete disconnection in the different strands of defence policy as declaratory policy largely divorced itself from military capability'.

In defence of the government in the early 1990s, the fall of the Berlin Wall had a profound effect on the international landscape, and it was not immediately clear how UK foreign policy should be altered to cope with the change. At the same time, the nation's worsening economic situation demanded cuts in expenditure across all government departments. Even though defence decision makers received little firm strategic guidance until the 1998 SDR, it is difficult to see what the politicians could have done differently. The only glaring error was perhaps the 1994 Defence Costs Study decision to focus on logistics capabilities, which had a significant effect on the armed forces' ability to support the medium scale expeditionary operations in Iraq and Afghanistan over the following decade.

The 1998 SDR began with the three defence roles first promulgated in the 1992 statement on the defence estimates, but then immediately rejected them. In their place, the review outlined eight new missions, which were intended to provide a more accurate and balanced statement of what the armed forces were for, and a clearer and more coherent basis for defence planning. Although the report implied that this alternative approach was a new idea, seven of the eight missions were almost directly lifted from the previous Conversative government's final statement on the defence estimates in 1996 (MoD, 1996, p 18). The only new mission introduced in the 1998 SDR was defence diplomacy, which was added to reflect the importance to UK security of building and maintaining trust together with preventing conflict, particularly in Europe.

The missions were deliberately not presented in any order of priority. For planning purposes, a further level of detail was considered necessary. This information was offered in the form of 28 military tasks, all of which were assigned to a mission and focused, as far as possible, on outputs (such as peace enforcement) rather than inputs (for example, elements assigned to a particular NATO force category). The full list of missions and associated military tasks is set out in Table 4.1 (MoD, 1998a, p 19).

Confirming the eight missions and 28 military tasks was the first step in translating the review's policy framework into a detailed basis for determining the UK's defence needs. In the SDR's supporting essay on future military capabilities, a comprehensive set of planning assumptions was also presented (MoD, 1998b). While not specifically output targets, these planning assumptions were the most detailed guidance for the generation and maintenance of military capability ever included in a defence review.

The first element of the planning assumptions was a scale of effort baseline for the UK's contribution to expeditionary operations. This was a level of forces over and above those required for day-to-day tasks, such as military aid

Table 4.1: Military missions and tasks from the 1998 Strategic Defence Review

Mission	Military task
Peacetime security	MT1: Military aid to the civil power in Great Britain
	MT2: Military aid to the civil power in Northern Ireland
	MT3: Counter drugs operations
	MT4: Military aid to other government departments
	MT5: Military aid to the civil community
	MT6: Military search and rescue in peacetime
	MT7: Nuclear accident response
	MT8: Integrity of United Kingdom waters in peacetime
	MT9: Integrity of United Kingdom airspace in peacetime
	MT10: Intelligence
	MT11: Hydrographic, geographic and meteorological services
	MT12: Evacuation of British citizens overseas
	MT13: Public duties and VIP transport
Security of the overseas territories	MT14: Security of the overseas territories
	MT15: Security of the Cyprus Sovereign Base Areas and territorial waters
Defence diplomacy	MT16: Arms control, non-proliferation, and confidence and security building measures
	MT17: Outreach
	MT18: Other defence diplomacy activities
Support to wider British interests	MT19: Support to wider British interests
Peace support and humanitarian operations	MT20: Humanitarian operations and disaster relief outside the United Kingdom and overseas territories
	MT21: Peacekeeping
	MT22: Peace enforcement
Regional conflict outside the NATO area	MT23: Regional conflict outside the NATO area
Regional conflict inside the NATO area	MT24: Regional conflict inside the NATO area
	MT25: Major regional conflict inside the NATO area
	MT26: Military home defence
	MT27: Nuclear forces
Strategic attack on NATO	MT28: Strategic attack on NATO

Source: *The Strategic Defence Review 1998 – Modern Forces for the Modern World*, Cm 3999

to the civil power in Northern Ireland. The review included four principal scales of effort, detailed in Table 4.2 (MoD, 1998b, p 3).

The planning assumptions also included guidance on readiness, endurance, concurrency and recuperation. A level of readiness was the notice period within which units must be available to deploy for a given operation. Endurance was the likely duration of operations, including the potential

Table 4.2: Scales of effort from the 1998 Strategic Defence Review

Scale of effort	Description
Small scale	A deployment of battalion size or equivalent. Examples include the ARMILLA patrol in the Persian Gulf, the UK contribution to United Nations Forces in Cyprus (UNFICYP), and the RAF operations enforcing the no-fly zones over northern and southern Iraq.
Medium scale	Deployments of brigade size or equivalent for warfighting or other operations. An example would be the UK contribution to the NATO-led Intervention Force (IFOR) in Bosnia.
Large scale	Deployments of division size or equivalent. The nearest recent example in 1998 was the UK contribution to the Gulf War coalition in 1990/91, although on that occasion the British division deployed with only two of its three brigades. Large scale is the maximum size of force the UK would plan to be able to contribute to peace enforcement operations, or to regional conflicts outside the NATO area.
Very large scale and full scale	These comprise all the forces the UK plans to make available to NATO to meet significant aggression against an ally. This is the most serious single scenario that the UK might now face. The two scales differ primarily in the warning time available in response to the emergence of a major threat, and in the size of that threat. In both cases, it is assessed that the warning time available would be many months or even years.

Source: *Supporting Essay Six – Future Military Capabilities to the Strategic Defence Review 1998*

need to sustain a deployment for an indefinite period. Concurrency was the consideration of the number of operations, of a given scale of effort and duration that the armed forces should be able to conduct at any time. Finally, recuperation was the time needed after an operation to rehabilitate units, so they were capable of being deployed again. Taking all the planning assumptions together, the SDR concluded that the size and shape of the post-review force structure were dictated by the following two main requirements:

• The challenge of conducting two concurrent medium scale operations, one a relatively short warfighting deployment, the other an enduring non-warfighting operation. For many elements of the force structure, this was considered to be the most demanding scenario.
• A full-scale operation, which was the most demanding scenario for the remainder of the force structure. (MoD, 1998b, p 4)

The armed forces were also expected to be able to retain the ability, at much longer notice, to rebuild a bigger force as part of NATO's collective defence should a major threat re-emerge in Europe. Tellingly, the government did not consider that the new scales of effort would require significant changes to the strength of the UK's regular forces. It also expected the force structure to be configured such that, as well as responding to major crises, force elements would be able at other times to carry out day-to-day defence activities, as well as several 'small but perhaps long-running commitments' (MoD, 1998a, p 32), and respond to minor contingencies.

Following the events of 11 September 2001 (9/11), the government re-committed to its focus on military capabilities for expeditionary operations (Boyce, 2002). The 1998 SDR's missions and military tasks were simplified by the then defence secretary Geoff Hoon in the 2003 Defence White Paper *Delivering Security in a Changing World*. The number of military tasks was reduced to 18, which were grouped under the four generic headings of: standing strategic commitments; standing home commitments; standing overseas commitments; and contingent overseas commitments. A new defence aim was also introduced. It was based on the 1998 SDR defence mission but recognized explicitly the threat posed by international terrorism. The defence aim was 'to deliver security for the people of the United Kingdom and the Overseas Territories by defending them, including against terrorism, and to act as a force for good by strengthening international peace and security' (MoD, 2003, pp 4–5).

The 2003 Defence White Paper also refined the concurrency guidelines in the defence planning assumptions. This was considered necessary to reflect the level and frequency of deployments for the more complex and demanding pattern of operations in the post-9/11 era. The new concurrency assumptions were:

- That as a norm and without creating overstretch, the armed forces should be able to mount:
  - an enduring medium-scale peace support operation simultaneously with an enduring small-scale peace support operation and
  - a one-off small-scale intervention operation.
- That the armed forces should be able to reconfigure forces rapidly to carry out:
  - the enduring medium-scale peace support operation and
  - a small-scale peace support operation simultaneously with
  - a limited duration medium-scale intervention operation.
- That, given time to prepare, the armed forces should be capable of undertaking:
  - a demanding one-off large-scale operation while still maintaining a commitment to
  - a simple small-scale peace support operation.

- Additionally, the armed forces must also take account of the need to meet standing commitments with permanently committed forces, for example quick reaction alert aircraft for integrity of UK airspace and contingent forces. (MoD, 2003, p 7)

The Early Expeditionary period was a time of reset for the armed forces as they switched from focusing on a single major threat in Western Europe to being prepared to intervene in trouble spots around the globe. Predictably, the strategic direction given to defence decision makers, especially in the immediate aftermath of the end of the Cold War, was slow to catch up with the changing geopolitical situation. That said, the 1998 SDR's approach to developing a force structure to meet the military's emerging expeditionary role was comprehensive and well thought through. The introduction of scales of effort, supported by credible planning assumptions, provided ample direction for defence planners to begin investing in appropriate expeditionary capability across all three environments. Moreover, the willingness of the Labour administration to make this information publicly available throughout its time in office had a positive effect on the translation of strategic direction into military capability, and was a major influence on the transition from a threat-based to a capability-based defence policy.

Quinquennial review of defence missions and tasks

The Labour government was committed to holding an SDR immediately after the 2010 general election. In preparation, defence secretary Bob Ainsworth published a Defence Green Paper – *Adaptability and Partnership: Issues for the Strategic Defence Review* (MoD, 2010a). The paper re-affirmed the 18 tasks from 2003. In addition, with only minor updates to reflect the latest terminology within the MoD, the concurrency assumptions were also unchanged. The very large/full scale of effort was removed, and explanations for each service's commitment were added, as detailed at Table 4.3 (2010a, p 49). These figures formed the start point for the 2010 SDSR.

The 2010 SDSR was the first defence review undertaken alongside the development of an NSS. In simple terms, the SDSR was designed to set out the ways and means to deliver the ends identified in the NSS (HM Government, 2010a, p 9). The NSS's two strategic objectives – ensuring a secure and resilient UK and shaping a stable world (HM Government, 2010c, p 22) – informed a set of new cross-cutting national security tasks and planning guidelines (HM Government, 2010a, pp 11–12), which, in turn, directed the military tasks and planning assumptions of the 2010 SDSR. The 18 missions in the previous government's Defence Green Paper were reduced

Table 4.3: Scales of effort from the 2010 Defence Green Paper

Scales of effort	Description by service
Small scale (for example, Sierra Leone in 2000)	• RN: task group containing approximately one submarine and 10 ships • Army: one battlegroup • RAF: one expeditionary air group comprising approximately 25 fixed wing, and 10 rotary wing aircraft
Medium scale (for example, Kosovo in 1999)	• RN: task group containing approximately two submarines and 20 ships • Army: one brigade • RAF: one expeditionary air group comprising approximately 75 fixed wing, and 20 rotary wing aircraft
Large scale (for example, Iraq in 2003)	• RN: task group containing approximately three submarines and 40 ships • Army: one division • RAF: up to three expeditionary air groups comprising approximately 130 fixed wing, and 50 rotary wing aircraft

Source: *Adaptability and Partnership, Issues for the Strategic Defence Review*, Cm 7794

Table 4.4: Military tasks from the 2010 Strategic Defence and Security Review

Defence review	Military tasks
Securing Britain in an Age of Uncertainty – The 2010 SDSR	• Defending the UK and its Overseas Territories • Providing strategic intelligence • Providing nuclear deterrence • Supporting civil emergency organizations in times of crisis • Defending our interests by projecting power strategically and through expeditionary interventions • Providing a defence contribution to UK influence • Providing security for stabilization

Source: *Strategic Defence and Security Review 2010 – Securing Britain in an Age of Uncertainty*, Cm 7948

to seven tasks by the Conservative/Liberal Democrat coalition, detailed in Table 4.4. That said, this was more of a streamlining exercise, and did not significantly alter the outputs expected of the armed forces.

The 2010 SDSR did include a considerable change in policy concerning planning assumptions. It made no reference to scales of effort, but envisaged that the armed forces of the future would be sized and shaped to conduct:

• An enduring[1] stabilisation operation at around brigade level (up to 6,500 personnel) with maritime and air support as required, while also conducting a non-enduring[2] complex[3] intervention (up to 2,000 personnel) and a non-enduring simple[4] operation (up to 1,000 personnel).

Or alternatively:

- Three non-enduring operations, if the armed forces were not already engaged in an enduring operation.

Or:

- For a limited time, and with sufficient warning, committing all of Defence's effort to a one-off intervention of up to three brigades, with maritime and air support (around 30,000 personnel).

Although the pre- and post-2010 SDSR commitments may appear similar at first glance, they did have significant differences. Firstly, the requirement to undertake concurrent medium-scale operations was abandoned in the 2010 SDSR, replaced by a single task, which was, in itself, limited to a stabilization operation only at around brigade-level. Furthermore, a non-enduring simple operation of up to 1,000 personnel proved to be far too unrealistic to plan against, in terms of both numbers involved and complexity. For example, the relatively simple operation to evacuate British nationals from Libya in 2011 required input from the maritime, air, logistics and special forces components, as well as command and control from the UK's extremely high-readiness operational headquarters, the Joint Force Headquarters (Sutherland, 2012). Moreover, at its height, it involved the deployment of approximately 1,200 servicemen personnal.[5] Finally, the one-off intervention commitment was less than two-thirds of the force deployed to Iraq in 2003 and, crucially, did not require the army to operate at divisional-level. With no supporting justification, and little scrutiny from the defence media or academia, the 2010 SDSR directed a sizeable reduction in the UK's ambition to conduct expeditionary operations.

The 2010 NSS and SDSR benefitted from a clear, hierarchical structure. It started at the top with a single sentence[6] that defined the strategic approach, flowed down to two complementary strategic objectives,[7] supported by a strategic policy framework – the adaptable posture, which was populated from the output of the NSRA. The adaptable posture was a simple construct designed to guide defence and security decision making. It had three principal elements:

- Respond to the highest priority risks[8] over the next five years.
- Be prepared to respond to the low probability but very high impact risk of a large-scale military attack by another state.

- Pursue an over-arching approach to respond to growing uncertainty about longer-term risks and threats. (HM Government, 2010a, p 10)

The MoD's interpretation of the adaptable posture was included in a permanent secretary and CDS endorsed *Strategy for Defence*, as follows:

We will remain ready to use armed force where necessary to protect our national interests, but we will be more selective in its use and focus our armed forces more on tackling risks before they escalate, and on exerting UK influence, as part of a better coordinated overall national security response. (MoD, 2011c, p 2)

Although the adaptable posture concept was praised by the HCDC (2011a, p 38), it received very little academic attention, and there is no evidence that its guidance was ever embedded within the MoD's decision-making processes. For example, it was not referenced in any of the versions of the DOM released between 2011 and 2015. However, it did set the requirements for the SDSR's outline force structure – Future Force 2020 (FF20) – which was designed to provide the requisite and affordable UK military capability for the 2020s (HM Government, 2010a, p 19).

As well as accepting its requirements from the adaptable posture, FF20 also drew on the military tasks and planning assumptions. It contained three broad elements:

- The **Deployed Force** – forces engaged on operations.
- The **High Readiness Force** – forces available to react rapidly to crises.
- The **Lower Readiness Force** – forces focused on recovery (having recently returned from operations) and those preparing to enter a period of high readiness.

This was the first time that a defence review had attempted to define a force structure as an aiming point for the armed forces, although, as can be seen in Figure 4.1, the report was extremely short on detail. As an example, it simply allocated 'combat ready fast jets' to the air component of all three elements of FF20; enduring high-readiness and all lower-readiness forces of the land component were merely labelled 'multi-role brigade', and joint enablers, that is intelligence, logistics, medical and communications were completely excluded (2010a, p 20). Even accepting that certain information, for example numbers of platforms held at readiness, had to remain classified and should be made available only to those within the government and the MoD who needed to know,

Figure 4.1: Future Force 2020

	Deployed Force (High Readiness)	High Readiness (One off)	Enduring	Lower Readiness			Extended Readiness
Maritime	Surface Ships (Frigates/Destroyers) Submarines (Trident and Attack)	Maritime Task Group Aircraft Carrier; Amphibious Ships; Submarines; Mine Hunters; Frigates; Destroyers	Surface Ships (Frigates/Destroyers)	Surface Ships (Frigates/Destroyers)	Surface Ships (Frigates/Destroyers)	Surface Ships (Frigates/Destroyers)	2nd Aircraft Carrier; Amphibious Ship
Land	Special Forces; Explosive Ordnance Disposal; CBRN defence units	Special Forces | 16 Air Assault Brigade | 3 Commando Brigade	Multi-Role Brigade	Multi-Role Brigade	Multi-Role Brigade	Multi-Role Brigade	Land Force Elements
Air	Combat Ready Fast Jets	Combat Ready Fast Jets	Combat Ready Fast Jets	Combat Ready Fast Jets	Combat Ready Fast Jets		

Increasing Readiness

Reserves — Reserves — Reserves — Reserves — Reserves

Allies and Partners

Source: *Strategic Defence and Security Review 2010 – Securing Britain in an Age of Uncertainty*, Cm 7948[12]

the high-level, broad-brush approach adopted by the report did little to enhance its credibility.

The adoption of a defined force structure also prompted questions around FF20's military capability, affordability and the critical mass of the armed forces. When questioned a year after the SDSR, all three single service chiefs declined to confirm that the UK's national ambition out to 2015 could be defined as being a full spectrum capability. In contrast, David Cameron was unequivocal in his assertion that the UK remained a 'full spectrum defence power' (HCDC, 2011a, p 31). Although there is not a universally agreed definition of full spectrum capability, Cameron defended his position by referring to the nation's £33 billion defence budget, and it being the fourth largest in the world. In a different approach, Nick Harvey, who was minister for the armed forces at the time, suggested that if having a full spectrum capability meant the UK was militarily capable of doing anything it wanted in any theatre in the world whilst being totally self-reliant, 'it had been decades since we retained that sort of definition' (2011a, p 33). Instead, he suggested that FF20 would have a wide spectrum of capability, which the then vice chief of the defence staff (VCDS), General Nick Houghton (2011a, p 62), confirmed would meet the 'National Security Council's adaptive posture in its considerations of the time' and, therefore, be 'full spectrum within sensible bounds'. This debate flowed into concerns raised at the time regarding the critical mass[9] of the armed forces. Significantly, the HCDC (2011a, p 63) was not convinced that from 2015, well before the future force construct had been implemented, the armed forces would be able to 'maintain the capability to undertake all that is being asked of them'. It considered that the path to FF20 may not be realizable, given the anticipated commitment levels of the armed forces during the period, and the capability gaps that had been directed by the SDSR.

In addition to the nervousness over military capability and critical mass of the armed forces, the affordability of FF20 was also being seriously questioned. Without a real-term increase in the defence budget after 2015, former CDS Jock Stirrup (2011a, p 65) concluded that 'Future Force 2020 would be completely unaffordable, and the armed forces would have to be substantially smaller than is currently planned'. Although both the prime minister and the defence secretary had confirmed that the level of ambition set out in the SDSR would require year-on-year, real terms growth in the defence budget in the years beyond 2015, there was no guarantee that this would be realized. Indeed, Oliver Letwin, the minister of state at the Cabinet Office in 2011, had confirmed that the government could not set expenditure decisions across that time period, and James Blitz, the *Financial Times*' Whitehall Editor, agreed, saying: 'I don't see the prime minister's commitment with the statement on the SDSR as a bankable commitment in any way' (2011a, p 65). Even though, in July 2011, the government agreed to a budgetary uplift of 1 per cent above real terms for equipment and equipment support from FY 2015–16, and to commit to a ten-year equipment programme that the MoD could plan on (HCDC, 2011b, p 25), it is questionable that the force structure aspirations of FF20 were ever affordable.

The 2015 SDSR changed some of the terminology from its predecessor. Strategic objectives became national security objectives, and military tasks became armed forces missions. The 2010 objectives were simplified and added to, becoming: protect our people; protect our global influence; and promote our prosperity (HM Government, 2015, pp 11–12) . The number of armed forces missions was increased to eight (from seven in 2010), listed in Table 4.5, and divided into 'routine' and 'be prepared to' activity (2015, pp 27–9). That said, apart from being slightly more specific in its potential kinetic contributions to the government's response to crises, these changes were superficial.

In a stark change from both the 2010 SDSR and the Labour government's 1998 SDR and follow-on white papers, the 2015 SDSR report included considerably less detail on planning assumptions. Apart from confirming that the maximum size of a single expeditionary force would be 50,000 (compared with around 30,000 planned for in FF20), it offered little insight into the type, quantity and duration of operations the armed forces would be sized and shaped to conduct. Instead, it simply identified that

Table 4.5: Armed forces missions from the 2015 Strategic Defence and Security Review

Defence review	Armed Forces missions
A Secure and Prosperous United Kingdom – 2015 SDSR	Routine missions: • Defend and contribute to the security and resilience of the UK and Overseas Territories • Provide the nuclear deterrent • Contribute to improved understanding of the world through strategic intelligence and the global defence network • Reinforce international security and the collective capacity of our allies, partners and multinational institutions 'Be prepared to' missions: • Support humanitarian assistance and disaster response, and conduct rescue missions • Conduct strike operations • Conduct operations to restore peace and stability • Conduct major combat operations if required, including under NATO Article 5

Source: *Strategic Defence and Security Review 2015 2015 – A Secure and Prosperous United Kingdom*, Cm 9161

when not deployed at the maximum number above, the armed forces would be able to undertake many smaller operations simultaneously, which might include:

- A medium-scale operation, often drawing mostly on just ·one service, such as the counter-ISIL [Islamic State of Iraq and the Levant] mission in Iraq.
- Multiple additional operations, ranging from specialist missions, such as counter-terrorism or counter-piracy, through to broader, more complex operations, such as the military support to tackle Ebola in Sierra Leone.
- A wide range of defence engagement activities, such as training teams and mentoring. (HM Government, 2015, pp 29–30)

These broad examples contained insufficient direction for defence decision makers to make informed decisions on the procurement and sustainment of military capability, nor were they intended to. This is because the government now considered that planning assumptions information concerning operational definitions, frequency and concurrency of operations and recuperation periods should be protected. To that end, it was consigned to a classified *Defence Strategic Direction* document. This was in accordance with the DOM guidance at the time, which stated:

> Each SDSR generates a Defence Strategic Direction document, which translates the outcome [of the SDSR] into long-term planning direction for us. In rare circumstances, this document can be reviewed between SDSRs. The interpretation of this direction for the next five years, particularly in terms of allocating resources, is set out in the annual Defence Plan. This in turn provides the direction for each TLB's yearly Command Plan, which is the delivery agreement between PUS [the permanent secretary at the MoD] and the TLB holder. (MoD, 2015b, p 14)

The eye-catching increase in numbers of the SDSR's best-effort combined force received the most positive academic attention in the months after the review (see Chapman, 2016; Keohane, 2016; and Molinelli, 2016), even though this new output target was to be achieved with no increase in the size of the army and only an extremely modest uplift to the RN and RAF (HM Government, 2015, p 6). However, the single-most significant output target in the review was the return to divisional warfighting, an aspiration the army had coveted since its abandonment in 2010 (Carter, 2013). As Anthony King (2019, p 34) noted, the ability for the army to operate at the divisional level was vital to ensure both its standing and its interoperability with its closest battlefield partner, the US Army. This point was also recognized by the HCDC (2017, p 4) when it agreed that a 'fully-manned and fully equipped warfighting division is central to the credibility of the army'.

In accordance with extant DOM guidance, SDSRs were expected to include details of a new and affordable force structure. This future force, based on the review's updated planning assumptions, should be deliverable within ten years (MoD, 2015b, p 14). This had first occurred in the 2010 SDSR with FF20. The 2015 SDSR announced a new future force – Joint Force 2025 (JF25) – as outlined in Figure 4.2 (HM Government, 2015, p 28).

Following the same approach as it had taken with planning assumptions, the report was short on detail regarding JF25, although the information it did include was an improvement on the 2010 SDSR's detail around FF20. In addition, the adaptable posture had not gained any traction within the MoD and was quietly dropped. A MoD-produced, SDSR defence key facts document did provide slightly more substance on the planned capabilities of JF25:

- By 2025, the armed forces will be able to deploy a force of around 50,000 drawn from:
  - Maritime task group of around ten to 25 ships and 4,000 to 10,000 personnel.
  - Army division of three brigades and supporting functions of around 30,000 to 40,000 personnel.
  - Air group of around four to nine combat aircraft squadrons, six to 20 surveillance platforms and five to 15 transport aircraft, and around 4,000 to 10,000 personnel.
  - Joint forces, including enablers and headquarters, of around 2,000 to 6,000 personnel.
- The composition and balance of the force would be dependent on a number of variables, including:
  - The adversary and their capabilities.
  - The region of the world into which UK armed forces were deploying.
  - The extent to which allies and/or multinational organisation such as NATO, are engaged.
  - The amount of logistic support, basing and access offered by a host nation. (MoD, 2015c, p 6)

In 2018, the MoD's MDP report re-affirmed the 2015 SDSR's three national security objectives and eight armed forces missions. It then went on to catalogue 25 tasks that defence fulfilled to help deliver the national security objectives (MoD, 2018d, p 18). These tasks formed the start point for the 2021 IR.

Figure 4.2: Joint Force 2025

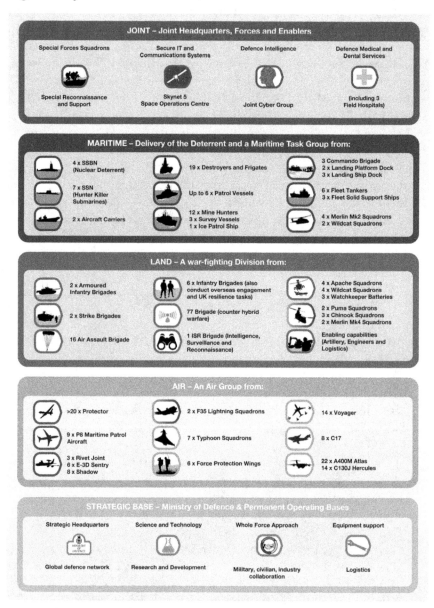

Note: See https://assets.publishing.service.gov.uk/government/uploads/system/uploads/attachment_data/file/478933/52309_Cm_9161_NSS_SD_Review_web_only.pdf

Source: *Strategic Defence and Security Review 2015 – A Secure and Prosperous United Kingdom*, Cm 9161.[13]

The 2021 IR looked beyond the boundaries of the previous two SDSRs, and delivered a report that covered security, defence, development and foreign policy. It introduced a strategic framework with four overarching and mutually supporting objectives (HM Government, 2021b, p 18). Most of the output targets for Defence were included in the third objective – strengthening security and defence at home and overseas. Here, the government committed to three high-level goals, which were broken down into sub-goals, each supported by priority actions detailed in Table 4.6 (2021b, pp 69–85).

Table 4.6: Defence-related goals and priorities from the 2021 Integrated Review

Goal	Sub-goals and priority actions
Counter state threats at home and overseas	Defending the UK and our people, at home and overseas • Secure British territory against physical incursions • Support the Overseas Territories and Crown Dependencies in deterring and defending against state and non-state threats • Enhance the support and assistance available to UK nationals overseas Defence and deterrence through collective security • Reaffirm the UK's commitment to leadership in NATO, supporting it adaption to threats above and below the threshold of war under international law • Improve interoperability with Euro-Atlantic allies • Modernize the UK armed forces • Improve the UK's ability to manage and de-escalate a multi-domain crisis • Sustain the UK's commitment to collective security beyond the Euro-Atlantic Countering state threats to the UK's democracy, society and economy • Take a whole-of-government approach to protecting democracy in the UK • Bolster the UK's cross-government approach to countering state threats • Ensure the future security of the UK telecoms network • Strengthen cyber security capacity and cooperation with like-minded partners • Enhance efforts to counter disinformation at home and overseas • Use the UK's armed forces to detect, understand and deter state threats below the threshold of war through persistent engagement overseas • Put diplomacy at the centre of international efforts to counter state threats

(Continued)

Table 4.6: Defence-related goals and priorities from the 2021 Integrated Review (continued)

Goal	Sub-goals and priority actions
Tackle conflict and instability	Tackle conflict and instability • Establish a more integrated approach to government work on conflict and instability • Establish a new conflict centre within the Foreign, Commonwealth and Development Office • Build momentum on efforts to prevent sexual violence in conflict • Tighten the focus of the cross-government Conflict, Stability and Security Fund
Enhance UK homeland security by tackling transnational security challenges	Countering radicalization and terrorism • Strengthen the UK's counter terrorism (CT) system • Reinforce the UK's approach to countering homeland radicalization and terrorism • Reduce the operational capabilities and intent of those involved in Northern Ireland-related terrorism • Address the conditions that give rise to terrorism overseas • Disrupt the highest-priority terrorist groups overseas using the full range of UK CT capabilities • Prevent terrorist activity online • Strengthen aviation security worldwide Serious and organized crime (SOC) • Bolster the UK's response to the most pressing threats faced from organized criminals • Strengthen the National Crime Agency • Increase regional and local policing capacity • Strengthen international efforts to disrupt and dismantle SOC networks • Tackle SOC within the UK's territorial sea Strengthening global arms control, disarmament and counter-proliferation • Reinforce international governance of state access to chemical, biological, radiological and nuclear weapons, materials or related technology • Reduce tensions in South Asia • Counter proliferation to states • Counter proliferation to non-state actors • Balance the opportunities of new technologies with controls

Source: *Global Britain in a Competitive Age – the Integrated Review of Security, Defence, Development and Foreign Policy*, CP 403

More direction for the armed forces was provided in the 2021 DCP (MoD, 2021b, p 8), which included a high-level explanation of how Defence would contribute to the Integrated Review's overarching objectives. It also confirmed the IOpC as the cornerstone of the armed forces' future evolution, which was explained under headings of: persistent engagement overseas; crisis response; warfighting; defending the UK and our territory; and the nuclear deterrent (2021b, pp 15–22). While not specifically stated, these five headings were far closer to the traditional defence roles than the goals and sub-goals of the Integrated Review.

The 2021 DCP also included a chapter on modernizing the armed forces. Its new aiming point was the Integrated Force 2030 (IF30). Multi-domain integration[10] was confirmed as the underpinning concept for how the armed forces would operate and fight, which required force elements to be integrated across domains[11] and across government. The same chapter confirmed that military capability in the future would be less defined by numbers of people and platforms than by information-centric technologies, automation and a culture of innovation and experimentation (2021b, p 39). Perhaps unsurprisingly, therefore, neither the 2021 IR nor the DRP included any planning assumption information. No details were given on the number and size of operations that the IF30 would be expected to undertake, nor any indication of readiness, endurance, concurrency or recuperation. Indeed, while the accompanying graphic on the IF30, reproduced as Figure 4.3, was certainly busier than those that had described FF20 and JF25 in the 2010 and 2015 SDSR reports, it contained less useful information, and no numbers at all (2021b, p 40).

The defence tasks and missions included in the reviews of the Quinquennial Review period have continued to focus on expeditionary activity. While not unexpected, this continuity is helpful for defence decision makers as it has resulted in an extended period to consolidate the acquisition of relevant military capability (for example, carrier strike). However, the methodology and reduced levels of supporting detail included in all three quinquennial reviews have undone much of the previous good work around force structure planning. There will, of course, always be a tension between how much planning information should be made publicly available and how much must be withheld for national security reasons. But choosing to omit all future force planning assumptions from the 2021 IR was too heavy-handed and will make external scrutiny of defence decision making in the future unnecessarily challenging.

How have defence roles, missions and tasks affected military capability choices?

During the Cold War, the defence secretary's task of articulating output targets for the armed forces was relatively simple. The most significant one – the size of the defence budget – was agreed at Cabinet level, either because of a manifesto commitment or as part of government-wide spending priorities. In addition, the enduring approach of defence against, and deterrence of, the Soviet Union narrowed considerably the options for defence roles, missions

Figure 4.3: Integrated Force 2030

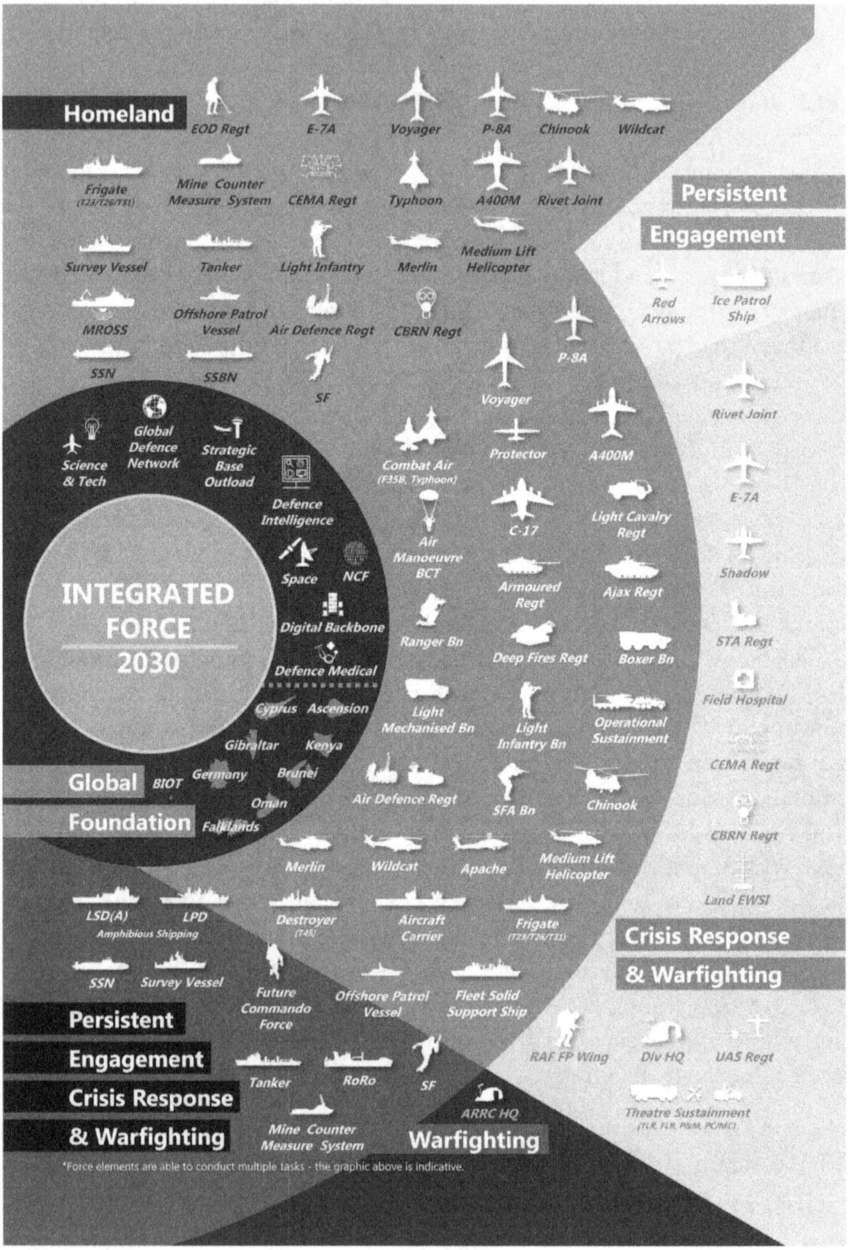

Note: See https://assets.publishing.service.gov.uk/government/uploads/system/uploads/attachment_data/file/974661/CP411_-Defence_Command_Plan.pdf

Source: *Defence in a Competitive Age*, CP 411.[14]

and tasks. Prior to the decision in 1968 to withdraw completely from East of Suez, account had to be taken of the UK's collective defence commitments outside NATO, but, in the main, safeguarding Europe was the overriding concern. As retrenchment continued into the 1970s, the government was forced to concentrate UK defence effort in those areas where it believed it could make the most significant contribution to the nation's security and that of NATO. This resulted in Mason's four defence roles, which, by and large, endured from 1975 until the end of the Cold War.

The effect on UK national strategy of the geopolitical upheaval caused by the fall of the Berlin Wall in 1989 was covered in Chapter 3. Of course, it also influenced the output targets given to defence decision makers by their political masters in the reviews of the Early Expeditionary period. UK defence budgets were dramatically reduced as both Conservative and Labour governments reprioritized spending commitments during the 1990s. By way of example, the level of GDP allocated to defence dropped from 3.7 per cent in 1991 to 2.5 per cent in 1999 (SIPRI, 2021). Although the opportunity for the defence budget to produce savings was obvious, it proved difficult to achieve. Christopher Coker (1992, p 73) put the blame on the Thatcher government in the late 1980s, suggesting that 'Defence spending declined significantly in Mrs Thatcher's last years, as the Conservatives struggled to bring down the level of state spending. One of the reasons why there was no immediate peace dividend when the Cold War came to an end was that the government had largely spent it.'

The removal of the threat from the Soviet Union also meant the UK government had to reconsider its strategic ends, and give appropriate direction to defence decision makers. As Asteris (1994, p 43) suggested, once the security of the UK and its surrounding seas had been allowed for, the nature of military provision became much more a matter of choice. The result was an initial re-calibration of defence missions that focused on territorial protection, insuring against external threats, and contributing to the maintenance of international peace and stability. The first defence review to be wholly focused on expeditionary operations – the 1998 SDR – developed these into a comprehensive list of eight missions and 28 supporting military tasks. Also, and no doubt influenced by the Labour Party's manifesto commitment to more open government through a freedom of information act (The Labour Party, 1997), the 1998 SDR also included comprehensive direction on what the armed forces must be capable of. This was built around planning assumptions that included scales of effort, as well as readiness, endurance, concurrency and recuperation limits. It is arguable whether the armed forces were ever adequately resourced to meet the planning assumptions; nevertheless, the 1998 SDR was a high watermark for the articulation of output targets for defence.

The three quinquennial reviews since 2010 have seen a dramatic reduction in the level of detail around output targets for Defence. While the government has little choice over declaring expenditure limits, the amount of planning assumption information it decides to include in a defence review report is entirely within its own gift. Of course, it must be wary of the messages that its overt strategic direction for defence decision makers sends to both allies and potential adversaries. As a specific example, a four-star defence decision maker was concerned that the 2015 SDSR's output target for the realization of its future force essentially confirmed that the UK would be unable to undertake major warfighting at scale against a peer adversary until ten years after the date of the review. He considered there was a risk in:

> 'Publishing white papers and defence reviews ... which say, "We are weak in the following areas and we're going to get better." I think an important part of deterrence is what's behind the curtain, what's not known and what's not said. We want to create dilemmas in our opponents' minds which says, "We don't know what the UK is actually capable of. We know what they say they're capable of but maybe there's more". I think maybe we need to be careful about being too honest, if you like.'

Nevertheless, there must be a reasonable level of detail available in the public domain to allow for an appropriate scrutiny of government policy and associated defence decision making. This issue was tackled by the HCDC in the immediate aftermath of the 2015 SDSR. In an oral evidence session, one of the expert witnesses, Patrick Porter, observed, 'I would like to see a clear articulation of what we think we should be able to do, but also an acknowledgement of things we will not be capable of, and to then place that in the template of the risk table [within the strategy document]' (HCDC, 2015b, p 11). He did, however, also recognize the obvious limitations of articulating potentially classified strategic guidance in a publicly available document, and that the generalization of some of the content was inevitable. When asked about the problem of having to tackle sensitive issues in a document with such a wide audience, he responded:

> I would say there is a difficulty. If the architects of this kind of document believe that the document suffices to create a National Security Strategy, there does have to be something off-camera where people are having much more precise conversations about what really does count as a ranked threat and a ranked priority ... I hope that these conversations are happening. There almost has to be a two-level process here. It is important to articulate something to the people who pay for these

things. There has to be some consideration of the democratic context. But not all of it can be open and explicit. (HCDC, 2015b, p 4)

Although recent reviews have reduced the amount of planning assumption detail they contain, they have also increased the information included around future force structures. There are two reasons why this is not necessarily a good thing. As we know, all the quinquennial reviews have outlined a force structure for the future, based on planning assumptions, and deliverable in 10 years' time. The 2010 SDSR detailed FF20; the 2015 SDSR detailed JF25; and the 2021 Integrated Review has just detailed IF30. A five-year review and update of the intended force structure's direction of travel may seem like a good idea, but the result is that every force structure ends up abandoned mid-creation. None is ever delivered. As I observed in an essay in a King's College London review of the defence and security aspects of the 2021 IR (Devanny and Gearson, 2021b), the decennial force structure cycle is fundamentally undermining the armed forces' management of military capability.

The second problem is that the decennial force structure cycle created a programmatic aiming point, rather than a conceptual one. That is to say, it created a task organization for the new force structure but provided no direction on how the force elements contained therein should actually fight. As an army major general observed:

'[W]hy would all of these capabilities we were buying, or the skills we were developing in our people, or the organizational design of our structures, or any of those cross DLODs … add up to a different way of warfare? We've never put that down [in writing], so we've never had a unifying operating concept that has applied to our defence strategic direction.'

As a result, over and above the simple direction on FF20 and JF25, detailed in Figures 4.1 and 4.2 respectively, the 2010 and 2015 SDSRs provided no conceptual vector for defence decision makers to assist them in developing the DLODs of the military capabilities for each force structure, to ensure that they would actually be capable of operating against current and future threats. Instead, the single services have had the latitude to choose the outcomes that reinforce their own bias and prejudice, instead of developing capabilities that may not always be in the interests of a particular service but are necessary for a joint force. The effects of this situation are examined further in Chapter 7.

This problem has finally been recognized by the MoD and, in September 2020, it responded by publishing the IOpC. This new concept provides the IF30 with a conceptual aiming point through the articulation of the UK's new approach to the utility of armed force in an era of persistent competition and a rapidly evolving character of warfare (MoD, 2020c, p 1).

Billed as the most significant change in UK military thought in several generations, it is expected to lead to a fundamental transformation in the military instrument and the way it is used (2020c, p 1). However, the 2021 DCP still included a graphic depicting all the anticipated force elements of the IF30 (see Figure 4.3). This would suggest either the new concept had been fully realized within six months of its publication, or the single services remain fixed on their current equipment plans. It is inconceivable that, given the current pace of technological change, the UK's force structure ten years from now can already be known. In all likelihood, some of the capabilities that will be fielded in 2030 have not even been invented yet. If the armed forces are truly to modernize for the threats of tomorrow, defence decision makers must become more flexible in their approach to developing military capability, and cannot be constrained by narrow-focused process of their own making.

In summary, therefore, the roles, missions and tasks articulated in defence reviews and associated policy documents have an important part to play in the translation of strategic direction into military capability. As we've seen with the UK's approach to strategy, the future will be considerably more complicated than the past. Fortunately, this has been recognized within Defence and the IOpC should provide the conceptual input into capability planning that was missing from both the 2010 and 2015 SDSRs. Nonetheless, the move towards multi-domain integration, and especially the addition of space and cyberspace in five new operating domains, will present some difficult capability choices for defence planners in the near term. The more detail politicians are prepared to commit to regarding Defence's roles, missions and tasks, the less problematic those choices will be.

5

Defence Reviews

Michael Quinlan (1992, p 160) recognized that focusing on the specific content of the UK's defence programme following a defence review is of far less value than studying the reasons why the related decisions were made in the first place. In line with his thinking, this chapter concentrates less on the 'what' and more on the 'why' of defence review decision making. In doing so, it balances academic commentary on the process of defence reviews from the last 75 years with the views and observations from recent practitioners. These inputs from senior officials within the MoD are, understandably, almost exclusively focused on the Quinquennial Review period.

Individual defence reviews methods regularly attract scrutiny from the defence academic community, sometimes to the point where process has overshadowed outcome. For instance, Andrew Dorman (2001a, p 24) suggested that 'many of the novel features of the [1998] SDR surround its conduct rather than its findings'. Nevertheless, there has been little academic analysis of pan-defence review processes and whether they all have a cyclical connection, or common attributes. One exception is research undertaken by Paul Cornish and Andrew Dorman (2010, pp 395–6), which concluded that UK defence reviews throughout the Cold War and Early Expeditionary period followed a flawed, four-phase, policy development process. Cornish and Dorman argued that policy failure was followed by policy inertia, which led to policy formulation, and, finally, policy mis-implementation. Furthermore, they contended that this resulted in an as-yet inescapable cycle of incomplete and unsustainable defence reviews. More recently, they developed this thinking to identify ten unwritten rules that influence the character and quality of defence reviews, which can be summarized as follows:

- Reviews are quickly overtaken by events.
- Governments find it difficult to sustain the logic of their own strategy review.
- Reviews are inevitably underfunded.

- Reviews are constrained by the capability decisions by which they are immediately preceded.
- In any review, certain areas will be considered 'off-limits' for party political, domestic or international reasons.
- The unanimity of service chiefs cannot be maintained, as their allegiance to their respective service takes precedence over their commitment to Defence overall.
- Allies and partners will attempt to influence the outcome of the review directly and will also be drawn in by the individual services.
- The threat of cuts to military capability leads to inter-service rivalry.
- The government will be subject to intensive media scrutiny, both prior to and during a review.
- On completion of a review, the government will claim to have gained control of defence inflation and cost overruns. (Cornish and Dorman, 2015, pp 359–64)

The ad-hoc cycle of defence reviews, taken to task by Cornish and Dorman, was replaced at the 2010 SDSR by the quinquennial review process (HM Government, 2010c, p 35). This process underpinned the MoD's operating model and control framework up until 2020 (see MoD, 2012c; and MoD, 2015b); however, it was arguably undermined by Boris Johnson's decision, in February 2020, to undertake an integrated review to include foreign policy and international development, in addition to defence and security (GOV.UK, 2020c). Nevertheless, to date, there has been no follow-up academic investigation to determine if any of these new ways of working are proving more successful or have broken Cornish and Dorman's flawed cycle. Moreover, the validity of their unwritten rules, formulated between the 2010 and 2015 SDSRs, have not been subject to any further scrutiny. Cornish and Dorman (2010, p 407) concluded that 'it has proved all too easy for a gap to develop between overall defence policy on the one hand and its implementation in the form of military equipment programmes on the other'. This would suggest a fundamental flaw in the way strategic direction is transmitted by politicians and received by defence decision makers.

If it is accepted that defence reviews are an examination by the UK government of its defence and security commitments and associated resources to ascertain whether they are still appropriate and, if necessary, initiate corrective action (the definition agreed in Chapter 2), then undertaking one should, on the face of it, be a reasonably simple, linear task. The ideal, as Quinlan (1992, p 160) suggested, should be 'one starts by identifying one's commitments; one assesses professionally what forces are needed to meet them; one costs these; and then one sends the bill to the treasury, which pays up'. However, all my research indicates that reality is somewhat different from Quinlan's ideal, with a multitude of internal and external factors making defence reviews far from simple or linear. Moreover, as defence reviews have become the most significant part of a government's strategic direction, it behoves us to understand how their complexity affects the military capability choices made by defence decision makers. To that end, this chapter steps through the main aspects of defence reviews that impact the opening chapter's translation of strategic direction into military capability model. It begins by examining the way in which reviews are undertaken, which has seldom followed a common standard. It then moves on to explore the impact that contemporaneous events, from seemingly insignificant activities to major strategic shocks, have had on defence reviews. The rest of the chapter is devoted to the two most significant contributors to the translation of strategic direction into military capability model: politicians and defence decision makers. The contribution of, and the relationship between, those giving and those receiving the strategic direction delivered through a defence review is a key part of the process. Defence reviews have always been more confrontational than collegiate, as both politicians and defence decision makers strive to avoid unfavourable outcomes that are particularly difficult to recover from.

The process of defence reviews

As there was no set standard for a Cold War defence review, it should be no surprise that there was no set methodology for undertaking one either. Furthermore, processes both matured over time and developed in line with revisions to the central organization of Defence – most notably the establishment of a unified MoD in 1964 (HM Government, 1963). Prior to the 1957 review, prime minister Harold Macmillan believed the power of the single services had to be reduced. As William Jackson and Edwin Bramall (1992, pp 314–15) explained, 'he was convinced that no major changes in the status quo would be negotiable unless the Minister of Defence was given the power to overrule the special pleadings of the Admiralty, War Office and Air Ministry'. To that end, he extended defence minister Duncan Sandys' responsibilities to include 'deciding all questions on the size, shape, organisation and disposition of the forces'. A second significant factor in how the 1957 review was undertaken was Sandys himself. His forcefulness, determination and personal political ambition underpinned the process of the review; indeed, it was these very attributes that prompted Macmillan to appoint him in the first place. Sandys retained close control throughout the short, two-month process, which, according to Richard Powell, also included personal involvement in the actual drafting of the document (ICBH, 1988, p 15). While Sandys' character is regularly cited as fundamental to the outcome of the 1957 review, Macmillan's contribution should not be overlooked. After all, he appointed Sandys, increased his ministerial authority, and backed him throughout. In his first speech as prime minister, he promised that 'no vested interest, however strong, and no traditions, however good, would obstruct the government's reassessment of defence policy' (Self, 2010, p 162). The strength of the two politicians working together was summed up by Ewen Broadbent (1988, p 20), who observed that 'they [defence review outcomes] were brought about by Mr Sandys' willpower and strong views reinforced by the knowledge of the prime minister's full support'.

Although the outcomes of Denis Healey's subsequent defence reviews were arguably no less controversial than Sandys', the way they were undertaken appears to have been far less divisive. According to Phillip Darby (1973, p 298), this was due to 'the primacy of the Treasury in determining the shape of the review', which trumped even the fierce inter-service rivalry that accompanied the process. That said, the efficacy of the process itself was questioned by Malcolm Chalmers, who reinforced his point with a telling quotation from Richard Crossman, a minister in Harold Wilson's Cabinet:

> I never suspected that when I got inside O.P.D [the Cabinet Subcommittee on Overseas Policy and Defence], and discovered what was actually being done by those colleagues it would be so crude, so unskilful − a futile attempt to remain Great Britain, one of the three world powers, while slicing away our defences. (Crossman, cited by Chalmers, 1985, p 86)

In contrast to Crossman's observations about the process that supported Healey's reviews, the way in which Roy Mason undertook his 1975 review is widely applauded. Michael Cary, the MoD's permanent undersecretary of state at the time of the review, said it was 'the best managed review in which I have been involved' (Cary and Foxley-Norris, 1976, p 1). David Greenwood saw both good and bad in the way the review was conducted. He recognized that the simultaneous scrutiny of claims, commitments and capabilities − without preconceived cost ceilings or pre-determined effectiveness criteria − testified to a logically sound appreciation of the defence resource allocation problem. That said, he was particularly critical of the lack of analysis surrounding the impact of the review on UK industry. Nevertheless, he concluded that 'over the last decade the procedural aspects of setting defence priorities have greatly improved' (Greenwood, 1975, p 226).

A strong CDS supported by a capable central staff within the MoD certainly improved the military contribution to the 1975 review. However, the input from the service chiefs remained relevant, particularly their contribution to, and acceptance of, the Critical Level, which was defined by Tom Dodd (1993, p 8) as 'the minimum military contribution to NATO that Britain's alliance partners would find credible and which the country could, at the same time, afford'. Although the adoption of the Critical Level was generally seen as positive in 1975, it had a distinctly negative impact six years later, during the Nott review.

John Nott's approach was compared by Jackson (1990, p 159) to Duncan Sandys': 'Like Duncan Sandys, John Nott completed his own assessment in a rush ... after a whirlwind tour of the Services, consultative visits with Britain's principal NATO allies and long and fraught discussions with the Chiefs of Staff.' Other commentators, however, have questioned the involvement of the service chiefs. In 1981, the service chiefs argued that the strategic landscape had not altered since Mason's review and, therefore, the Critical Level identified therein could not be reduced further. Nott disagreed, but the service chiefs would not back down. As a result, they were sidelined, and Nott sought advice elsewhere. Dorman (2001b, p 102) asserted that: 'As a result of the impasse between the services, the CDS and Nott, the work of the Capabilities Group, which included the chief scientific advisor and the deputy chief of the defence staff (operational requirements) had a much greater influence than it might otherwise have had.' This conclusion is supported by Michael Carver (1992, p 135) who observed: 'Cm 8288 [the 1981 defence review command paper] reflected the views of the scientists and civil servants in the Ministry more than it did those of the chiefs of staff committee.' It can never be known if the full involvement of the service chiefs would have yielded a different result, but that is not of consequence. The point here is there can be no guarantee that a principle previously established by a government will be honoured in the present, or the future, especially by a different political party.

The defence reviews of the Cold War all followed the same retrenchment approach. Even the 1981 review, which was undertaken against the backdrop of a 3 per cent increase in defence spending (MoD, 1981, p 2), still included significant cuts to military capability. Given this, it is unsurprising that the accompanying civil military relationship was often fraught. When strong-willed and ambitious politicians attempt to force unwanted change on service chiefs, whose allegiance to their respective service is near-absolute, the atmosphere will always be abrasive. The most obvious example of this was the complete lack of empathy between Duncan Sandys and the service chiefs at the time of the 1957 defence review. Richard Powell suggested that the service chiefs positively hated Sandys (ICBH, 1988, p 9) and, during the same seminar, Arthur Drew confirmed that General Gerald Templer, the Chief of the Imperial General Staff, actually struck Sandys after a dinner party (1988, p 18). Nevertheless, a defence review is a political process, driven by politicians. It is they who set the agenda and it is they who ultimately own the outcome. As a result, for the defence decision makers of the Cold War, defence reviews were rear-guard actions, often bitterly fought, to protect what existing capability and future programmes that they could.

Unfortunately for their successors, as the rest of this chapter's analysis will confirm, not much has changed.

The various reviews of the Early Expeditionary period were undertaken in considerably different ways. In 1990–91, the government's narrative was that Options for Change was a two-phased, MoD-led process: the first being an analysis by ministers; the second an evaluation of the resultant broad assumptions against several options for each capability area and defence role (Mottram, 1991, p 22). However, this opinion was not shared by all, with the alternative view being that it was a treasury-led pursuit of expenditure reductions (see Perkins, 1992, p 65; and Self, 2010, p 172). In contrast, the 1994 Defence Cost Study process attracted far less controversy. Indeed, Dodd (1994, p 2) described a relatively simple construct of a secretary of state-led steering group, giving direction to a minister of state for defence procurement-chaired executive group, overseeing 33 separate studies, which each sought to examine a particular support area across services lines. He also identified that the Defence Costs Study report maintained every recommendation was examined against one major criterion: would it directly or indirectly reduce the operational capability of the armed forces. If the judgement was made that a proposal would damage the operational capability of the armed forces, it was rejected. Both reviews were carried out by a Conservative government, which remembered the acrimony that had surrounded the Nott review and was determined not to repeat it. This is more evidence that defence reviews are inherently political in nature.

The processes that the Conservative government of the early 1990s used to underpin its reviews were like those used in the Cold War; however, the Labour government that followed was prepared to adopt a far more innovative approach. In the first instance, it established a policy baseline, in conjunction with the FCO. This was followed with an 'analysis of defence needs and the drawing up of a force structure to meet them' (Dodd, 1997, p 9). The work involved a wide range of academics, industrialists, civil servants, politicians and opinion formers. It was also supported by several seminars held around the country. Colin McInnes (1998) recorded some telling observations regarding the 1998 SDR process. In the first instance, he recognized how easy it was to be cynical about the consultative approach adopted, as it was unclear how much influence those external contributions had in determining specific policy outcomes. He also suggested that those within the armed forces, but not involved with the review process, suspected that 'when the tough decisions over resources and force structures were made, it would be "business as usual", with civil servants and the three services fighting protracted bureaucratic battles within the MoD and perhaps with other Whitehall departments (especially the Treasury)'. His conclusion, however, was most relevant, as he wrote:

What has happened is that the culture of defence policy has been opened up. It is no longer solely the preserve of military officers, civil servants and government ministers; decisions are no longer simply promulgations by Whitehall. Of course, the extent to which the process has been opened up is limited, but a start has been made, Defence is becoming more open and accountable, and the culture is not ruled by the assumption that Whitehall knows not only what is best but what can be legitimately discussed as part of the defence debate. (McInnes, 1998, p 830)

The openness and inclusivity of the 1998 SDR marked a significant deviation from previous Cold War reviews to the extent that, at the time, the novel features surrounding its conduct received more attention than its findings, which were considered rather conventional (Dorman, 2001, p 24). Furthermore, the time taken to complete the review – 14 months – was more than double the anticipated period, and considerably longer than all its predecessors. Increasing the number and diversity of contributors was bound to lengthen the review's timeline; however, McInnes (1998, p 829) also recognized the sheer scale and complexity of the review as a contributing factor. This confirms the considerable amount of time needed to complete such a wide-reaching and strategic review, time which politicians may not always be willing, or able, to give.

As the opening decade of the twenty-first century was ending, a new approach to defence reviews began to take shape. This approach had been developed by the incumbent Labour government through a series of reforms aimed at bringing together the plans and objectives of all departments, agencies and forces responsible for national security. The reforms covered strategic, structural, resource and legislative elements, and culminated in the production of the UK's first NSS in 2008. This all-inclusive approach to national security signalled that the government no longer intended to consider principal defence matters in isolation; furthermore, all three major political parties confirmed a similar approach in their 2010 general election manifesto (see The Conservative and Unionist Party, 2010a; The Labour Party, 2010; and The Liberal Democrat Party, 2010). The effect this had on the UK's approach to strategy was covered in Chapter 3; its effect on the process of future defence reviews is explored below.

The 2010 general election was dominated by the economy, education and employment (*The Telegraph*, 2010), with debate around defence issues concentrated predominantly the conflict in Afghanistan (Brown et al, 2010). Away from current operations, all the main political parties promised to focus on the welfare of servicemen/women and their families, and to retain the nuclear deterrent (Dorman, 2010). In addition, even before party manifestos were released, both Labour and the Conservatives had committed to hold a defence review immediately after the election (see MoD, 2010a; and The Conservative and Unionist Party, 2010b). The outcome of the election was a Conservative/Liberal Democrat coalition government, which, on its very first day in office, established an NSC and appointed an NSA (Devanny and Harris, 2014, p 6). Thereafter, it began the Conservative's manifesto commitment to undertake a SDSR, publishing a new NSS on 18 October 2010 (GOV.UK, 2010b), and an associated SDSR the following day (GOV. UK, 2010c).

As research in previous chapters has identified, defence reviews normally follow a general election,[1] with the newly elected government drawing on its manifesto commitments to provide initial direction for the review. However, in May 2010, the coalition government had two manifestos to consider, which were not aligned on several key policy issues. The solution was the publication of the coalition's *Programme for Government*, which Cornish (2010, p 4) suggested could be seen as a *post*-election manifesto. The document was published on 20 May 2010, eight days after the coalition government formed. It confirmed the creation of the NSC, and the appointment of the NSA. It also confirmed that the SDSR had already commenced, together with the development of a new NSS. All review activity would be overseen by the NSC, 'with strong Treasury involvement' (HM Government, 2010d, p 24). In the section on Defence, the coalition outlined only two strategic assertions: it would maintain Britain's nuclear deterrent (even though the Liberal Democrats would 'continue to make the case for alternatives') and it would 'aim to reduce the MoD's running costs by 25 per cent' (2010, p 8). In Cornish's opinion, commencing an SDSR in the first week of taking power was a bold undertaking, but had to happen to be able to influence the government's forthcoming spending review. The SDSR took no more than five months to complete, considerably less time than the previous review in 1998. However, as Chalmers (2010, p 12) pointed out, although there may have been some complaints from within the defence community about the haste in which the SDSR was conducted, if it had not taken place simultaneously with the spending review, it would have been constrained by budgetary allocations that had already been fixed. Specifically, the full implications of different scenarios for defence cuts could be considered before financial allocations were made, which spared the MoD savings originally envisaged of between 10 and 20 per cent. The strong treasury involvement in the SDSR, promised in the coalition's *Programme for Government* document, was an early warning of the prominence that finance would be given in the review. To that end, curtailing input from research institutes and academia, through a foreshortening of the process, could be viewed as a price worth paying to be able to influence the decisions of the spending review. There was, however, a downside to the swiftness of the review's completion. The SDSR failed to deal with a whole range of difficulties confronting Defence;

instead, it commissioned a series of further studies, which delivered their findings piecemeal over the next 12 to 18 months (Cornish and Dorman, 2012, p 216). These included: a review of the defence acquisition process (MoD, 2013a); a study of reserve forces (Houghton et al, 2011); a report of the Military Covenant Task Force (Strachan et al, 2010); a white paper on science and technology (MoD, 2012b); and the Defence Reform Report (MoD, 2011a). Each of these studies had a considerable impact on the output of Defence, yet this approach meant they were all considered in isolation, rather than in conjunction with the other major decisions that had been announced in October 2010. The most noteworthy changes included the disaggregation of capability management from MoD head office to the single services and the creation of JFC, following the Defence Reform study. In the summer of 2011, the MoD also undertook a 'Three Month Exercise', which tackled other issues that had been overlooked in the SDSR. Its most significant outcome was a further reduction of 12,000 personnel in the size of the regular army (MoD, 2012a, p 42).

The 2010 SDSR marked a significant change in scope over its predecessors, being the first that included a specific examination of security issues alongside the traditional scrutiny of defence. As analysis in Chapter 3 recognized, the driver for this change was the previous government's decision to introduce an NSS in 2008. This decision positioned Defence in a more over-arching security policy context. Michael Clarke (2008, p 4) recognized that, by commissioning an NSS, the government had taken a conceptually new approach to national security, setting defence within an even wider spectrum of governmental activity, covering all aspects of the physical, economic, social and psychological well-being of British society. In the view of Cornish and Dorman (2011, p 339) this new approach provided the strategic framework within which defence policy would be considered, with '[the NSS] setting out the purpose of national strategy and … [the SDSR] … showing how these goals were to be achieved'. Another by-product of the introduction of an NSS, and, in particular, the choice of its framework, was to move the SDSR away from being capability-led – a feature of reviews of the Early Expeditionary period – to a risk-based approach (Dorman, 2011, p 5).

As well as encompassing security for the first time, the 2010 SDSR was also the first in several other areas. It was the first to be conducted under the oversight of the newly created NSC (Devanny and Harris, 2014, p 24); it was the first review process owned by the Cabinet Office and not the MoD (Taylor et al, 2011, p 26); and it was the first to be presented to parliament by the prime minister, rather than the secretary of state for defence (HM Government, 2010a, cover page). Cornish and Dorman (2011, p 339) saw these firsts as the 'beginnings of what might be described as a formal and transparent national strategic process in the United Kingdom', which they concluded as being the review's 'most significant achievement'. In contrast,

Mark Phillips (2012, p 28) condemned the tactical delivery of the review, suggesting that 'preparations were hampered by a lack of consensus in how it [the review] should be conducted and a poor conceptual understanding of the task'. Furthermore, he did not believe the Cabinet Office had provided sufficient direction to prepare for a possible cross-government review process. He concluded that, outside the MoD, most other government departments prepared poorly, perhaps on the assumption that Defence would dominate. If this was the case, the usefulness of broadening the traditional defence review process, to encompass the totality of national security, and then handing it over to the Cabinet Office to manage, is questionable. Is a well-executed, defence-specific review better than a poorly produced, cross-government one in providing the strategic direction necessary to make the right choices concerning the procurement and maintenance of military capability?

On 7 May 2015, to the surprise of some both nationally and internationally (see T.W., 2015; and Jamieson, 2015), the Conservative Party secured a 12-seat working majority at the general election. Three weeks later, during the state opening of parliament, Her Majesty the Queen announced that the government would hold a full strategic defence and security review (Hansard, 2015a), thus confirming the previous Conservative/Liberal Democrat government's commitment to undertake a SDSR, and produce a new NSS, every five years (HM Government, 2010c, p 35). This news was not unexpected; indeed, before the election, Cornish and Dorman (2015, p 351) had suggested that 'the machinery of government has once again entered the "phoney war" stage of the defence cycle: preliminary work and positioning has begun prior to the formal start of the review process'. Moreover, in January 2014, prime minister David Cameron had confirmed the scope, structure and timing of the next NSS would 'span the period of the next election' and 'We should be starting now' (JCNSS, 2015, p 9). It is impossible to confirm exactly how much preparatory work was undertaken by the Cabinet Office and relevant government departments prior to the formal announcement of the 2015 SDSR, although one of the benefits of mandating a regular cycle of reviews should be the ability to identify long lead-time analysis necessary to support the anticipated decision making, and then schedule it appropriately. What is known is that the 2015 SDSR was published six months after the election, as opposed to the five months it took to complete the 2010 review, and the updated NSS and SDSR outcomes were distributed as a single command paper (HM Government, 2015).

The 2015 SDSR replicated all the original features that had appeared in the first quinquennial review. Perhaps as a result, it attracted only limited academic commentary regarding its process. That said, there were still disagreements over its usefulness. On the one hand, Tim Street (2016, p 3) was critical, suggesting that the review had simply repeated mistakes of the past and thus 'continued with business as usual'. On the other, John

Louth (2016, p 1) observed that 'as an exercise in engagement management it appears almost peerless'. Chalmers was clear in his view that the 2015 process was significantly more integrated than in 2010; he was also clear as to the reasons why:

> At the heart of this [more integrated] approach was strong central leadership from an experienced prime minister and chancellor, with a close political relationship, who were determined to lead the SDSR from the centre, using the combined power of the National Security Secretariat and the treasury to ensure that departments worked together to achieve centrally set objectives. (Chalmers, 2016c, p 10)

Prior to the 2015 SDSR, the HCDC published two reports in which it made several process-related recommendations regarding the next review (see HCDC, 2014; and HCDC, 2015c). However, the two most meaningful – undertaking wide consultation and establishing constructive challenge – were not implemented by the government. In Street's view (2016, p 3), the review lacked any 'serious consultation or engagement with civil society and alternative viewpoints', an opinion that was also shared by elements of the national press (see Stanton, 2015; and Farmer, 2015). In addition, there is no evidence of the establishment of independent groups to provide a shadow process or 'red team' challenge of the review's outcomes. To that end, it would appear the review process, which had undergone a fundamental change in 2010, did not benefit from any substantial additional development in the build up to, and execution of, the 2015 review.

In its first annual report on the 2015 NSS and SDSR, the government, while recognizing that 'the world can appear more uncertain and challenging than it has for many years', confirmed that 'the principal threats to our national security remain the same' (HM Government, 2016). Accordingly, it made no reference to the need for a refresh of the NSS or a new SDSR. However, less than six months after the annual report was published, the UK underwent another general election (The Electoral Commission, 2019). Although no party won a majority in parliament, prime minister Theresa May was able to form a Conservative government with the support of the Democratic Unionist Party through a confidence and supply agreement (GOV.UK, 2017a). Of the three main political parties, only Labour included a commitment in its manifesto to undertake a complete SDSR if elected (The Labour Party, 2017, p 20). The Conservative manifesto made no mention of any additional investigation into UK defence and security policy; however, one month after the election, the government announced that it had begun work on a review of national security capabilities (GOV.UK, 2017b), which would become the NSCR.

The government intended the NSCR to be carried out alongside the ongoing implementation and monitoring of the 89 principal commitments set out in the 2015 NSS and SDSR. The review was planned as an 'examination of the policy and plans which support implementation of the National Security Strategy, and help to ensure that the UK's investment in national security capabilities is as joined-up, effective and efficient as possible, to address current national security challenges' (GOV.UK, 2017b). That said, Chalmers (2018, p 3) was convinced the defence element of the review would be 'the most consequential, substantively and politically'. He also questioned the decision of aiming for a cost-neutral outcome, based on budgets agreed during the 2015 Spending Review, given the government's intention to hold a further spending review in 2019.

The review consisted of 12 separate work strands,[2] which were progressed by cross-department government teams, overseen by the NSA. The process lasted eight months and concluded with the publication of a report in March 2018, which was endorsed by the prime minister and included the government's second annual report of the 2015 NSS and SDSR (UK Parliament, 2018). The report stepped through each of the 12 work strands, but none included any significant new developments. Instead, the narrative mainly re-emphasized the government's existing approach, for example, 'We will continue to implement the National Security Cyber Security Strategy and ensure it keeps pace with the threat'; or made bland and non-contentious statements, such as, 'We will take a whole-of-government approach to serious and organised crime' (2018, p 21). The section on defence was limited to a mix of re-stating elements of the 2015 SDSR report, for example listing the JF25 force structure, and highlighting recent achievements in the equipment programme. The only new initiative generated by the NSCR was the introduction of the Fusion Doctrine, discussed in Chapter 3.

On 1 November 2017, Michael Fallon resigned as secretary of state for defence to be replaced the following day by Gavin Williamson. In January 2108, even though the NSCR was still running, Williamson persuaded the prime minister to support a concurrent, defence-focused study – the MDP. The aim of the MDP was to 'deliver better military capability and value for money on a sustainable and affordable way' (Hansard, 2018a). Williamson justified it by stating that 'we must do more to ensure that we use our resources effectively and deliver the efficiencies that the Department has committed to, so that they can be reinvested in the capabilities we require for our Armed Forces' (Hansard, 2018a). The target completion date for the MDP was July 2018; however, it was December 2018 before Williamson was able to provide a final update to parliament (Hansard, 2018b), and the report was published (MoD, 2018d).

The MDP was divided into four work strands: organizational development and reform; efficiency management; commercial and financial management; and capability development. It was the final work strand – capability development – that the HCDC's preliminary report on the MDP identified as the most significant (HCDC, 2018, p 17). However, apart from not announcing any cuts to specific capabilities, the report failed to tackle capability development issues at all. Indeed, the four work strands were completely absent in the final report, which instead coalesced around three new themes: mobilize, modernize, and transform. Under these themes, the MDP broadly described what would be prioritized:

> We will mobilise, making more of what we already have to ensure our Armed Forces are best placed to protect our security. We will modernise, embracing new technologies and assuring our competitive edge over our adversaries. We will transform, radically changing the way we do business and staying ahead of emerging threats. (MoD, 2018d, pp 15–16)

In a briefing paper for parliamentarians, Louise Brooke-Holland (2018, p 1) described the MDP report as 'a relatively short document that firstly recounts developments in Defence since 2015 and assesses current and future threats before identifying three broad areas it will now prioritise'. In general, however, the lack of detail in the report attracted widespread criticism (see, for example, Makin-Isherwood, 2018; and Guest Contributor, 2019). Howard Wheeldon said it had 'hardly a specific detail of anything that really matters' (Wheeldon, cited by Chuter, 2018); Trevor Taylor's observation was equally blunt:

> The formal MDP document was conspicuously spread over less than 30 pages, many of which were taken up by photographs, blank pages and material summarising current and past activities of the armed forces. Material about the future was addressed in just around seven pages of generously sized and spaced text. (Taylor, 2019)

Cornish (2018, p 15) suggested that one of the new defence secretary's first tasks should be to 'challenge the notion that national security and defence can be achieved "on the cheap" and to argue that the defence budget cannot take any further reductions without accepting the strategic risk that must, inevitably, be associated with reduced capability'. However, the MDP ducked this issue as well, choosing instead to defer to the government's CSR, planned for 2019. Indeed, the report made no fewer than five separate references to the forthcoming spending review (Brooke-Holland, 2018, p 5), with Williamson confirming 'it is going to be very important for the Department to make sure that we get the right investment going forward'

(Hansard, 2018c). This led to my own assertion in a 2019 article for *The RUSI Journal* that it was hard to conclude that the MDP report was anything more than an exercise in 'kicking the can down the road'.

The Conservative manifesto ahead of the December 2019 general election did not include a commitment to undertake a defence review (The Conservative and Unionist Party, 2019). However, during the election campaign, prime minister Boris Johnson revealed that he wanted to hold 'the deepest defence and security review since the Cold War' (Maddox, 2019). That translated into an Integrated Security, Defence and Foreign Policy Review, which was confirmed in the post-election Queen's Speech as a reassessment of the nation's place in the world, covering all aspects of international policy from defence to diplomacy and development (Hansard, 2019). In February 2020, Johnson offered more details on the scope of the Integrated Review, and how it would be undertaken (GOV.UK, 2020c). He confirmed that a wide range of foreign policy and national security experts, inside and outside government, would be involved to ensure the UK was equipped to meet the global challenges of the future. He also insisted the review would be policy-led and go beyond the parameters of a traditional review by considering the totality of global opportunities and challenges the UK faces. It would then determine how the whole of government could be structured, equipped, and mobilized to meet them. As with the SDSRs of 2010 and 2015, the Integrated Review was intended to be run in parallel with a government spending review, to ensure relevant departments would be allocated the resources needed to enact the review's recommendations. Little information regarding the process of the review was forthcoming, although it was revealed that there would be a cross-Whitehall team, which would report to the prime minister. Decisions on the review would ultimately be made by the NSC. Submissions of evidence were invited from the public (GOV.UK, 2020b), although no details were ever provided on the process for the evaluation of what was subsequently received, or indeed if it had influenced any of the review's outcomes.

Even before the prime minister made his announcement, there was widespread speculation, both in the media and from defence commentators, that the review was experiencing difficulties. Evidence was emerging that at least two of Cornish and Dorman's unwritten rules were about to re-surface (see Parker and Warrell, 2020; and Fisher, 2020). Then the COVID-19 pandemic struck, and on 9 April 2020, the deputy NSA, Alex Ellis, announced a formal pause to the review that would last for almost three months (see Chuter, 2020b; and Roberts, 2020). The review re-started in July, but it remained far from transparent. The government confirmed that work was concentrating on the following five thematic workstreams: resilience, foreign policy, defence, science technology and data, and strengthening government systems (Brooke-Holland, 2020, p 5).

Ellis (2020) also revealed that, as a result of the pandemic, the government had conducted new 'horizon scanning and fresh analysis' and focused on 'intensified geopolitical competition'. Nevertheless, the lack of transparency resulted in ongoing media speculation, most of which was pessimistically focused on potential reductions in capability (see, for example, Shipman and Tipley, 2020). The lack of detail was also highlighted by the HCDC, which called for much more clarity on how the review was being conducted (HCDC, 2020a, pp 54–9).

In November 2020, at the same time as he announced an uplift in defence spending of circa £24 billion over the next four years, the prime minister confirmed that the Integrated Review would conclude 'early next year' (Hansard, 2020b). The 2021 IR was finally published on 16 March 2021 and included:

- The prime minister's vision for the UK in 2030.
- The government's current assessment of the major trends that will shape the national security and international environment to 2030.
- A strategic framework that establishes the government's overarching national security and international policy objectives, with priority actions, to 2025.
- An outline of the approach to be taken to implementing the strategic framework.
- A list of spending review decisions that support the Integrated Review, and a description of the evidence and programme of domestic and international engagement that supported the review. (HM Government, 2021b, p 12)

The implications for Defence of the 2021 IR were laid out in a separate command paper, which was released six days later on 22 March 2021. According to defence secretary Ben Wallace, it was an honest assessment Defence can and will do (MoD, 2021b, p 3).

At the time of writing, academic reaction to the 2021 IR and associated DCP has not moved much beyond newspaper articles and a few short analysis pieces on think-tank websites (see, for example, Anelay, 2021; Barry et al, 2021; and Jessett et al, 2021). One exception is the series of essays published in July and October 2021 by the Centre for Defence Studies at King's College London (see Devanny and Gearson (eds), 2021a; and Devanny and Gearson (eds), 2021b). Understandably, observations have been focused mainly on the policy aspects of the review, and the impact of cuts in military capability. To date, little thought has been given to process aspects, and how they may affect future defence reviews. That said, the government's approach of revealing less detail than has hitherto been seen appears to hold true for the mechanics of the wider, Integrated Review process.

The most obvious conclusion to draw from analysis of the defence review process is there is no standard. As I shall explore further later in this chapter, defence reviews are politically driven and the default choice for a politician is always to maintain maximum freedom of action. Defence decision makers, on the other hand, are much more comfortable with pre-defined procedures that make it easier to coordinate the large bureaucracy that supports them. This mismatch of approach replicates the problems with making and undertaking strategy identified in Chapter 3. Expectation management is also a major issue during defence reviews. Politicians expect their ideas on how a review should be run to be accepted and implemented across Whitehall without question. However, senior officers and civil servants in the MoD generally want to repeat the process from past reviews, with which they are familiar. When aligned with the reality that defence reviews almost always bring about cuts in capability, this guarantees the process's confrontational nature, which has been a constant throughout the research period. The subsequent tension does little to help the translation of strategic direction into military capability.

The irregularity of defence reviews during the Cold War and Early Expeditionary period also presented problems for defence decision makers. For example, the financial pressure on the defence budget in the late 1980s forced the CDS and the service chiefs to initiate an internal review of military spending before the government committed to the Options for Change exercise in 1990. Then, only a few years later, with the outcomes of the Options for Change exercise still nowhere near delivered, they had to support a further review – *Front Line First: The Defence Costs Study* – and take responsibility for the delivery of its recommendations as well. For defence decision makers, reviews are stressful and time-consuming; moreover, they are always followed by the implementation of their outcomes, which invariably involves reductions to capability and the unpopular decommissioning of ships and the disbandment of regiments and air squadrons. It is no surprise that few in Defence look forward to the defence review process.

The impact of contemporaneous events and strategic shocks on defence reviews

Contemporaneous events and strategic shocks are often instinctively cited as external factors that affect defence reviews. Given the interrelation between defence reviews and strategic direction, it is reasonable to expect they also influence the translation of strategic direction into military capability model. While a contemporaneous event is self-explanatory, what constitutes a strategic shock is open to debate. Stan Anton (2013, p 58) suggests that 'strategic shocks rock the usual conventions in such a way that require the affected institutions to fundamentally reorient their strategies, missions, investment policies, etc, by definition, strategic shock being unexpected and unpredictable'. A more defence-orientated definition was included in a recent US Army War College special commentary piece: 'Strategic shock results when the defense enterprise abruptly refocuses and retools to respond to an unexpected strategic-level challenge. Shock, as the word suggests, is fundamentally disorienting to the entire defense enterprise. Shock suddenly alters plans, priorities, and operations in ways that result in wide-ranging institutional change' (Freier et al, 2020, p 2). Since the end of the Second World War, there have been at least three strategic shocks that required the UK 'to fundamentally reorient' its national strategy: the Suez Crisis in 1956; the fall of the Berlin Wall in 1989; and the COVID-19 pandemic that began in 2020. An argument could also be made that the UK's economic decline in the second half of the 1960s and the global economic crisis of 2008 also fit Anton's definition.

In all these cases, there is evidence to suggest that the strategic shock impacted on, or, in some cases, was the catalyst for, a concomitant defence review. In an observation on Sandys' defence review in 1957, Dorman stated that, 'The failure of the Anglo-French expedition [in Suez in 1956] served as a trigger for a major reconsideration of British defence policy'. A similar, but broader, view was put forward by Michael Dockrill (1989, p 65), who wrote, 'The Sandys White paper was the culmination of attempts since 1952 to reduce Britain's defence expenditure; the devastating financial and political consequences of the Suez crisis in 1956 provided the impetus for a vigorous effort to achieve this'. The aftermath of events in 1956 was noted by John Baylis (1989, p 61), who confirmed 'the cornerstone of the Macmillan government's foreign and defence policy after Suez was therefore to try and re-establish close ties with the United States'. Writing a year after the unification of Germany, Richard Mottram (1991, p 22) identified the driving force behind the 1991 Options for Change defence review as international change and 'particularly the impact of development in Soviet foreign and defence policies under President Gorbachev over a number of years'. This view was supported by Robert Self (2010, p 171) who wrote: 'The revolutionary events in Eastern Europe in 1989, which culminated with the dissolution of the Soviet Union in December 1991 ... fundamentally transformed the environment in which British external policy was formulated. These momentous events made demands for the already long overdue defence review almost irresistible.' The impact on the 1991 review was unmistakeable. In addition to significant equipment reductions across all three services, military manpower fell by 18 per cent and UK forces in Germany were halved (HCDC, 1998a). At the time of writing, the COVID-19 pandemic is still affecting much of our daily lives. Therefore, to quote Zhou Enlai's apocryphal observation on the French Revolution, it is too early to say how it will affect future government's strategic direction or defence decision makers' subsequent military capability choices. That said, it was clearly to the fore during the 2021 IR. Indeed, it was the underpinning theme of the prime minister's *Forward* to the Integrated Review report, which included the promise to 'build back better, ensuring that we are stronger, safer and more prosperous than before' (HM Government, 2021b, p 3).

Throughout the last 75 years, there is plenty of evidence to suggest that contemporaneous events also played their part in the shaping of UK defence policy through defence reviews. During Healey's tenure as defence secretary, for example, Carver (1992, p 88) identified two external events that impacted on UK defence policy. Both had a Gallic connection. The first was French president Charles de Gaulle's decision to withdraw his country from the military organization of the North Atlantic Alliance (NAA) in March 1966, and his subsequent demand for the removal from French territory of all its installations and member states' forces. The second was prime minister Harold Wilson's decision to apply for a second time to join the European Economic Community in 1967, following his predecessor's failed attempt four years earlier[3] (The National Archives, 2003b). The outcome of both events was the UK government felt it increasingly necessary to be seen as a committed member of the NAA, by both the US and its fellow European members. To that end, it had no leeway in fulfilling its extant Brussels Treaty obligations regarding the maintenance of agreed troop levels and a tactical air force in Northwest Europe.

Contemporaneous events have continued to influence defence reviews during the Quinquennial Review period. During the 2010 SDSR, two events stand out. The global economic crisis of 2008, which is considered in Chapter 6, and the ongoing conflict in Afghanistan. Although UK military operations in Afghanistan had begun in 2001, with British forces deploying as part of Operation *Veritas* in support of the US Operation *Enduring Freedom*, it was the deployment to Helmand Province in 2006, under Operation *Herrick*, that saw activity increase to an enduring, medium-scale effort (Elliott, 2015, pp 129–42). By 2010, the UK armed forces, and in particular the army, had adopted a campaign approach to Operation *Herrick* (Richards, 2014, p 287) and, when the SDSR was published, had in the region of 9,500 personnel in Afghanistan. Furthermore, it was recognized, by both the government and the UK media, as Defence's main effort[4] (see HM Government, 2010a, p 15; and Channel 4, 2010). Dorman (2011, p 80) categorized this as the 'elephant in the room', and believed that, even though other reviews had had wars and conflicts in the background, the war in Afghanistan was far more prominent and influential in determining the outcomes of this SDSR. For example, he suggested that it was the argument deployed by the army for excepting it from most of the cutbacks. Although some commentators believe the post-Afghanistan bar for committing UK forces to enduring interventions will be considerably higher than during the Early Expeditionary period (see Chalmers, 2011, pp 26–7; and Dover and Phythian, 2011, pp 434–5), a precedent may have been set. With all three services committed to significantly more operations in the post-campaigning era – albeit predominantly at a reduced scale of effort than both Iraq and Afghanistan – the influence of participation in extant operations may well be substantial in defence reviews of the future. This, in turn, could have a direct impact on decisions regarding future military capability.

In addition to the COVID-19 pandemic, contemporaneous events also influenced the 2021 IR and, more noticeably, the associated DCP. In its chapter on the future battlefield, the command paper makes clear that tomorrow's operating environment will be defined by complex and integrated challenges, which are driving significant changes to the character of conflict (HM Government, 2021b, pp 9–10). These conclusions are regularly discussed in public forums by defence decision makers (see, for example, GOV.UK, 2021b; and GOV.UK. 2021c) and were drawn from the examination of ongoing conflicts in such places as Syria, Libya, Ukraine and in the Nagorno-Karabash region.

As well as the external events discussed above, several other, less obvious, events also influenced defence reviews. For example, the ongoing troubles in Northern Ireland, and the resultant strain of maintaining high force levels in the province, was recognized by Jackson (1990, p 138) as a significant reason as to why none of the army's infantry units were disbanded in the 1975 defence review. Also relevant during this period was the increase in prominence of public perception. Mason recognized the importance of convincing people not only of the need for resources in security, but also of the impact any decisions in the review might have on jobs. At the same time, he acknowledged the importance of unions, conveners and shop stewards – very much a sign of the times – and summed up a key aspect of this issue with the following:

> [I]t is one of the paradoxes of defence policy that, once you have attained peace, you soon lose – in the eyes of all too many people – the justification for maintaining military forces, or anything more than a minimal state of readiness for resisting political and military pressures from other countries. (Mason, 1975, p 220)

Finally, there are also lower-profile occurrences, which are easily forgotten but nevertheless focus the minds of decision makers at a specific moment in time. One example was the Options for Change strapline: 'forces which while smaller, are well equipped, properly trained *and housed*, and well-motivated' [italics added] (MoD, 1991, p 6). The 'and housed' was included because of actions forced on the government at the time, in response to extensive criticism in the media over the woeful standard of married quarters that some service personnel were having to live in. In a year that was considered 'the most momentous for Defence since the end of the Second World War' (1991, p 5), it is unlikely that anyone anticipated having to include a reference to service accommodation in the secretary of state's introduction to the statement on the defence estimates. It may be impossible to predict the future, but it is possible to predict that future strategic shocks and contemporaneous events will regularly impact on defence reviews. Moreover, as defence reviews are now the most significant part of a government's strategic direction, if future strategic shocks impact defence reviews, they will also have an effect on military capability decision making.

The political aspects of defence reviews

In a construct that is driven so heavily by strategic direction, it is axiomatic that politics will play a significant part in the process of defence reviews. That includes internal party politics. For example, both Healey and Mason had to cope with dissent from their fellow MPs and the wider Labour Party. The Labour government's increased majority after the 1966 general election enabled its backbenchers to become far more vocal in their opposition to the government's determination to maintain Britain's world-wide role and retain its independent nuclear deterrent (Chalmers, 1985, p 85). Darby (1973, p 322) also discussed this issue, pointing to MP Michael Foot's querying the validity of his own government's defence savings by saying 'Healey's £100 million turns up like a free coupon in every package'. Nine years later, large sections of the Labour Party did not believe that the 1975 defence review had got the balance right between the conflicting pressure of security interests and economic growth, and pressed for larger cuts in defence spending. Prior to the 1974 general election, a resolution had been overwhelmingly passed at the Labour Party conference calling for cuts of at least £1 billion a year to defence spending (Mason, 1999, p 123). Even after the 1975 review, Labour's National Executive's defence study group demanded a further 20 per cent cut in planned defence spending to fulfil their manifesto target (Chalmers, 1985, p 96). Michael Chichester and John Wilkinson (1982, p 48) suggested that Mason did well to withstand the pressures from within his party and maintain a credible outcome to his review.

The unusual political situation that followed the 2010 general election also unquestionably affected the 2010 SDSR. In addition to the process aspects of the coalition government's approach discussed previously, the politics within both the Conservative and Liberal Democrat parties also played their part. Dorman (2011, p 5) recognized the dilemma facing David Cameron over what to do with a close rival – in this instance, Dr Liam Fox – and how he chose to follow a 'traditional Tory leader policy' by giving him the 'poison chalice of the defence portfolio'. This keeping your enemy close approach meant that Fox would be fully occupied in a difficult role, which could also undermine his popularity within the Conservative Party due to the cuts to Defence he would be forced to make. In addition, Fox would have to observe Cabinet collective responsibility. The leader of the Liberal Democrats, Nick Clegg, also faced internal, party-political issues, primarily over the probable like-for-like replacement for the nuclear deterrent, which many of his party colleagues opposed. In addition, any defence review decisions that went against the RN were unlikely to be well received in the traditional liberal heartlands in the southwest of England. For Clegg, therefore, the SDSR centred on domestic politics, and how its outcomes would affect his party in the next general election.

An examination of the political aspects of the 2015 yielded a fascinating cross-section of responses from senior officials. One four-star officer, when asked if he could talk about the political influence on that review, responded 'No, I don't think so. I mean, there was a lot, but I'm not going to talk about anything.' In contrast, another four-star officer suggested there was undue influence from 'two people in particular, one the prime minister and two the chancellor'. A third believed that the biggest influence on the whole shape of the SDSR outcome was 'what Number 10 and Number 11 wanted'. Moreover, he also suggested that there was a significant trade-off game being played:

'It is the case that right up until a few days before the outcome [of the 2015 SDSR] that many of the things that Defence wanted, Number 10 and 11 would not agree to unless we gave them more of what they wanted, which were different to what Defence wanted. That was the trick in the final stages.'

David Cameron's hands-on approach was confirmed by an air marshal, who was in a key SDSR appointment outside the MoD at the time of the review. In his view, the prime minister was heavily involved in the detailed decision making. This opinion was supported by another senior official who confirmed that: 'There was also a savings option against annual pay increments for military personnel, which was removed at the last minute by the prime minister himself.' A final observation on the roles of the prime minister and the chancellor of the exchequer in 2015, made by a major general, reinforces the significance of both contemporary events and personalities as factors in the translation of strategic direction into military capability:

'The political guidance was interesting, because at the time Mr Cameron was the prime minister, Mr Osborne was the chancellor, and the working assumption, I think, was that Osborne would take over from Cameron in due course. So that had an influence on their view of what Defence's priorities were. The chancellor's letter of direction to the secretary of state [for defence] – so that's the first thing, the PM and chancellor [were] both giving direction – was pointing in a different direction. It was more about prosperity and capabilities for the long term ... [it] felt a bit like "I want to make sure Defence is in good order when I ascend to the throne" as it were. There was definitely a divergence. In terms of unity of direction, I didn't see it. In fact, I saw the opposite.'

Another major source of tension during defence reviews was the influence of small and large 'P' politics. An RAF two-star officer suggested that the MoD was regularly restricted in its force structure decision making because of lobbying at the political level; the example he gave was the debate during the NSCR about the value of amphibious forces. A high-profile media campaign in defence of the Royal Marines was initiated as soon as it became clear that reductions to the UK's amphibious capability were being considered (see BBC, 2018; and Farmer, 2018). That prompted a report by the HCDC (2018b), which, in the opinion of the same senior official, undoubtedly influenced future amphibious capability programming decisions:

'You can make a perfectly rational, reasonable case that you shouldn't spend the money on landing craft that move at four knots and are sitting targets in a modern world with guided weapons. Therefore, you should spend it on something else. But the small and large 'P' politics have played a part in that, and has got us to a position where actually, it's become untenable to even talk about any kind of reduction in amphibious capability. I'm not saying it is, but even if that were the logical lower priority for us to go at.'

The same official recognized that opinions in parliament could have a similar effect on capability choices that defence decision makers may wish to make:

'The problem is that you have got a Tory backbench principally, but there are others, who see any adjustments in anachronistic, archaic structures and capabilities as an assault on British manhood. Therefore, [they] will fight in the Commons, and fight dirty, to prevent us from doing things that are quite obvious or would be quite reasonable or sensible to do. That's going to make life bloody difficult. The danger is you end up not taking out things you want, which are some of the photogenic capabilities, in order to invest in the glue and the enablers, because of the politics of the situation. I think that's a real threat to us.'

The difficulties of convincing politicians to support capability decisions that favour enablers over ships, planes and tanks was highlighted by a two-star officer serving in JFC. His view was 'you have to really convince people they want to [procure enabling capability], because no parliamentarian is going to be photographed in front of a server'. Although frustrating to the military practitioner, this approach by politicians reinforces the point about dissimilar worlds and should not be a surprise. Political influence in defence decision making has a long history. For example, as McInnes (1998, p 831) pointed out, even though ministers emphasized that no options should be ruled out of the 1998 SDR, several programmes, including Eurofighter Typhoon, were effectively ring-fenced. More recently, a former three-star civil servant highlighted, at the outset of the 2010 SDSR, 'Number 10 had decreed that [reducing the British Army to 80,000] was politically off the table'.

A commonly held view among senior officials was that an SDSR will always be more about politics than strategy; indeed, a former senior civil servant suggested of an SDSR report that 'wherever you get rough edges in it, the political sandpaper comes out to make it not look so rough-edged'. The significance of a new government's manifesto promises, another regular influence on defence reviews already identified in this investigation, was also recognized. One RAF four-star officer posited that defence reviews would always be underpinned by tangible manifesto requirements, regardless of any imperative considered by defence planners at the time. He believed that 'it's always going to be an outcome, which is shaped by manifesto commitments, which may or may not bear a contact with reality'. While many senior officials acknowledged that politicians would always want their manifesto commitments delivered, one army general cautioned about reading too much into a manifesto commitment. Having studied the defence and security aspects of successful parties' manifestos throughout his considerable time in service, he concluded that:

'A commitment to the deterrent is only a commitment to "x" number of boats of a certain type, if that's what it says [in the manifesto]. If it's just a commitment to a deterrent, that could be just one bomb in a bunker somewhere. So, there is a bit of a tendency for people to read too much into a commitment. It's very definitely the words on the card.'

The conclusion reached in Chapter 3, that politicians and the military occupy dissimilar worlds, is reinforced in this section. Defence reviews have subtly different audiences in the different worlds and aspire to achieve subtly different outcomes. What the military is looking for is explored further in Chapter 7; what the politician is seeking may be more akin to this thought offered by a former three-star civil servant: 'I think that what politicians are trying to do is to come up with something crafty, that spills the least amount of political blood, whilst trying to keep the most number of people [as] broadly happy as possible'.

The role of defence decision makers in recent defence reviews

The Quinquennial Review period has seen SDSRs in 2010 and 2015, as well as the Integrated Review in 2021. It has also included the NSCR and the MDP study, both of which reported in 2018. The window for my elite interviews lasted from May 2016 until March 2018. Therefore, while some of the observations recorded in this section may well be relevant to all activity within the Quinquennial Review period, it should be recognized that they were raised only in discussions specific to the 2010 and 2015 SDSRs.

Although the reviews of 2010 and 2015 were both strategic defence and security reviews and sought similar goals, most defence decision makers recognized there were considerable differences between both the context and the way they were conducted. The common view was that the 2010 SDSR had been dominated by finance, and the need for the defence and security community to contribute to the coalition government's plans to bring the budget deficit under control. One four-star army general described the driving function of the 2010 SDSR as a 'withdrawal in contact with austerity'. Similarly, an air marshal, who was closely involved with his service's contribution to the 2015 SDSR, observed:

> '2010 was very clearly arguing about who got a slice of a smaller pie. That created a lot of angst and difficulty ... '10 and '15 were very, very different in context terms, and clearly in outcome terms. It's hard to draw too many parallels between one and the other.'

A simple interpretation of the feedback from senior officials was '2010 SDSR – bad, 2015 SDSR – good'. A typical summary of the 2010 SDSR experience was offered by a senior civil servant who said: 'it just felt like a train wreck. It felt like you went in in chaos, and you came out in just a different flavour of chaos.' In comparison, reaction from those close to the 2015 SDSR process was far more upbeat. The RN view was that 'It worked really well from a Navy Command Headquarters perspective'; a senior army officer suggested, 'I think absolutely one would see it [the 2015 SDSR] as a positive ... [it] broadly got the army to where it wanted to be'; and an air marshal confirmed that 'overall, as an airman, I don't think we could have come out of '15 any better'. However, when considering how the Quinquennial Review process affected the translation of strategic direction into military capability, many of those interviewed believed there was considerable scope for improvement.

The idea that there has never been a standard process for a defence review was reinforced by several senior officials. Furthermore, as I recognized in a 2019 article for *The RUSI Journal*, that is unlikely to change, as it is not in the interests of politicians to reduce their own freedom of manoeuvre. This supports the view that defence reviews and their outcomes are inherently political. One recently retired RAF three-star officer believed that reviews become political footballs, and that 'They are very much of their time, and if elections or situations within government are at a certain point in time, the SDSR has to just take its place as part of that argument or process'. A similar view was offered by one of his four-star colleagues:

'[W]hat tends always to happen in defence reviews is something which matches political required outcomes, which is focused on force structure. In other words, what the government will announce out of the defence reviews is not some conceptual thing. It will be, "We're going to buy more ships, tanks, aircraft", or something like that.'

This is at odds with an understanding expressed by a number of senior officials that a defence review is about 'balancing the books', or is 'a once-in-a-five-year opportunity to reset the programme', or even 'an opportunity for the government of the day to restate what its strategic defence and security policy is … to either revalidate what they've already said, or to tune it'. These views accord with the MoD's own official definition prior to 2020, which confirmed the SDSR's remit as identifying the means (resources) and ways (courses of action) across government, needed to deliver the ends described in the NSS (MoD, 2015b, p 14).

However, while these views, and the MoD's official definition, may well represent a reasonable expectation of the outcomes of a defence review, one RAF four-star officer, who was very closely involved with the Defence input to the 2015 SDSR, took time during his interview to explain what he considered the reality of the review process to be. He argued that it was exceptionally rare for a defence review to result in a radical change to policy, pointing out that Healey's reviews of the late 1960s and the Options for Change exercise in 1991 were the only two occasions in the last 75 years where this may have occurred. In his view, there was seldom an appetite within government to undertake a radical redefinition of defence policy, as that would require a radical redefinition of foreign policy, which would mean re-visiting the question of Britain's place in the world. He went on to suggest that 'governments generally aren't up for that and, by and large, the world doesn't need it either'. This view was supported by a fellow army four-star officer who suggested that the only time real change in defence policy would be countenanced was when the government faced a 'massive money crisis' or the military has had 'a major thrashing'. The conclusion drawn by the first officer was that doing the conceptual thinking was not wrong, but Defence should always be focusing its efforts on the decisions that the government wanted to make, for example what was the political appetite and what did the politicians actually want to do? This approach was needed because, ultimately, what happened in the decision making of the defence review process was a fusion of what Defence thought it needed to do for the future and what the government actually wanted to do for the future.

One of the obvious advantages of working to a pre-agreed cycle for defence reviews was the opportunity for prior preparation. In the words of a two-star, defence review expert, ' you need to give yourself enough time to get on top of the context, to ensure that you have cleared the ground and you know what you're doing for an SDSR'. However, if the reality of the situation argued in the previous paragraph is accepted, then there is a real danger of the MoD undertaking considerable amounts of nugatory work in the build-up to an SDSR. For example, the logical preparations for Defence to invest effort in would be to focus on the future operating environment and strategic trends. This, of course, it does – MoD's global strategic trends analysis being the most obvious example (see MoD, 2010c; MoD, 2014c; and MoD, 2018b). Nevertheless, the outcome from this activity may be completely irrelevant in the context of a defence review, because, if the preparatory work leads to the conclusion that a radical redefinition of policy is required, the analysis above has confirmed that the government generally 'isn't up for that'. As the same air marshal cited above observed: 'In the preparations [for a defence review], there needs to be a degree of purity in the thought process, but we should not confuse that purity of doing ... the intellectual process, with what's actually going to happen in the actual reality of the decision making.'

The line of analysis followed above led to several discussions about how defence decision makers view defence reviews. One RAF two-star officer, in an influential MoD head office appointment, believed that all defence reviews were a negotiation. This view was reinforced by two of his colleagues who were closely involved in MoD head office's initial preparations for the 2015 SDSR; in particular, the defensive position adopted by the department prior to the government's 2 per cent (of GDP) defence spending commitment in the July 2015 budget (Hansard, 2015b). Both discussed the extreme concern felt because of the expectation that the MoD was going to have to accept a reduction in its budget. They also confirmed the pre-budget focus was predominantly on making a case to counter that. One suggested, 'had we been told that the best [financial settlement] we could have hoped for was flat-real, or even a reduction, then we would have spent a considerable part of the SDSR working up arguments to try and move that decision'. On a broader front, a recently retired four-star officer suggested that the 2015 SDSR was a 'battle from the start' and that 'we were shying away from the true state of Defence across the piece'. This adversarial, us-and-them evidence suggests that the defence decision makers' view of defence reviews was far from a collegiate, all-of-one-team event. Instead, it was more akin to a fraught, high-stakes battle involving all the defence- and security-related government departments, while acknowledging the most dangerous opponent was almost certainly the treasury.

Recognizing the confrontational nature of the cross-government SDSR process outlined above, the MoD has responded by building and operating internal ways of working that have successfully prepared it for participation. With regard to the 2015 SDSR, this revolved around preparing and presenting options for the Defence Strategy Group[5] (DSG) to endorse and feed up into the macro-SDSR decision-making cycle. The options were developed from internal conceptual analysis around the capabilities the MoD believed it needed for the outputs it thought were expected of it, input from allies (notably the US and France), and the priorities initially identified by the prime minister and the chancellor of the exchequer. This generated a short list of key capabilities (around six or seven) that needed to be addressed. The next step was to identify and cost the capability improvements that would provide the best value for money and operationally significant enhancements to the key capabilities, which generated a prioritized list of approximately 130 options. At the same time, savings and efficiency measures were being developed to provide the resource to underwrite the capability improvements. The two parts came together to present a decision-making matrix to the DSG, which identified how much money could be generated, to reach how far down the priority list, to enable how much capability enhancement.

Notwithstanding the effect of the political direction injected into the process, the methodology outlined above could be considered a credible defence input into the cross-government review process. However, it was not without flaws. As I've already argued, capability decisions are shaped by the existing force structure, or, in other words, what Defence already has. The baseline for the conceptual analysis at the start of the process will always be the existing force structure. As a former incumbent of MoD head office's most senior capability management appointment observed:

'It would be tempting to say, "every defence review, a blank sheet of paper – what do we need for the future?" Then we'd put together an investment plan which achieves that. Then we'd look to see how that matches up with what we're already planning to do. In a pure world, you'd be absolutely right, but we're not [in a pure world]. The reality is here's the force we've got. That in many ways defines the defence policy and the whole process.'

Furthermore, regardless of the thoroughness of the analysis and the trustworthiness of the associated costings, the reality was that in 2015 defence decision makers were constantly being pressured to realize more savings, to buy more capability enhancements, and to progress further down the priority list. This pressure was the source of many of the concerns raised by senior officials about the overall affordability of defence, which is explored further in the next chapter.

Defence is not a single, homogenous construct, and, therefore, it was no surprise that the views of senior officials generated conflicting evidence concerning Defence's approach to the Quinquennial Review process. It was suggested that, from the outset, Defence's interaction with the 2015 SDSR was deliberately established as an MoD, centre-led process, with only 'relatively light touch consultation' with the service commands. This approach was seen differently by senior officers in single service appointments. The RN view was that the single services were kept out of the process for too long; the response from the army was that the single services felt slightly ostracized by the process and would have preferred to have been more fully engaged; and the RAF considered that the service chiefs had had very little influence over the process.

There was, however, congruence between the single services and MoD head office on pre-budget views over finance, with one army four-star officer commenting, 'people imagined that SDSR and CSR 15 would be about a mega-savings exercise. So, I think a lot of people were preparing themselves for a knife fight in a phone box.' Even when the initially feared budgetary restrictions failed to materialize, the single service reading remained that finance was the driving factor, with one RAF four-star officer confirming: 'What was clear from our viewpoint [was] there was going to be a pot of money, which the individual chiefs were invited to pitch for, for want of a better phrase.' Officers from all the single services asserted that they prepared and delivered a proposition for the 2015 SDSR to the DSG. However, this approach inevitably led to an element of inter-service confrontation, as, even with the chancellor's relaxing of the purse strings, there was never going to be enough money to go around. This was corroborated by an air marshal who, when asked whether there was 'protectionism from the services', answered:

'Protectionism is the wrong word. Was there ambition? Yes, and I can tell you that the army wanted two-star divisional warfighting, two-star divisional command, was their name. They wanted Scout; they wanted the two strike brigades. The navy wanted protection of the carriers, they wanted more frigates than they ended up with, and they wanted more people. I think their bid was about 2,500 and they got 400. So, there are games played in that space, in terms of affordability, you know, pushing programmes left and right, and finding headroom within them. So, that's half the problem. The next problem is, the services then, sort of eye each other across the table, and go, "Well, I want this, and you want that, and I want the other". So, there is a game within a game. Personally, I would prefer if all those positions were just laid on the table. Of course, it's right and proper of a service chief, as the expert of his field, to put a case for what he believes he needs to meet the strategy.'

Even during an SDSR when, as one three-star civil servant from MoD head office confirmed, 'the debate became how the money should be best spend', it was clear the single services all believed that they were in a contest, which would have winners and losers. In fact, very much a one–step–down position from where MoD head office considered itself, within the overall review process. Moreover, in a contest where the politicians call the shots, the single service winner would be the one that best understood the political appetite and could provide the capability choice that best supported what the politicians wanted to do. This analysis was confirmed by an air marshal, who was closely involved with his service's preparations for the 2015 SDSR. He explained that the RAF's pitch did not include a big idea, whereas the army's presentation was built around the new strike brigade concept, which caught the eye:

'The lesson I took from it is that it is ultimately about politics, and the prime minister was going to stand up in the House of Commons and announce this thing. He needed stuff that would catch the eye. If you read his transcript, he led with strike brigades. I guess the deduction from that is that it's all very well being steady, stable, logical, rational, which are, I think, important factors in it, and using evidence that is understood and seen. But you also need to have an eye to the announcement, something that will get them.'

A senior army officer, working in the DE&S offered an extremely pertinent comment about the 2015 SDSR during his interview. He said, 'I came away from [SDSR] 15 thinking "oh, we might be alright" [but] what we'd done is, we'd put the difficult decisions off until tomorrow'. Over the last few years, more and more post-2015 SDSR problems have emerged. The most obvious of these are in the financial management space. One TLB holder confessed: 'the financial reality was, the year of the SDSR … just closed out, effectively in moratoria to get there, and I was nowhere near closing out years two and three, they were a billion quid adrift in each year.' The UK's decision to leave the EU undoubtedly contributed to Defence's budget challenges; however, as one army three-star officer pointed out, decisions taken as part of the 2015 SDSR were equally to blame: 'We didn't want to make large changes to the balance of the programme, so we just balanced the books on paper by giving ourselves wedges.' Notwithstanding the resource management improvements that the DRP was designed to engender, until Defence adopts a more robust and credible approach to its financial management, future reviews are likely to unravel as swiftly as the 2015 SDSR has done.

A further, sizeable constraint, identified by interviewees from all backgrounds, was the time allocated to complete recent defence reviews. All who expressed an opinion about either the 2010 or 2015 SDSR confirmed that the process was conducted too hastily, and outputs suffered as a result. One former three-star civil servant believed that the limited time allocated to SDSRs led to immature thinking; others considered that it resulted in the need to reverse engineer some decisions. One RAF two-star officer commented that 'it felt like there were a series of pre-conceived conclusions that had been reached [and] that this work was now about evidencing them'. Another former three-star civil servant, who was close to the political process in 2010, believed the time to deliver that SDSR was very constrained, and the defence secretary 'simply didn't have enough days for him to devote a lot of attention to each and every report'. This observation was reinforced by another civil servant who confirmed that many of the supporting studies commissioned by the MoD for the 2010 SDSR simply 'ended up on the cutting room floor'. A similar situation occurred five years later when the Cabinet Office team for the 2015 SDSR was seeking to secure direction from the NSC. An air marshal, working on the review externally to the MoD, reported that only three sessions of the NSC were devoted to reviewing SDSR documentation, with all other information having to be circulated out of committee. His recollection of the process was:

> 'You have to deliver your key points to the National Security Council; you've probably got five bullets to discuss in a very short period for their business. This is what we're doing. Here's where we're going. Key points are the following. Key issues and worries. Are you happy with the progress?'

A final point discussed by defence decision makers concerned potential changes for future reviews. Views fell broadly into three groups. The greatest number of comments concerned an increased role for the single services, which, unsurprisingly, accords with analysis earlier in this section. The second group of comments focused on changes outside Defence; for example, achieving a consensus on the national vision for the UK's place in the world, generating a political climate where an honest review about the state of UK defence could take place, or receiving a credible fiscal envelope to plan against. One senior official argued that the secretary of state should be legally obligated by parliament to create a balanced programme and demonstrate that it was so. The final, and smallest, collection of comments concentrated on changes that could be made within Defence to improve the process. Here, there was a recognition that good internal process or documentation was often not fully exploited or, in some cases, was ignored completely. Examples given were MoD joint doctrine and risk management procedures. One three-star officer also acknowledged that the Defence approach to the Quinquennial Review process needed to be more agile, particularly to be able to accommodate politicians' preferences for last-minute decision making. Accepting the political nature of the process and abandoning the military's desire to confirm courses of action as early as possible, were, in his view, essential internal improvements that needed to be made.

How have defence reviews affected military capability choices?

Throughout the Cold War and Early Expeditionary period, defence reviews did not follow any pre-ordained timeline. Instead, they were undertaken at a time that suited the government of the day. The only defence review in the last 75 years that kept to its expected schedule was the 2015 SDSR, which adhered to its predecessor's commitment of holding a review of defence and security policy every five years. Even though the 2021 IR began in 2020 and may appear to have kept to the cycle, it was never portrayed by the Johnson government as the third quinquennial review. Indeed, the prime minister went out of his way to distance his review from the previous two SDSRs, by using different terminology, widening the scope to include development and foreign policy, and promising that it would be the deepest since the end of the Cold War. Similarly, the methodology used to undertake defence reviews has never been standardized. This also includes the content and format of the accompanying documentation. From the go-it-alone method of Duncan Sandys and John Nott to the all-encompassing, collegiate method of George Robertson, the process of a defence review has always aligned with the general approach to governing and policy aspirations of the incumbent government. As it is not in the interests of politicians to reduce their own freedom of manoeuvre, that is unlikely to change. For the same reason, it is doubtful we will see the defence review process ever codified through legislation.

The reason for this lack of standardization in both timing and process is simple. Defence reviews are fundamentally political undertakings and will always be guided by the political instincts of the government of the day. My definition of a defence review, tweaked from Lawrence Freedman's original over 30 years ago, is: an examination, by the UK government, of its defence and security commitments and associated resources to ascertain whether they are still appropriate and, if necessary, initiate corrective action. To use operational planning parlance, the politicians are the supported command, the military are supporting (NATO, 2010, pp 6–7).[6] However, while this relationship is reasonably well known by those defence decision makers who have been closely involved in the high-level workings of defence reviews, it is not necessarily understood by senior officials outside MoD head office. Some defence decision makers do not appreciate the political realities of the translation of strategic direction into military capability. This situation is not helped by Defence's insistence on trying to codify its end of the process. The military way is to create and document standard procedures to show the way for busy staff officers at all levels in the chain of command. However, when it comes to defence reviews, the military's carefully crafted regulations have no political socket to plug into. This mismatch is troublesome, but by no means disastrous. Much of the MoD's pre-defence review preparations play a useful role in informing the debate; however, the fact remains that, in the eyes of defence decision makers, too much of their input either fails to get the desired traction or is ignored completely.

The traditional approach to defence reviews was accurately, though somewhat depressingly, summed up by Edward Hampshire:

> Defence reviews have the reputation of being focused on cutting capabilities and commitments, of cancelling defence projects, of reducing numbers of troops, and then being accompanied by the wailing and gnashing of teeth by retired generals, think-tankers and Conservative backbenchers as Britain's international power and influence is seen to be shrinking and the UK is accused of withdrawing from its world role. (Hampshire, 2015)

Today's defence decision makers have lived through every defence review since the end of the Cold War. Many, like the current secretary of state for defence, Ben Wallace, will only have been a junior officer at the time of the Options for Change review in 1991 (MoD, 2021b, p 1); nonetheless, they have first-hand experience of post-Cold War cuts to manpower and equipment. The dominating paradigm of their formative years in the military aligns completely with Hampshire's view. This was very evident during the elite interviews conducted for this book, and it clearly affected the defence approach to both the 2010 and 2015 SDSRs (while I cannot offer any firm evidence, that is probably the case for the 2021 IR as well).

The current cohort of defence decision makers see defence reviews as battles, which they have fought on two distinct, but inter-related levels. At the higher level, the MoD battles with the treasury to secure the largest possible share of public funds for Defence. On the same plane, it is in a contest with other government departments for as much cross-Whitehall security funding as it can secure, from sources such as the Conflict, Stability and Security Fund (HM Government, 2021a). At the same time, the MoD is trying to gain Downing Street backing for new capabilities, while also fighting to safeguard existing capabilities that it wants to maintain. The result is a messy series of decisions, almost always centred on equipment, that brings together what Defence thinks it needs to do for the future and what the government wants to do in the future.

One level down, the single services battle between themselves for the largest possible slice of the defence budget. Threats of cuts always lead to inter-service rivalry (see, for example, Wyatt, 2010); moreover, as Cornish and Dorman (2015, pp 362–3) have identified, during defence reviews the unanimity of service chiefs cannot be maintained, as their allegiance to their respective service will take precedence over their commitment to defence overall. Lobbying groups and retired senior officers add their voices to the mix, as public support is sought to defend historic regiments or traditional equipment types reported to be facing the axe. Capabilities often survive because of who shouts the loudest, rather than how well they might contribute to the future force structure. To return to my definition, today's defence reviews are far from an examination of defence and security commitments and associated resources to ascertain whether they are still appropriate and, if necessary, initiate corrective action. They are neither dispassionate nor collegiate. Instead, they have become a multi-level, confrontational negotiation, involving central government, the MoD and the single services, that focuses on resources and outputs, rather than considering a conceptual view of the application of military capability to meet policy aims. In the context of translating strategic direction into military capability, this really matters. As I have repeatedly observed in this chapter, defence reviews are the most significant part of a government's strategic direction. If they are undertaken badly, and deliver poor outcomes, this can only lead to tougher military capability choices for defence decision makers.

The Affordability of Defence

Existing analyses of early defence reviews are dominated by the impact that economics has had on decision making. John Baylis (1986b, p 443) cited the titles of several books and journal articles on the subject[1] to reinforce what he believed was a commonly held, or conventional, view that a continuous process of contraction and decline was the most apt description of the trajectory of post-Second World War UK defence policy. This historiographic orthodoxy that economic constraints on defence expenditure precipitated the UK's post-1945 relative decline remains the dominant paradigm. In the academic examinations that followed all the Cold War defence reviews, cutbacks in capability were regularly attributed to the deterioration of the economy, which forced the government of the day into reducing defence expenditure (see Chichester and Wilkinson,1982, pp x–xvi; and Rees, 1989, p 218). For some, even the first consideration of nuclear weapons in the 1957 defence review was influenced by economic factors (see Dorman, 2001c, pp 188–92). Specifically, Martin Navias (1989, p 408) asserted that '[in 1957] nuclear strategic thinking was very much a secondary consideration in a larger formula that sought major financial savings'. Evidence that this thinking endured throughout the Cold War period can be found via both commentators (Healey and Cross, 1969, p 15) and practitioners (Jackson, 1990, pp 3–22). Revealingly, in 1975, defence secretary Roy Mason (1975, p 218) observed that 'the imperatives of economics, no matter how illogical this may be, do in fact exercise a commanding influence over the level of the resources which we can devote to defence'.

There are alternative points of view. Recalling the consequence of the UK's tardy rearmament decision in the 1930s (Dunbabin, 1975), John Slessor recognized the significance of the prevailing economic situation in the 1950s, but sounded the following words of caution:

There are those in Britain who ... are sceptical of the validity of the claim that Britain cannot afford to be strong. They remember the days when, little over a year before the outbreak of World War II, the material basis of British defence planning was a ruling by the government of the day that this country could not afford more than £300 million a year for all three services over the five years 1937–1941 … And they reflect with some bitterness upon the number of millions a year we had to pay in the ten years after 1939 for the luxury of being weak in 1939. This appeal to economics is a hand that can be overcalled. (Slessor, 1957, p 555)

Phillip Darby (1973, p 317) suggested that, during the Labour government's reviews of the 1960s, neither short- nor long-terms savings were so significant as to argue that the final shape of the UK's footprint East of Suez was economically motivated. Instead, he attributed the decision to other non-economic factors, notably increasing scepticism among government ministers about the effectiveness of the UK's military posture in the Middle and Far East, as well as an increasing groundswell of opinion (especially driven from within the Labour Party) towards redefining the UK's role as one within Europe, rather than maintaining world power aspirations. There is, however, one academic who is synonymous with a questioning of the enduring orthodoxy that a diminishing economy was the reason for the contraction of the UK's military capability since the end of the Second World War: David Greenwood.

Greenwood's revisionist approach to explaining how the UK budgeted for defence during the Cold War was so distinctive that it spawned its own term, 'Greenwoodery' (Baylis, 1986b, p 457). He was highly critical of the viewpoint that capability reduction was made inevitable by force of economic circumstances; instead, he argued that the government of the day always had a choice regarding its resource allocation for Defence. In Greenwood's view, economic constraints may have been influential, but they were never decisive. On this point, he asserted:

> The state of the economy does not force governments to make defence cuts, it merely defines the limits of policy choice. What a government decides to do when faced with various economic problems reflects its own values and priorities. It is, strictly speaking, a question of political choice, not of economic necessity. (Greenwood, cited by Baylis, 1986b, p 452)

Although Greenwood's assessment may be literally correct, others have recognized that cuts and reductions in declaratory defence policy have often been made by the government of the day with the utmost reluctance. For example, Malcolm Chalmers (1985, p 87) argued that, right up until the final moment, ministers continued to believe the 1968 decision to withdraw completely from East of Suez by 1971 could have been avoided 'by sleight of hand or a sudden improvement in the economy'. By contrast, Chalmers also pointed out that, at the 1974 general election, the incoming Labour government was elected on a manifesto pledge to 'progressively reduce the burden of Britain's defence spending to bring costs into line with those carried out by [the UK's] main European allies' (1985, p 95). Therefore, even though the state of the UK economy was so parlous that, according to William Jackson (1990, p 134) 'no government – Labour or Tory – could have left Defence unscathed in the economic and political chaos that engulfed the country in the spring of 1974', the Labour Party had already committed to realizing several hundred million pounds per annum of savings from the defence budget (Chichester and Wilkinson, 1982, p 14). Even though Greenwood's hypothesis that 'the UK can devote to Defence what is chooses to devote to it' (1968, p 328) may be technically correct, this suggests the economic situation throughout the Cold War forced UK politicians frequently to translate his choice characteristic as no choice at all.

Beyond the general reference to Greenwood's individual approach to defence budgeting, Greenwoodery was also associated with his particular contribution to the argument concerning a purported funding gap in the UK defence budget in the late 1980s (Baylis, 1986b, pp 454–6). Greenwood argued that, from the 1983 general election until the end of the decade, the UK defence programme was continuously underfunded, creating a gap between declaratory defence policy and the actual military capability necessary to achieve stated policy goals. In his view, this was primarily because the treasury and the MoD used overly optimistic assumptions about inflation in their public expenditure planning, but also because of 'that persistent tendency of costs in the defence sector to rise faster than prices in general' (Greenwood, 1991, p 40). As a result, military resources and political commitments became out of balance. Rather than reconsider commitments, the Conservative government of the time chose to take short-term savings measures, such as reducing military activity levels and elongating delivery schedules for new equipment. For example, not only was the introduction into service of the European Fighter Aircraft (since designated the Eurofighter Typhoon) delayed, but it also went on to replace rather than supplement – as had been originally planned – the Tornado F3, which itself had only entered service in 1987. In addition, rigorous efficiency drives were pursued across defence in an effort to reduce costs (Hobkirk, 1987). According to Baylis (1986b, p 455), Greenwood believed that, although efficiency measures did yield some savings, the size of the funding gap would reach approximately £3.7 billion, or almost 20 per cent of the entire defence budget, by 1989. This concern about the shortfall in the defence budget was not limited to Greenwood (see Coker, 1992; and Dunn, 1992); moreover, as Michael Asteris (1994, p 43) pointed out, it was only resolved by the fortuitous demise of the Soviet Union and the subsequent disbanding of the Warsaw Pact.

The end of the Cold War also saw the end of the Greenwoodery debate. Reductions in military capability in the early 1990s, following the Options for Change and the Defence Cost Study reviews, appeared to have closed the funding gap (Mottram, 1991). Scholars became far more preoccupied with what defence activity would look like in the post-Cold War era. This change in academic focus was evident not only in the content, but also the titles of journal articles of the time (see, for example, Bolton, 1991; Bellamy, 1992; Quinlan, 1992; and Sabin, 1993).[2] However, the underlying problems that created the funding gap have not gone away. Public expenditure planning remains vulnerable to over-optimistic assumptions, and defence inflation still exists (Hartley, 2010). These factors continue to place strains on government attempts to balance defence resources and policy commitments articulated in defence reviews, an issue I will return to later.

This chapter is divided into two main areas: the impact of the economy on defence reviews and contemporary affordability issues. The previous chapter confirmed the relevance of defence reviews to the interpretation of the translation of strategic direction to the military capability model; therefore, recognizing how finance and the economy have shaped defence reviews is a critical part of understanding why the UK has the military capability that it has. The second part of the analysis in this chapter focuses on the more tactical financial concerns of defence decision makers as they go about their business-as-usual management of military capability. Undoubtedly the biggest concerns expressed by senior officials in this area were the over-commitment of the defence budget and the ever-expanding list of efficiencies they were expected to deliver to help keep it in check.

The impact of the economy on defence reviews

Writing just before the end of the Cold War, Paul Kennedy (1988, p 482) observed that the 'divergence between Britain's shrunken economic state and its overextended strategic posture is probably more extreme than that affecting any other of the larger powers, except Russia'. Ron Smith (1990, p 76) was more focused when he suggested that 'economic performance was a constant constraint on [UK] defence policy'. Analysis confirms that finance and the economy had a considerable impact on all defence reviews from the end of the Second World War to the present day.

All four defence reviews of the Cold War had to contend with financial and economic issues, and all four ministers approached them in a different way. In 1957, Duncan Sandys recognized that the UK's internal economy and export trade underpinned its military power and global influence:

> Britain's influence in the world depends first and foremost on the health of her internal economy and the success of her export trade. Without these, military power cannot in the long run be supported. It is therefore in the true interests of defence that the claims of military expenditure should be considered in conjunction with the need to maintain the country's financial and economic strength. (MoD, 1957, p 1)

Wyn Rees (1989, p 226) concluded that Sandys knew the struggle against the Soviet Union would be long and drawn out and, therefore, only a healthy economy would be able to support a prolonged effort. To that end, Sandys' broad-brush measures of success were not numbers driven;[3] instead, he predicted that the full implementation of his defence plan would 'appreciably reduce the burden on the economy … releasing badly needed scientists and technicians, for employment in civilian industry. Both exports and capital investment will gain' (MoD, 1957, p 10).

In the 1960s, Denis Healey also understood the primacy of the economy, confirming that 'military strength is of little use if it is achieved at the expense of economic health' (MoD, 1966, p 1). However, in his review he elected to set a financial target for defence spending[4] even though, as Chalmers (1985, p 81) noted, the actual figure was 'arbitrary and chosen without any real consideration of the possible implications for commitments and programmes'. Regardless of whether monetary target-setting is the best method by which to focus a defence review, Healey had no doubt as to the importance of the financial context when undertaking defence decision making, as he explained during a lecture at RUSI towards the end of his tenure at the MoD:

> If I were to identify one lesson, which a Minister must learn when he is in office, it is the way in which financial constraints must limit a government's freedom of choice – even the richest country in the world. No Minister of Defence can hope to acquire every military capability which is desirable on purely defence grounds. (Healey and Cross, 1969, p 15)

The parlous state of the UK economy in the mid-1970s impacted on all the government's budgetary decisions, and Defence was no exception. In his memoirs, Mason (1999, p 123) observed that 'the country simply couldn't afford to go on spending such sums [on defence] – 5.7 per cent of GNP [gross national product] in 1973 – when the economy was in such poor shape'. Before the 1975 defence review, rather than set a specific monetary target, the government instead directed that the UK should not spend more on defence than its principal European trading competitors (Dodd, 1993, p 8). Nevertheless, as Michael Cary and Christopher Foxley-Norris (1976, p 2), recognized, although this had the advantage of not prejudicing the review's analysis of commitments and priorities, the resulting figures 'at least had to come out in the right ballpark'. Greenwood was similarly sceptical about the lack of an explicit financial limit:

> Getting defence's share of GDP down to around 4–5 per cent was undoubtedly regarded as a clear minimal obligation. Since a 'working projection' of future national income is an integral part of public expenditure planning, this means that, in practice, a budgetary target of about £3,750 million (at 1974 prices), to be achieved by the end of the planning period, was implicit in the exercise. (Greenwood, 1975, p 225)

In 1981, the problem facing John Nott was notably different to his predecessors. Even though, at the time, the government was committed to an annual 3 per cent increase in real terms to the defence budget, the MoD's ten-year programme was unrealistic and unfunded (Carver, 1992, p 134). According to Michael Quinlan, who was the deputy undersecretary of state (policy) in the MoD at the time, 'the programme and the budget were out of sync' (ICBH, 2001, p 36). The purpose of Nott's review was to bring them closer into line. As a result, the reductions in Nott's review were not driven by the state of the economy; instead, as Andrew Dorman (2001d, p 116) asserts 'the cut in the defence budget in terms of the long-term costings was merely money that was hoped for, but which was never likely to be realised'. This was a most salutary caution that presaged the outcomes of both the 2010 and 2015 SDSRs.

Apart from the Nott review, all the Cold War defence reviews were predicated on the need to reduce government spending because of the prevailing economic situation. Moreover, although Nott may argue that the poor state of the economy did not directly drive his review, the poor state of budgetary planning in the MoD definitely did (Dorman, 2001b, p 99). This suggests that finance and the economy are perennial factors in defence reviews. Furthermore, although Sandys, Healey and Mason adopted different methods to cut defence spending, none of them achieved any long-term success. Although spending did reduce in the immediate aftermath of all three reviews, according to the Stockholm International Peace Research Institute (SIPRI), within a few years it was on the rise again (see Table 6.1). This supports Smith's (1990, p 78) assertion that defence

Table 6.1: UK defence spending, 1950 to 1989

Year	Cash by £ billion	As % of GDP	As constant (at 2018) USD billion	% change to constant (at 2018) USD billion	
1950	0.849	6.4	28.272		
1951	1.149	7.4	33.289	+17.8	
1952	1.561	9.3	42.583	+27.9	
1953	1.681	9.8	47.310	+11.1	
1954	1.569	9.0	44.915	-5.1	
1955	1.567	8.1	42.766	-4.8	
1956	1.615	7.7	41.975	-1.9	
1957	1.574	7.1	40.533	-3.4	Sandys' Review
1958	1.591	6.8	39.470	-2.6	
1959	1.589	6.5	39.271	-0.5	
1960	1.655	6.3	40.083	+2.1	
1961	1.709	6.1	40.044	-0.1	
1962	1.814	6.2	40.558	+1.3	
1963	1.870	6.0	41.251	+1.7	
1964	2.000	5.8	42.368	+2.7	
1965	2.091	5.7	42.495	+0.3	
1966	2.153	5.5	42.268	-0.5	Healey's Review
1967	2.276	5.5	43.348	+2.6	
1968	2.332	5.2	42.731	-1.4	
1969	2.303	4.8	40.381	-5.5	
1970	2.607	4.6	41.594	+3.0	
1971	2.815	4.5	41.501	-0.2	
1972	3.258	4.6	44.144	+6.4	
1973	3.512	4.4	44.291	+0.3	
1974	4.160	4.5	44.303	0.0	
1975	5.571	4.8	46.544	+5.1	Mason's Review
1976	6.132	4.6	45.862	-1.5	
1977	6.810	4.4	43.861	-4.4	
1978	7.616	4.2	45.255	+3.2	
1979	9.029	4.2	46.670	+3.1	
1980	11.542	4.5	49.765	+6.6	

Table 6.1: UK defence spending, 1950 to 1989 (continued)

Year	Cash by £ billion	As % of GDP	As constant (at 2018) USD billion	% change to constant (at 2018) USD billion	
1981	12.144	4.5	48.747	-2.1	The Nott Review
1982	14.870	4.8	53.147	+9.0	
1983	15.830	4.8	55.510	+4.5	
1984	17.511	4.9	58.263	+5.0	
1985	18.352	4.8	58.811	+0.9	
1986	18.639	4.5	58.084	-1.2	
1987	19.269	4.2	57.451	-1.1	
1988	19.290	3.8	55.416	-3.5	
1989	20.868	3.6	55.904	+0.9	

Source: Stockholm International Peace Research Institute, Military Expenditure Database

reviews do no more than outline a future policy that fails to materialize, or chart a way forward that is rapidly reversed.

The simple reason why spending did not continue to reduce over time was that the reviews were successful in restraining the growth in defence costs, but failed to reduce the defence budget's total demand on national resources. Defence costs grow because the MoD always plans to maintain its extant force laydown to meet its extant commitments. The effect of this was ably articulated by Mason in his review: 'the cost of these forces was bound to increase progressively over time to keep pace with the constant development of technology and the growing sophistication of modern weapon systems' (MoD, 1975, p 2). Research by Keith Hartley (2016) attributes this growth to defence inflation[5] and intergenerational cost escalation.[6] A 2011 defence economic research paper, based on 1955–2011 data, estimated intergenerational real cost escalation of 2.9 per cent for submarines, 3.8 per cent for aircraft carriers, and 5.8 and 5.9 per cent for combat aircraft and main battle tanks respectively (MoD, 2011b, p 22). This evidence suggests that defence costs growth is enduring and, as such, will continue to impact on reviews in the future.

In 1991, defence secretary Tom King recognized that the dissolution of the Soviet Union and disbanding of the Warsaw Pact allowed the government to 'make some reductions in Defence but only in a carful and prudent way' (MoD, 1991, p 6). In reality, talk of a peace dividend started almost before the last of the Berlin Wall's concrete blocks had hit the ground (Greenwood, 1991, p 63). However, although this strategic shock was the obvious driver for the Options for Change review, the impact of financial decisions taken during the 1980s was also a significant factor. Phillip Sabin (1993, p 275) pointed out that there had been a real decline in equipment spending of around 20 per cent between FYs 1984–85 and 1990–91. The seriousness of the defence funding situation in the late 1980s was confirmed by the service chiefs' instigation of an in-house review because, in conjunction with the CDS, they believed that 'the procurement programme had become so far removed from the rest of policy that a review was needed to bring it back into line and force the government to make some politically difficult decisions' (Dorman, 2001d, p 21).

As the 1990s progressed, the UK's worsening economic position forced the Conservative government to re-examine its defence commitments, even as it was still in the process of major restructuring resulting from Options for Change. As we've already learned, the MoD's response was *Front Line First: The Defence Costs Study*, which sought to find the necessary savings without reductions to front line capabilities. The financial influence over the study was confirmed by the then defence secretary Malcolm Rifkind, who announced that the subsequent report was 'the culmination of a major exercise to review the possibilities for reducing costs and increasing efficiency across the whole of the MoD's support and administrative activities as [Defence's] contribution to the government's campaign to contain public expenditure' (MoD, 1994, p 1). The reduction in defence spending over this period can be seen in Table 6.2.

Although the 1998 SDR did not explicitly state the need for financial savings, it was undertaken within the constraints of the Labour government's commitment to maintain the previous Conservative government's spending plans for its first two years in office (The Labour Party, 1997, p 4). However, although academic reflection on the 1998 SDR is largely positive (see, for example McInnes, 1998; Codner, 1998; and Self, 2010, p 273), as Tom Dodd (1997, p 18) observed, 'whatever its construction, the defence review takes place, as with any previous review, within a resource context'. The Labour government in 1998 also faced the same problem as its predecessors, leading Humphry Crum-Ewing (1998, p 326) to record: 'at the very heart of the political arguments about the SDR lies the push and pull between the need for a sufficient defence budget and the need to contain that budget in order to provide for other desired public expenditure purpose'. Lawrence Freedman (1999, p 98) saw that this was further exacerbated by the lack of military experience amongst Labour MPs, with their interests being overwhelmingly in domestic affairs. He suggested they were not hostile in the defence secretary's battle to defend his budget, but indifferent.

The 2010 SDSR may have embraced several firsts, as discussed in Chapter 5, but from a financial perspective it was depressingly familiar. David Kirkpatrick (2010, p 4) identified a principal driver for the review, which was that the level of expenditure required to meet MoD aspirations

Table 6.2: UK defence spending, 1990 to 2009

Year	Cash by £ billion	As % of GDP	As constant (at 2018) USD billion	% change to constant (at 2018) USD billion	
1990	22.287	3.6	55.983	+0.1	
1991	24.380	3.7	56.630	+1.2	Options for Change
1992	22.850	3.5	52.894	-6.6	
1993	22.686	3.2	50.478	-4.6	
1994	22.490	3.0	49.089	-2.8	Defence Costs Study
1995	21.439	2.8	46.043	-6.2	
1996	22.330	2.6	45.602	-1.0	
1997	21.612	2.5	43.983	-3.6	
1998	22.477	2.4	44.127	+0.3	Strategic Defence Review
1999	22.548	2.3	43.891	-0.5	
2000	23.552	2.3	44.862	+2.2	
2001	24.874	2.3	46.541	+3.7	
2002	26.991	2.4	49.427	+6.2	SDR – A New Chapter
2003	29.338	2.4	52.975	+7.2	Delivering Security in a Changing World
2004	29.524	2.3	53.568	+1.1	
2005	30.603	2.3	53.995	+0.8	
2006	31.454	2.2	54.278	+0.5	
2007	33.486	2.2	55.960	+3.1	
2008	36.431	2.4	58.510	+4.6	
2009	37.425	2.5	59.766	+2.2	

Source: Stockholm International Peace Research Institute, Military Expenditure Database

was significantly higher than its extant budget allocation, even before the anticipated reductions to support the government's deficit reduction strategy, following the 2008 global economic crisis. This over commitment, primarily in the equipment programme, and generally accepted to be in the region of £35 to £38 billion over ten years (see, for example, Taylor, 2010b, p 12; and Cornish and Dorman, 2011, p 342) was seen by many as the most pressing factor for the review.

Specifically, Chalmers (2011, p 20) recognized that the reduction in the MoD's core budget of 7.5 per cent, in real terms, in the four years following the 2010 SDSR had to result in a period of 'radical retrenchment and reform' for UK defence policy. In his view, 'the elastic ha[d] snapped'. Moreover, he believed that, to balance the books, the MoD would have to seek even greater cuts, possibly as high as 13 per cent. Mark Cavanagh (2011, p 7) suggested that savings of this magnitude would require reform rather than expenditure, that is to say not what the MoD spends its money on, but how it spends it. However, from an economics-based position, Hartley (2010, p 4) argued that the 2010 SDSR was 'the typical outcome of various interest groups in the military-industrial-political complex'. His view was that all defence reviews are subject to budget constraints and uncertainty, cost and budgets are central to every nation's defence policy. This approach accords with Greenwood's argument in the 1970s and 1980s that ultimately it is a question of political choice rather than economic necessity (Greenwood, 1976). Simply put, 'high and rising costs of modern defence equipment together with falling defence budgets mean that no nation can avoid difficult defence choices' (Hartley, 2010, p 4). In this regard, the opposing positions in the secondary literature about the financial influence on defence reviews were as entrenched in 2010 as they were throughout the Cold War and Early Expeditionary period.

Notwithstanding the differing academic viewpoints, the government's position regarding the significance of the economic situation was made abundantly clear during the 2010 SDSR. Statements such as: 'Our ability to meet current and future threats depends crucially on tackling the budget deficit' (HM Government, 2010c, p 4), and 'Our most urgent task is to return the nation's finances to a sustainable footing' (2010c, p 14) are difficult to misinterpret. Moreover, this urgency obviously flowed down to the MoD as the then CDS, Air Chief Marshal Jock Stirrup, identified in evidence to the HCDC (2011a, p 29): 'the strategy was to eliminate the deficit ... the requirement to reduce expenditure overrode just about everything else.' The impact of the government's response to the economic crisis on defence spending is plain to see in Table 6.3.

Analysis of every defence review since the end of the Second World War has exposed the substantial impact that finance and the economy have had on defence decision making. In the build-up to the 2015 SDSR, it appeared that this trend would be continued. Even though the UK government had been a strong supporter of efforts to encourage all NATO member states to meet the alliance's target of spending at least 2 per cent of GDP on Defence, reiterated in the Wales Summit Declaration in 2014 (NATO, 2014), Chalmers (2015b, p 10) identified that the UK was projected to spend only 1.95 per cent of its GDP, or £37.4 billion, on Defence in FY 2015–16. Furthermore, he estimated that by FY 2019–20, meeting the NATO target would require the MoD to be provided with an additional £5.9 billion in annual spending, compared with 2015 assumptions. In his view, in the context of wider austerity in public spending, such an increase was not plausible and his

Table 6.3: UK defence spending, 2010 to 2019

Year	Cash by £ billion	As % of GDP	As constant (at 2018) USD billion	% change to constant (at 2018) USD billion	
2010	37.645	2.4	58.962	-1.4	2010 SDSR
2011	37.608	2.3	56.813	-3.6	
2012	36.808	2.2	54.524	-4.0	
2013	36.217	2.1	52.355	-4.0	
2014	35.850	1.9	50.996	-2.6	
2015	35.087	1.9	49.838	-2.3	2015 SDSR
2016	35.866	1.8	49.912	+0.2	
2017	36.324	1.8	49.412	-1.0	
2018	37.758	1.8	49.892	+1.0	NSCR and MDP
2019	38.205	1.7	49.916	+0.1	

Source: Stockholm International Peace Research Institute, Military Expenditure Database

pessimistic analysis of all three major political parties' spending plans prior to the 2015 general election suggested the MoD could face a 10 per cent real-terms budget cut over the next four years.

The reality was somewhat different. In the July 2015 summer budget, the government committed to provide the MoD with real-terms increases of 0.5 per cent per annum through to FY 2020–21 (Hansard, 2015b). Furthermore, in an examination of defence and security budgets after the 2015 CSR, Chalmers (2016b, p 4) identified that, when the MoD's allocation from the Joint Security Fund[7] (JSF) was considered, core spending on Defence would increase by 3.1 per cent in real terms over the four years from FYs 2015–16 to 2019–20. He also suggested that, with the MoD basing its forward plans beyond 2020 on the assumption that the total core budget would continue to grow at 0.5 per cent per annum in real terms, and allocations from the JSF would be maintained broadly equivalent to pre-FY 2020–21 levels, and the department could continue to make savings broadly comparable to those identified up to FY 2010–21, the overall defence budget would have been successfully stabilized (2016b, p 8). This, in turn, would allow the government to make the commitments for spending beyond FY 2020–21 on which its £178 billion equipment plan was based (HM Government, 2015, p 27).

Prior to the July 2015 summer budget, the general view amongst defence analysts was that the MoD would have to accommodate further cuts as an outcome of the 2015 spending review (see, for example, Cornish and Dorman, 2013; De Waal, 2014; and Reeve, 2015). Indeed, Chalmers had suggested that further reductions in overall government spending could see the defence allocation falling to between 1.5 per cent and 1.6 per cent of GDP in FY 2020–21 (Chalmers, 2014, p 10). Dorman et al (2016, p 48) summed up the situation well when they wrote: 'To many commentators, the government's overall deficit reduction pledges appeared to presage inevitable and significant UK defence budget cuts.'

The government decision in July 2015 to meet the NATO 2 per cent of GDP target was, in the view of Dorman et al (2016, p 46), 'one of the more curious episodes in recent British defence policy'. In their view, four different factors came together to encourage this change. First, it was unprecedented for a US administration to have been quite so outspoken about the UK's budget plans, especially at the outset of a defence review. Specifically, General Raymond Odierno, chief of staff of the US Army, voiced concerns about the impact that defence spending cuts could have on US–UK divisional-level interoperability (BBC, 2015). Second, after being such a strong advocate of NATO's spending target at the 2014 Wales Summit, David Cameron would have risked both domestic and international accusations of hypocrisy if the UK then failed to meet it. Third, the severe reductions in military capability made in the 2010 SDSR were beginning to have an observable detrimental effect on UK defence output. For example, the need regularly to call on allies to track Russian submarines off the UK coast (Ward, 2015). Finally, prime ministerial legacy and successions also played their part in Cameron's decision making. My research has already uncovered considerable evidence that finance and the economy have been influential in all the defence reviews from the end of the Second World War. However, in 2015, David Greenwood's argument that the government of the day always has a choice regarding its resource allocation for defence predominated. Cameron and his chancellor, George Osborne, considered the necessity of applying further austerity measures to the defence budget against the factors identified by Andrew Dorman, Matthew Uttley and Benedict Wilkinson (2016, pp 49–50), and, in the view of the academics the 'cuts were less appealing and the volte-face more attractive'.

Confirmation that the UK would continue to meet the NATO target to invest 2 per cent of GDP on defence, and a commitment to spend £178 billion over the next decade on equipment and equipment support (HM Government, 2015, p 27) generated positive, if not entirely wholehearted, support in the secondary literature. For example, James de Waal (2015) wrote that the SDSR had largely succeeded in providing Britain with the tools necessary to deal with domestic and international threats to its security, and Chalmers (2016a, p 8) suggested that 'after five years characterized by reductions and retreat ... the UK's reputation as a credible military power has, in broad terms, been restored'. John Louth (2016, p 3) believed that, 'on a first reading, the SDSR is a credible and well-thought-out attempt to help the UK to address defence and security issues and risks from now into the 2030s and beyond'. However, he followed that assertion up with 'yet, on closer inspection, issues emerge around affordability'.

Concerns over the longevity of the 2015 SDSR's outcomes were shared by other commentators (see, for example, Keohane, 2016, pp 3–4; and Street, 2016, p 9), and these concerns have since proved to be legitimate. The MoD's 2016 Equipment Plan (2016, p 4–11) provided more detail around the 2015 SDSR commitment of £178 billion for equipment and equipment support, in the form of a ten-year spending plan. However, in its associated report, the NAO (2017, p 15) highlighted that the SDSR had added £24.4 billion of new commitments, all of which had to be funded from within the existing plan. Furthermore, it confirmed that the MoD had allocated all the plan's previously set aside financial headroom, removing its flexibility to accommodate additional capability requirements. It also needed to generate £5.8 billion of new savings from projects within the plan to meet its new commitments (2017, p 20). Added to this, Louisa Brooke-Holland (2017, p 4) pointed out that the equipment plan was vulnerable to foreign exchange rates, noting that approximately £18.6 billion would have to be paid in US dollars. On the same subject, the HC PAC (2017, p 3) stated it was 'very concerned that the MoD's equipment plan is at greater risk of becoming unaffordable than at any time since its inception in 2012'. One year later, in its report on the MoD's 2017 Equipment Plan (2017b), the NAO (2018a, p 29) confirmed that the plan was now unaffordable, with a minimum affordability gap of £4.9 billion and a potential affordability gap of £20.8 billion. Apprehensions in academia that the 2015 SDSR's financial vulnerabilities were reminiscent of the 1998 SDR, and would generate the same affordability pressures for military capability (see Dorman et al, 2016, p 51; and Hampshire, 2015), had been realized.

Under the quinquennial review process, the SDSR was the point in time where strategic decisions on both existing and future military capability were to be made. This part of the process should also have included a thorough review of long-term financial plans, with budgets reset as necessary to allow the following five-years' business-as-usual capability management to be overseen by defence decision makers with only a light touch on the financial tiller. This process was outlined and refined in early iterations of the DOM (see MoD, 2012c; and MoD, 2015b) and is relatively straightforward. The plan, however, never survived contact with the financial reality in Defence. Instead, throughout the Quinquennial Review period, capability managers have been forced to live from hand to mouth as short-term financial expediencies have ridden roughshod over often well-reasoned and viable capability management plans. Many of the reasons why are exposed in the following section. Needless to say, Defence's inability to live by its own financial rules has had a considerable impact on the translation of strategic direction into military capability.

Contemporary affordability issues

The effect of the economy on the affordability of defence understandably plays out more at the political level. As a result, much of the associated academic commentary is focused on its impact on defence reviews. However, when affordability issues are discussed with senior officials within the MoD, the subjects raised are invariably less strategic and concentrate more on the more day-to-day, or business as usual, activities that govern the acquisition and maintenance of military capability. The three most pressing concerns expressed during my research were: the rules and regulations governing the management of public money and the behaviours within the MoD that resulted from them; the ongoing over-commitment of the defence budget (modern-day Greenwoodery); and the increased department-wide focus on identifying, accepting and securing savings and efficiencies from the defence budget.

Opinions regarding the MoD's budgetary system were expressed both at the macro level and to a fine degree of detail. Overall, few were positive. Several senior officials recognized a problem with the balancing of ambition and resource, with one going as far as saying 'the budgetary system is fundamentally flawed because we are failing to match ambition with finance every time'. Although not completely supporting this view, an army general believed there were too many pressures in government to allow resource and ambition ever to be matched. As a specific example he offered:

> '[O]ne of the things we could have said in the SDSR is that warfighting at scale is beyond the nation. We're never going to do that [undertake warfighting at scale], because truthfully, we're very unlikely ever to find the resource ... Instead of saying that and accepting that at the policy level, with all the howls of political angst that would have generated, the government would rather set warfighting at scale as our ambition, and then find later in a much less obvious way that actually we couldn't do it.'

The same individual went on to assert that the ambition in all government departments always exceeded the level of resource available. Moreover, in his view, departmental levels of ambition were never regularized within strategy, so what eventually had to happen was a failure to deliver the government's strategy through lack of resource. A fellow officer came to a similar conclusion when he considered that the comprehensive analysis of the strategic context, undertaken during an SDSR, was never followed through when it came to designing and prioritizing appropriate capabilities, because of the need for Defence to fit inside a pre-prescribed financial envelope. He described this situation as 'the financial tail wagging the strategic dog'.

A similar degree of concern was expressed at the more detailed financial planning level. One RN three-star officer, with considerable experience in acquisition and support, suggested that the UK should adopt the legal obligation placed by the US government on SROs to confirm their programmes are fully funded, through life, prior to approval. He insisted that, in the absence of this remit, optimism bias was inevitable, which drove unaffordability into the equipment plan. Another admiral suggested that, although the rigid annualization approach to financial accounting worked well in the business as usual space, it regularly over-complicated and reduced flexibility in the management of protracted capital programmes.

The most serious failing in the MoD's financial planning process was, in the opinion of a four-star civil servant recruited from industry, a lack of accountability. He questioned when, if ever, an SRO had been sacked or publicly held to account for approving a programme plan where it was knowingly undeliverable. Furthermore, in his opinion, the MoD's financial planning was not nearly as rigorous as would be found in a commercial environment, and he suggested that, if forced into honesty, 'a large proportion of our very senior colleagues would openly "fess up" to the fact that they know they are part of a plan that is seriously underfunded'. He supported his concerns with the following:

> '[I]f I hired a top-notch, very senior and experienced chief financial officer from a FTSE20 company, and put them in charge of this financial planning exercise, and it was clear that if we end up delivering the wrong numbers, you will be publicly sacked [and] it will be all over the front pages of the *Financial Times*. I can guarantee to you it would be a totally different process that it would be running to. The primary reason is ... accountability.'

The contemporary relevance of Greenwoodery was recognized by several senior officials. It could be contended that Greenwood's funding gap in the late 1980s, brought about by an unwillingness of the Conservative government to underwrite the military capability necessary to achieve its stated policy goals, was replicated by the Labour government during its final years in office in the first decade of the twenty-first century. Moreover, evidence suggests that the underfunding in the 1980s was exacerbated by government decisions, in the latter part of that decade, to relax some of the more severe cuts in capability made during the 1981 defence review (see Dorman, 2001d, pp 114–16; and Greenwood, 1991, p 37). This approach was arguably replicated by the Conservative government following the 2010

SDSR with, for example, its decisions to return to divisional warfighting and regenerate a maritime patrol capability in the 2015 review. As Asteris (1994, p 44) confirmed, the 1980s' funding cliff edge was only avoided because the government was fortuitously able to reduce the UK's force structure at the end of the Cold War. However, the post-2015 SDSR affordability challenges discussed above prompted the hypothesis that Defence was heading towards a similar funding cliff edge, but this time with no serendipitous strategic shock to come to its rescue.

Most senior officials who explored this premise agreed there was the danger of an impending financial cliff edge. Significantly, this view was held by officers and civil servants in appointments right across Defence. Others recognized the hypothesis but cautioned against overstating the extant financial position. For example, a senior civil servant, with over thirty years' acquisition experience confirmed 'there's a cliff there to go over', but suggested 'there are [still] various things that could be done to avoid it'. A more detailed view was offered by a two-star officer serving in the centre of MoD:

> '[I]n the longer term, it's not as bad a situation. I don't think we are heading for a cliff. I definitely don't think we are stood on a precipice. To put that into some kind of context, if you believe what's in the papers, that we have a £20 billion black hole, which isn't the right number, but if you were to believe that, our budget over 10 years is £415 billion. We are talking about less than 5 per cent of our shortfall over 10 years.'

Of those who acknowledged that Greenwoodery remained an issue in defence expenditure planning, few had an answer to its underlying causes. Instead, it was suggested that over-optimistic assumptions were still widespread, and defence inflation was an ever-present factor. One of the more pessimist views confirmed that 'the gap is so huge between money available and ambition ... there is no way we're ever going to close that'. That said, two officials did suggest that the UK's departure from the EU had the potential to provide a strategic reset, with one commenting in 2017, 'we haven't got a Berlin Wall, but we do have a Brexit!'

Although the search for efficiencies had begun in the early 1980s during the Thatcher government (Dorman, 2002, pp 63–99), the first overt inclusion of specific goals for increasing efficiency was the 1994 Defence Costs Study (MoD, 1994, pp 5–8). Since then, all defence reviews have had an efficiency agenda. The 1998 SDR confirmed that 'the continuing push for greater efficiency is an integral part of our plans to drive down costs to pay for the modernisation of our forces' (MoD, 1998a, p 6). In the Labour government's 2004 budget, the MoD was committed to a target of efficiency improvements amounting to at least 2.5 per cent of the total defence budget for each of the three years of the spending review. This amounted to a target of £2.8 billion by FY 2007–08 (MoD, 2004, p 11). By 2015, the MoD, together with security and intelligence agencies and cross-government counterterrorism, had been given responsibility for delivering savings of more than £11 billion (HM Government, 2015, p 75). Against this demanding backdrop, it is unsurprising that finding efficiencies is a significant focus for today's defence decision makers.

Scrutiny of command papers suggests that little care is taken in high-level government policy documents to differentiate between cost savings and efficiencies; however, as one TLB holder was quick to point out, they are not the same:

> 'Efficiency is what is says. It's not a saving. The notion here is that we can do the same amount for less. So, we can somehow, for example, crew additional F-35 squadrons or P8 squadrons, without any extra manpower, because elsewhere in the RAF, we will find ways of not needing the existing manpower. That will generate the manpower cover to do these additional force elements … efficiency assumptions aren't related to the abandonment of certain types of capability, as it stands at the moment. They are pure efficiencies, i.e. they're not do less for less. The assumption is do the same for less. That's the notion of the efficiency space.'

This is significant, as all the defence decision makers who had efficiency targets to meet, were almost entirely focused on delivering within the same-for-less envelope. The TLB holder quoted above did recognize the less-for-less option and was also of the opinion that ceasing low priority activity might be viable. That said, I have been unable to find evidence of defence decision makers from any service approving reductions in output to reduce capability.

Opinions over Defence's ability to deliver the efficiencies outlined in the 2015 SDSR were unmistakably divided: those officers and civil servants in acquisition and support roles considered the targets to be attainable; everyone else who expressed a view, did not. The attitude from the procurement experts was that innovative approaches to managing military capability, for example changing behaviours or accepting different risk profiles, could unlock considerable new benefits. However, a regularly held view away from the MoD enabling organizations was that heroic assumptions had been made to underpin efficiencies without a credible supporting evidence base. To that end, many senior officials believed the existing portfolio of efficiency measures was simply beyond reach.

The default salami-slicing approach taken by the department to achieve efficiencies attracted considerable criticism, as did the perception that political interference often resulted in some defence outputs being considered off limits. One two-star civil servant suggested that traditional tactics, like cutting activity, needed to be replaced with a more productive methodology:

'[Y]ou have a very expensive machine, and you're de-tuning the carburettors, as it were, to make it go slower to save yourself five shillings and sixpence of fuel, but you're running a Rolls Royce ... Think about the value-additive efficiency that you can get through, for example, international aggregation, whereby you are able to produce more capability through collaboration.'

One change to the rules around efficiencies that attracted attention was the decision in the 2015 SDSR 'to allow the MoD to invest efficiency savings into the Armed Forces' (HM Government, 2015, p 27). At first glance, this appeared to be an extremely positive change. One three-star army officer pointed out, 'The reason why efficiencies have never worked [in the past] is that there was no incentivization in the individuals in the army, navy and air force to do anything about it'. However, it was soon recognized that the most significant factor in the affordability of the 2015 review was the delivery of efficiencies to pay for the already announced capability enhancements. As one four-star officer put it:

'[I]n order to pay for more equipment, what the SDSR did was say, all of you TLBs, you're going to make these vast efficiencies. Much higher than ever before, and so that's allowed us to persuade ourselves that there is the money to buy this new equipment, but of course if those efficiencies are not delivered then we have a new black hole emerging.'

Since 2015, it has become more and more obvious to most defence decision makers that the total efficiencies identified in the 2015 SDSR, plus others committed to in subsequent annual budget cycles, were unlikely to be delivered. A three-star civil servant confirmed that 'the efficiency assumptions that were made to provide the additional headroom turned out to be fundamentally flawed'. This was supported by a three-star admiral from one of the MoD enabling organizations, who said 'We have a hugely imbalanced programme today because of wildly optimistic efficiency prognosis made in SDSR 15'. By contrast, a RAF two-star officer argued this was a problem of Defence's own making, because all the service chiefs had agreed as part of the 2015 SDSR that they could deliver all of the enhancements necessary to build JF25. Furthermore, they had accepted the challenge that the delivery of those enhancements would require the provision of efficiencies within their TLB to a known amount of money. It is difficult to understate the impact that the 2015 SDSR's demand for efficiencies has had over the thoughts and actions of defence decision makers. In the opening remarks to his final evidence session to the HCDC in November 2021, the outgoing CDS, General Nick Carter, said:

> 'When I took over [as the CDS] on 11 June 2018, I realized pretty quickly that there was work to be done in terms of getting the defence budget into the right place … We were having a slightly hand to mouth existence in defence, because some rather optimistic assumptions in the 2015 SDSR had led to a realization that the efficiency that the Department was supposed to deliver was not necessarily going to equip us for what we needed in terms of the defence programme.'

The final contemporary affordability issue that has affected the acquisition and maintenance of military capability was Brexit. The day after the EU referendum, sterling fell to its lowest level against the dollar in more than 30 years, at one point its value had reduced by 13 per cent (Blitz and Lewis, 2016). *The Economist*'s economic intelligence unit predicted that UK GDP would contract by 1 per cent in 2017 (Street and Reeve, 2016, p 2). This was, in turn, reinforced by research in the *Financial Times* that revealed by the end of the first quarter of 2018, the UK economy was between 1 and 1.5 per cent smaller than it would have been without the EU referendum vote (Giles and Fray, 2018). The financial impact can be summed up thus:

> The implications of this currency depreciation and the likely economic contraction will be felt in British defence and security policy in terms of the affordability of the overall defence budget, currently pegged at 2.0% of GDP [and] the price of planned equipment purchases from abroad. (Street and Reeve, 2016, p 3)

Although the government's hedging on sterling provides some insulation from any drop of the pound, it only lasts two years and, for the defence budget, was no more than a short-term fix (Bond, 2017). By mid-2019, the sterling/dollar exchange rate was no more than four cents above the immediate post-EU referendum figure (Bloomberg, 2019). Consequently, the cost for new equipment acquired from US contractors has risen sharply. Trevor Taylor (2016a) initially predicted that the increase could be as much as 11 per cent, on an estimated annual outlay of $10 billion, although his follow-on calculations suggested the increased cost of Britain's defence imports could be lower, at £700 million per annum from FY 2018–19:

> With a defence budget of slightly more than £35 billion, the £700-million shortfall amounts to a 2 per cent cut in the purchasing power

of Britain's defence budget, and a much larger cut in the purchasing power of the equipment and support budgets. This must be a substantial challenge for defence planners and programmers. (Taylor, 2016b)

In the summer of 2020, the build-up to the 2021 IR was unnervingly like its 2015 predecessor. Influenced at least in part by the massive increase in expenditure forced on the government because of the coronavirus pandemic, the media view was the armed forces would have to swallow significant reductions as government spending tightened (see, for example, Beale, 2020; Chuter, 2020a; and Warrell and Parker, 2019). The most optimistic view from academia was the extra £1.9 billion that had already been allocated to the MoD would be incorporated into the 2020 spending review baseline, with a further 0.5 per cent real increase per annum added, because it had been included in the Conservative party's 2019 general election manifesto (Chalmers and Jessett, 2020, p 13).

Then, one week before the 2020 spending review was made public, the prime minister announced an increase in defence spending of £24.1 billion over the next four years, which would raise it as a share of GDP to at least 2.2 per cent (Hansard, 2020b). While some may have expected the additional funding to have reduced pressure on defence planners to find more widespread savings, it did not silence the debate around funding military capability (see Warrell, 2020). Moreover, as the 2021 DCP revealed, it also did little to stave off the anticipated cuts to the force structure (Brooke-Holland, 2021).

How has the affordability of defence affected military capability choices?

Of all the different type of events and influences that have had an effect on the translation of strategic direction into military capability, finance and the economy have arguably been the most prominent. From the Labour government's decision in the mid- to late-1960s to maintain the annual defence budget at £2 billion at constant prices, to the Conservative's pursuit of the peace dividend in the early 1990s, to the Conservative/Liberal Democratic coalition's austerity measures in 2010, affordability has been at the heart of defence decision making for the last 75 years. Whether one accords with Mason's view that the imperatives of economics significantly affect the level of resource that governments can devote to Defence, or supports Greenwood's assertion that the state of the economy does not force governments to make defence cuts – it merely defines the limits of policy choice – it is difficult to come to any other conclusion.

Greenwood was clear in his belief that the state of the economy defined the limits of a government's policy choices, but it did not in itself force defence cuts. A politician's interpretation of this is that the government can only allocate to Defence what it can afford. Affordability is a judgement and, in this instance, is a political judgement. In the mid-1970s, Jackson (1990, p 134) believed that the political judgement put re-establishing the national economy above national security. However, in 2015 it appeared that the reverse was true when, even though austerity was still a major factor in the chancellor's summer budget, the government signalled a real-term rise in defence spending, seemingly putting national security above the national economy. In both instances, it was a political call, and the realpolitik reality is that it probably always will be. What does this mean for the affordability of defence? It strengthens the point made by one senior official that defence reviews are a negotiation. It is, however, more complicated than the MoD just trying to secure the largest possible financial settlement, because Defence's output parameters are also on the negotiating table. A balance must be struck between what the government expects of the armed forces and how much that should cost. Ultimately if that balance is not achieved, everyone loses. This is because either Defence would be under-resourced and struggle to meet the tasks it is called upon to undertake, or the government had been profligate in its settlement with the MoD, and other departments' spending priorities would suffer. When viewed through this affordability-of-defence lens, most defence decision makers argued that, in both the 2010 and 2015 SDSR, an unbalanced financial settlement had been reached – or imposed – to the detriment of defence.

The impact of delivering efficiencies on the translation of strategic direction into military capability is a more recent phenomenon. During the reviews of the Cold War, it was not even considered by defence decision makers. Today, however, it is perhaps the most vexing issue within the boundaries of MoD financial management. The sums of money involved are considerable, and the way they have been managed to date puts budget holders on the back foot from the outset. Traditionally, efficiency targets were arbitrarily divided amongst the MoD's TLBs with budget totals commensurately reduced. This system is known within Defence as wedging. In effect, it takes money from capability managers before they can consider measures that could be enacted to manage the shortfall. Their default response is to make salami-slice cuts to budgets across all programmes, which generally leads to reductions in sustainability and training, or delivery delays and cost overruns. Notwithstanding this approach, Defence has regularly fallen short in its attempts to meet its efficiency targets, and the likelihood of it achieving those currently baked into its budget remains low.

In 2018, as part of the MDP, the MoD reappraised its approach to delivering efficiencies. It introduced a small number of high-level transformation programmes,[8] charged with delivering pan-defence efficiencies across their area of responsibility. It also accepted that efficiency targets should be managed above TLBs until those programmes could satisfactorily evidence the efficacy of their projects. Under this revised approach, appropriate downward adjustments would only be made to relevant budgets after a project was approved within MoD head office and accepted for delivery by the appropriate single service. This much improved methodology increases the likelihood of achieving externally imposed efficiency targets, both today and into the future.

Following the 2015 SDSR, the single services were encouraged to seek efficiencies within existing programmes, with the incentive that the savings generated would be theirs to reinvest. This has created an unfavourable consequence. A perceived efficiency today will produce a cost reduction profile that is projected over the relevant programme's budget for future years. Once the efficiency measure is accepted, the reduced budget figures are programmed into the overall TLB, seemingly creating headroom in the profile. However, that headroom only exists on paper until the efficiency is delivered, which is often a year-on-year occurrence. Consequently, the actual delivery of the cost reduction frequently cannot be confirmed until it happens. Nevertheless, to benefit from the efficiency, capability managers must plan to spend against the perceived budgetary headroom in advance and, in most cases, commit to that expenditure in the form of a contract. The result is guaranteed expenditure against a non-guaranteed efficiency. Consequently, if the anticipated cost reduction is not delivered, the budget deficit is increased. Evidence suggests this situation already exists across the single services; furthermore, as it is essentially internal TLB business, the effects may not be felt for years to come. Estimating its Defence-wide impact and instigating appropriate mitigation will not be easy. To that end, notwithstanding the MoD's more pro-active approach to managing transformational change, the post-2015 SDSR increased emphasis on delivering efficiencies across Defence has exacerbated the salami-slicing reduction of military capability and encouraged the adoption of guaranteed expenditure against non-guaranteed efficiency within TLBs.

Earlier analysis focused on the validity of Greenwood's funding gap hypothesis and whether it is likely to be relevant for Defence in the future. One of Cornish and Dorman's 10 unwritten defence review rules that we learned about in the previous chapter is that, on completion of a review, the government will claim to have gained control of defence inflation and cost overruns. This rule was corroborated by David Cameron in his *Forward* to the 2015 SDSR report. He wrote: 'In 2010, the total black hole in the defence budget alone was bigger than the entire defence budget in that year. Now it is back in balance' (HM Government, 2015, p 5). However, just four years later, in 2019, the MoD had, by its own estimate, a £7 billion shortfall in its ten-year equipment and support programme budget (NAO, 2019, p 5). Moreover, that figure assumed Defence would achieve all its share of the £11 billion efficiency target from the 2015 SDSR. At the time of writing, that is a long way from happening. This situation prompted the following pessimistic, but frank, assessment from an externally recruited four-star acquisition specialist:

> '[W]e are either knowingly, and probably in many cases unknowingly, allowing ourselves to be sucked even deeper into a piece of financial fiction that means that the most likely outcome is, at some stage, we will have a bust of some quite sizeable proportion in the ability to finance what has been positioned through government as a defence plan.'

The additional funding for defence announced by the chancellor in the 2020 Spending Round (HM Treasury, 2020b, p 7) will certainly ease the pressure on the MoD's budget. That said, defence inflation and cost overruns still threaten the credibility of its long-term financial planning, and the MoD's day-to-day running expenses will remain extremely taught. This is because the entire increase has been allocated to capital spending. Over the five years from FY 2019–20, capital spending is set to rise in real terms by 43 per cent, but spending on the MoD's running costs is expected to fall over the same period by around 2 per cent (Chalmers, 2021, p 3). Furthermore, the MoD is not allowed to reallocate capital spending to plug the gap (HM Treasury, 2020a, p 13).

Whether Defence's finances are heading for a cliff edge in the near or medium term is a moot point. The reality is, before the prime minister's largesse in November 2020, there was considerable pressure on the equipment and support programme, which only four years previously had been in balance. This would suggest either a lack of appreciation of the factors affecting the affordability of Defence, or poor capability decision making, or both. Less than two years ago, the NAO (2019, p14) highlighted that the MoD's business and financial planning risk of finding a sustainable, long-term balance between its available budget and the cost of its programme remained challenging. All my research supports the conclusion that this remains the case.

7

The MoD and the Single Services

Some may argue that the last 75 years has seen a steady erosion of the predominance of the single services within Defence. From the formation of the MoD in 1946 (HM Government, 1946), to the establishment of the CDS role and the Defence Board 12 years later (HM Government, 1958), the unification of the MoD under a single secretary of state in 1964 (HM Government, 1963), and, finally, the creation of a unified defence staff (MoD, 1984), the evolution of the central organization of Defence has progressively moved authority away from the single services. These changes have also driven a gradual reduction in the dominance of the service chiefs, since the high watermark of their defence policy and global strategy papers of the early 1950s (see Chiefs of Staffs, 1950; and Chiefs of Staff, 1952). Today's service chiefs are not members of the Defence Board, and their direct access to the prime minister is no longer explicitly stated in the DOM. Nevertheless, the post-2010 SDSR DRP did expand considerably the single services' responsibility for the acquisition and maintenance of military capability (MoD, 2011a, pp 36–43). The common shorthand across Defence for this disaggregation of responsibility from MoD head office to the single services, which was explained fully in Chapter 2, is the delegated model. The processes and procedures that underpin the delegated model, and the role played within them by the service chiefs and the single services, are fundamental to understanding why the UK has the military capability that is has.

This final data chapter explores the role played by the MoD and the single services in the translation of strategic direction into military capability. The first half of the chapter concentrates on the individual nature of the single services and the changing roles of the service chiefs. While the organizational construct of Defence has been regularly revised over the research period, the central framework of three separate military establishments that each concentrate on one of the three warfighting environments of maritime, land and air has remained constant. Crucially, it is this one-to-one relationship between the single services and their respective warfighting environment that gives them their strength and, therefore, is protected at all costs by the service chiefs. The second half of the chapter raises the focus to Defence-level process, procedures and decision making. How and why defence decision makers go about their day-to-day business is the final influencer to be considered in this journey to understand the translation of strategic direction into military capability model.

The individual nature of the single services

Prior to the DRP, capability management still operated under the principles of smart acquisition amended by the fundamentals of TLCM. Several officials who had held senior appointments within that construct highlighted both its advantages and its shortcomings. The clear strength of the pre-DRP methodology was its ability to consider capability management through a joint prism; its obvious weakness, as one lieutenant general observed, was that 'the single services had no responsibility, accountability or authority and simply acted as pressure groups in the process'. The result was often requirement creep, with capabilities over-specified to a point where their performance, time and cost envelope became unmanageable. The view from the single service was 'it's all being done to us', with the critical decisions being taken by the ECC in MoD and the DE&S's IPTs. Another common refrain was that 'the capability was simply being thrown over the wall for us to manage in service'. That said, the assessment from the delivery agent was little better, evidenced by this opinion shared by a former three-star civil servant, who had worked in DE&S:

> 'Having lived that period of time where, very vividly in my memory, each of the three services ... was betting the ranch on being able to steal money from the other two. And the entire game was around making sure that, one way or another, your ships were paid for out of the army's tanks. Because there was no other way on God's earth you were going to get them. Which I thought was a hugely destructive and nugatory way of expending energy.'

The process implications of the DRP are explored later in the chapter; however, some senior officials also expressed opinions on how the delegated model has played to the individual nature and separate interests of the single services. The common view was that the delegated model did tackle most of the negatives expressed in the previous paragraph. For example, the alignment of responsibility, accountability and authority for capability management to the single services was widely commended. In addition, any attempt to remove the conditions that led to inter-services disputes over resources was considered by one senior civil servant to be a real positive:

'[Under the delegated model] your money will be doled out at the beginning of term, and there's only one rule, you can only spend what you've got. And don't think for one millisecond that you're going to lay your hands on anybody else's ... I liked the ... accountability that came in the principle that came with that.'

However, even though the delegation of responsibility, accountability and authority down to the single services had created an environment where, in the view of an RAF two-star capability planner, 'the incentives are better aligned to deliver the output for the minimum input', a number of senior officials were concerned at the second- and third-order effects that the change had generated. In their collective opinion, the delegated model promoted single service advocacy to the detriment of 'jointery'. One army three-star officer was extremely forthright in expressing, 'I think ... a joint cultural approach has been diminished by Levine ... [it] has institutionalized single service parochialism. I think it has diminished the capacity and authority of the centre to both set strategic direction and then arbitrate between the single services.' This view was supported by a fellow defence decision maker, who believed:

'The flaw in the Levene outcome is that for the services ... this is a declaration of independence where every five years [they] gets some loose instructions through a defence review. Then they go away and do what they think they should be doing and report back success or failure, or whatever. That was clearly never the intention. That's not delegation, that's abrogation.'

While many senior officials recognized the benefits that delegation had brought, there was a definite view that capability should be planned on the basis of 'jointery by design'. In the eyes of one lieutenant general, the way to achieve that was to 'swing the Levene pendulum back to a more centrist position'. One army two-star officer observed that Defence 'should be designing a joint force, not environmental forces that may stack up to a joint force'. An RAF air marshal also suggested there was a view held by some very senior people in MoD head office that the single services made decisions in their own interests, rather than the wider interests of Defence. This opinion had some support during my research, although an army two-star officer did point out that the delegated model had been designed that way. To avoid this, a British Army general suggested that the single services should adopt an approach of 'altruistic intelligent jointery' to their capability planning. The balance between the potential for significant improvement in capability management, while, at the same time, increasing single service insularity, was seen by some interviewees as the key issue. This conundrum was summarized by one senior official as follows:

'What you have done … is you've just given a whole series of robber barons all the money. What's the outcome of that? Their behaviour, in protecting their own resource – regardless of whether they're making internal efficiencies or not – has become more stark, because you've given them more power to be more protective. It's a balance. The balance is, 'Is that less collegiate behaviour worth paying the price for a more efficient outcome at TLB level?' … I think the answer is, "The jury is still out".'

The single services are different. The environments within which they operate, the traditions they have assimilated over time to develop the culture and ethos they have today, and their visions for the future, are all distinct. The simple adage that the RN and the RAF man the equipment while the army equips the man is a powerful pointer to the contrasting approaches to capability planning. Some senior officials recognized the dangers of combining the naturally individualistic approach of the single services with a delegated model that, at the very least, provided latitude for nonconformist agendas to be pursued. Having spent the formative part of his career in an actively encouraged joint milieu, one three-star army officer expressed concern that the delegated model would lead to the three services 'veer[ing] away from each other over time'. Another army general posited that the delegated model was not strong enough to counter the single services predisposition to pursue their own goals, to the potential detriment of the joint force:

'[I]if you look at the history of British military capability, what you start with is originally two and eventually three powerful independent services where the idea of joint effect, if they recognize it at all – and they didn't for a very long time – is built bottom up on the basis of the stomach of the individual services to consent to collaboration.'

The tribal and often adversarial nature of the single services was regarded by some as a significant contributor to the way capability was being developed and delivered within the delegated model. One senior civil servant described some uniformed capability managers as 'evangelical'. The close-minded attitude of the single services was unsurprisingly highlighted as having a detrimental effect on the defence-wide management of military capability. A two-star officer working in JFC confirmed that, even though much of the command's capability was generated to enable others, he had experienced remarkably little coordination and cross-boundary work with the single services in developing those capabilities. Furthermore, at the highest levels of the single services, serious concerns were expressed over capability management interdependencies brought about by the lead command model,[1] which was the approach adopted to manage multi-use capability.

Understanding the deep-rooted nature of the differing single service positions was a line of discussion explored by several defence officials. Two extremely pertinent explanations were offered by one defence decision maker:

'The RAF was formed as an endeavour to make use of the third dimension in a way that we hadn't previously in warfare. At its absolute core, at its inception, were pilots. Manned flight. ... we didn't develop unmanned aerial vehicles in 1917 or whatever. We had a machine, and we had a pilot, and in due course we had navigators and engineers, but at the core of the existence of that service is the notion of the pilot. So, the notion that you might go to unmanned air vehicles, for example, which would be one really substantial way of cutting the cost of the Air Force, really cuts to the essence of the service. So, it's really hard to do.'

And:

'If you look at the army over time, it is vested in the infantry and the armoured corps. The infantry predates the armoured corps, and still dominates the army. Both in volume terms and in status terms, but the armoured corps was the thing that created success in the Second World War, as far as land is concerned. ... and then throughout the Cold War, what was the thing that was at the core of the army in the Cold War? It was tank divisions, to fight Soviet tank divisions. So, our history's been based on that for a really long time. Just as in the same way as the air force, consciously getting out of that game is really counterculture.'

Analysis of defence reviews is replete with examples of the single services acting in their own interests, particularly during reviews when resources were known to be scarce, for example Sandys' review in 1957 and the 2010 SDSR. Whether, in a presentation during the defence reviews of the 1960s, an RAF staff officer did deliberately reposition Australia hundreds of miles to the west of its actual location to strengthen his service's argument for land-based air power over carrier-based air power, remains an urban myth that may always be contested. Phillip Darby (1973, p 301) believed he did, Jeffrey Bradford (2010) thought otherwise. Either way, the fact that this is even considered a possibility shows how far the single services are prepared to go to protect their own current or future capability.

Notwithstanding this, some may argue that protecting capability is the raison d'être of the single services and, therefore, it is precisely what they should be doing. To illustrate the point, the RN's own website makes it clear that, in the first instance, the professional head of the navy – the first sea lord – is 'responsible for the fighting effectiveness, efficiency and morale of the Naval Service' (RN, 2019a). It then goes on to record that he also 'supports the management and direction of the Armed Forces'. Senior service enthusiasts may reasonably contend that looking after 'The Andrew'[2] should always be the first sea lord's priority, and his wider defence responsibilities should always be a secondary consideration. However, there were strong views among the elite interviewees that the delegated model had done too much to encourage single service parochialism and that the development of JF25 was suffering as a result. In particular, senior officers from all the single services expressed concern about the complexity of the lead command arrangements, as well as known capability management interdependencies. As an example, an RN four-star officer pointed out his service's reliance on both the MoD head office strategic programmes team and the Defence Nuclear Organization for the ongoing development and delivery of the Dreadnought programme:[3] 'Eventually, it's going to produce a submarine that I have to man, train, sustain and operate. How we keep the governance mechanisms in place, to enable that procurement programme to deliver what I need, is going to take some significant work.'

The differences between the three services are often seen as strengths and identified as a reason why the whole of Defence is greater than the sum of its parts. These strengths are deep-rooted in single service histories, from which their distinct culture and sometimes opposing ethos are generated. However, these environmentally specific attitudes also underpin how the single services manage themselves. They value their own esoteric knowledge and experience, advance their own champions, and safeguard their own continuance. There is a danger, therefore, that these strengths can also become weaknesses for Defence as a whole, encouraging the single services to pursue self-serving goals, increase their insularity and become less concerned about what is good for the future, integrated force. As one RAF two-star officer noted, when you introduce different organizational constructs and associated processes, you generate different boundaries and seams, which create a requirement to manage across those boundaries and seams. In increasing the single services' responsibility, accountability and authority for capability management, the delegated model has given them far more freedom to exercise their individuality. It has been designed to improve Defence's ability to develop and maintain military capability, but it has also introduced a tension around the needs of developing future forces versus the aspirations of the single services. To help reduce this tension, an equitable balance is required that affords the single services sufficient freedom of manoeuvre to manage capability, yet also provides MoD head office sufficient control to ensure that capability management delivers an appropriate integrated force. Such a balance will not be easily found. As a four-star general observed, 'successful translation of strategic direction into military capability needs to take account of the fact there's a deeply cultural thing in this space that gets in the way of doing the right thing'.

Although most of the debate on service culture, ethos and professions was concentrated on the single service side, some consideration was given to the issues from a broader, Defence perspective. Two senior officials observed that, traditionally, the balance of the defence budget had altered only very little since the Sandys review in 1957. Although it is difficult accurately to quantify this assertion over time, there is some evidence to support it, as detailed in Table 7.1.

In 2019, there was less than £4 billion, or just 2 per cent, difference in the total allocation of funding for the single services over the entire period covered by the equipment plan (a total of £186.4 billion over 10 years). Twenty-five years earlier, in FY 1994–95, even with a considerable element of the procurement programme committed to the Eurofighter programme, there was only a 12.4 per cent difference between the highest spend on the RAF and the lowest spend on the army. Finally, the method for presenting costs in the defence estimates of the 1960s does not allow a direct comparison to be made to contemporary equipment plans; however, an examination of the entire estimated Defence costs for FY 1965–66 shows an even closer alignment between the three services, with less than 1 per cent between the highest and lowest estimates. This situation was accurately, if rather pessimistically, summed up by Mr Brynmor John, the Labour shadow defence minister at the time of the Nott review, who said: 'The whole history of defence planning has been equality of misery – every Service has taken its proportionate share of cuts' (Hansard, 1981).

The individual nature of the single services has a significant impact on the translation of strategic direction into military capability, especially since the

Table 7.1: Comparison of single service and Joint Forces Command budget allocations

Figures in £ million and (% of total budget or outturn)	RN	Army	RAF	JFC
Equipment Plan funding allocated to FY 2027/28	32,500 (17.4)	30,200 (16.2)	34,000 (18.2)	30,200 (16.2)
Equipment Plan outturn for FY 2017/18	3,000 (19.8)	2,000 (13.2)	3,500 (23.2)	2,300 (15.2)
Main divisions of the procurement programme for FY 1994/95	2,488 (26.6)	1,875 (20)	3,033 (32.4)	N/A
Estimated cost of the defence programme for FY 1965/66	544 (25.7)	555 (26.2)	561 (26.5)	N/A

Source: *The Defence Equipment Plan 2018, Financial Summary Version 3; Statement on the Defence Estimates 1994*, Cm 2550; and *Statement on the Defence Estimates 1965*, Cmnd 2592

introduction of the delegated model. The RN, British Army and RAF will naturally favour capability choices that strengthen the delivery of military effect within their warfighting environments. What's more, Defence's current ways of working allow them to make those choices, with only limited scrutiny of their effect on the overall needs of both the current and future force. The alignment of responsibility, accountability and authority for capability management is a good model for Defence, and, in a complicated and multi-faceted bureaucracy, probably offers the best construct within which to develop and maintain military capability. Nevertheless, in its current form, it does not provide sufficient scrutiny on the decision making around what military capability should be acquired in the first place. More checks and balances need to be inserted before acquisition decisions are made, to ensure that the needs of Defence are prioritized over the aspirations of the single services.

The changing roles of the service chiefs

The role of a service chief has traditionally been seen as a role with influence. For example, no history of the Falklands Conflict would be complete without a stirring account of the then first sea lord Admiral Henry Leach's late-night meeting in the Palace of Westminster with Margaret Thatcher and John Nott the day after the Argentinean invasion, where he sought, and received, the prime minister's permission to form a task force to re-take the islands (Woodward and Robinson, 1992, pp 72–3). Leach's role in initiating the UK's response to the Argentine invasion was the high point of his career (see *The Telegraph*, 2011; and *The Times*, 2011), and a description of his meeting with Thatcher was even considered significant enough to be included in the book *Vulcan 607* – an RAF-centric account of the long-range bombing raids on Stanley airfield (White, 2012, pp 42–3).

However, the truism that the authority of the single services has been steadily eroded over the last 70 years equally applies to the service chiefs. We have already seen that, during the defence reviews of the Cold War and Early Expeditionary period, they were excluded from the inner circle of decision makers in 1957, 1981 and 1991; my research suggests those serving over the periods of the 2010 and 2015 SDSRs fared little better. Timothy Garden (1999, p 50) was in no doubt that 'compared with the heady days of the global strategy review when the single service Chiefs could produce government and NATO policy', the role of the service chiefs has been much reduced through successive measures to centralize Defence, up to and including the SDR in 1998. This view was supported by an RN four-star officer who confirmed that, during the period when each service had its own department of state, service chiefs had 'very significant control over their service's strategy'. In his view, each service chief was 'a CDS in his own right in those days'. That said, evidence from my research suggests that the service chiefs still wield considerable influence when it comes to the translation of strategic direction into military capability. Of the 32 senior officials interviewed, 11 had either first-hand experience as a service chief, or deputy, or were still on a career trajectory that could see them assume that role sometime soon. As a result, their opinions on the impact of changing roles of the service chiefs are particularly relevant.

A four-star army officer referred to a quotation from General Omar Bradley, the first chairman of the US Joint Chiefs of Staff, when discussing the current roles of the service chiefs: 'American armed strength is only as strong as the combat capabilities of its weakest service. Over emphasis on one or the other will obscure our compelling need – not for air power, not for sea power – but for American military power commensurate with our tasks in the world.' His point was the current British service chiefs had to work together to generate military capability and be prepared to compromise to ensure the right capability to meet future force structures was procured and maintained, regardless of the aspirations of the single services. However, one army two-star officer suggested that this was not the default for service chiefs. Referring to the Institute of Directors' direction on the role of a company's board, he pointed out that all board members individually should behave in the long-term interests of the health of the company. In his opinion, the service chiefs did not do that; instead, he suggested they 'feel the weight of history, tradition and precedent, and, as a result, are quite likely to be more narrowly focused'. Although the officer who had quoted Bradley was non-committal on this point, he did confirm that:

> '[I]if you have a single service chief of staff who fights his own corner with his service's self-interest at the forefront of what he does, agnostic of the potential displacement of his behaviour on other people's positions, then you will end up with, as Omar Bradley put it, British military power not being what it should be.'

The direction from the version of the DOM in circulation at the time of my research interviews was not overly conducive to a collegiate approach by service chiefs to the higher management of defence. It confirmed they had specific responsibility for identifying the most effective and affordable force structure and capabilities needed to realize defence requirements, and then developing their service to deliver them. This development included recruiting, educating, training, equipping, preparing, and sustaining (MoD, 2015b, pp 28–30). But it also confirmed that they had no specific responsibility for defence strategy, allocating resources or managing Defence at a business level (2015b, p 28). This encouraged the service chiefs to perpetuate a parochial approach to capability development, whilst absolving them of any formal, collective responsibility to do the same for Defence as a whole.

Even though the DOM was explicit about service chiefs' responsibility regarding delivering capability, one former service chief, who served after the introduction of the delegated model, was pragmatic about amount of influence he had been able to exercise during his tenure, specifically because of the legacy programme:

'The influence is [limited], because of course you are a victim of the legacy programming that's delivered what I've got now. You're also, to a certain degree, guided and being led down a path on those future programmes, which are also from legacy thinking. So, I don't have the ability to start steering this bloody super tanker through 90 degrees and reversing it. I am limited. It's a bit like the bridge watch keeper, when the captain of a ship goes to sleep. You're allowed plus or minus one degree off heading, otherwise give me a call. I think we're still in the situation where I've got sort of one, two degrees. Just given the scale of the investment already made and the plans that have been put in place.'

Moreover, given the considerable development period and subsequent prolonged in-service period of platforms within his service, he did not anticipate that influence increasing markedly for his successors in the short to medium term.

Most interviewees from the service chiefs sub-set had a view on the higher management of defence limitations placed on the service chiefs by the DOM. Although responsible for providing advice on the operational use of their service, some complained about not being part of the operational decision-making process. It was also suggested that being dependent on the CDS to represent their issues at the Defence Board was sub-optimal and resulted in one former service chief not always feeling 'as empowered as I would wish'. In a similar vein, a suggestion was also put forward that the service chiefs should have a greater input into the generation of Defence's output requirements, as they had been officially ordained as the pan-Defence experts for their warfighting environment. That said, a counter view was offered by a two-star officer serving in MoD head office that such a position would be as good as allowing the service chiefs to set their own homework. This groundswell of negative thinking was summed up by a former service chief who suggested, 'I have been likened by many external colleagues to the executive chairman of a FTSE 100 company. It doesn't feel like that.'

Recognizing the limitations on service chiefs to influence the higher management of Defence, some senior officials highlighted several pro-active measures that could be brought to bear to improve the situation. One four-star army officer confirmed that service chiefs must work very hard 'to make sure ministers know where [they are] coming from and what the potential capability of [maritime/land/air power] is, and the risks associated with [their] use'. He also stated that timely and targeted interaction with MoD head office was just as important, so that the individual service chief's views and direction on his service's capabilities were being adequately represented to the operations, finance and military capability staff to inform their day-to-day decision making.

While my research did not explicitly demand an examination of the macro-level structure of Defence, the subject was broached in several interviews. The default view was well summed up by this quotation from an RAF four-star officer:

'We have regularly challenged ourselves with that question [is the single service structure within Defence still fit for purpose?]. Each time we challenge ourselves, the requirement for expertise in the three environments to be the custodian of air power, as a professional airman, to be the custodian of British maritime power as a professional military maritime admiral, and the same in the land domain, remains valid.'

However, an alternative point of view was offered by an army general in an MoD head office appointment. He was in favour of rebalancing delegated authorities in favour of MoD head office, thus curbing the extant authorities and responsibilities of the service chiefs. He also questioned whether Defence still required four-star heads of service and suggested that three-stars under command of the CDS may be a better alternative. He argued:

'I think they could usefully re-examine the locus of the chiefs, writ large. What is the role and purpose of a service chief beyond his specific tribal responsibilities to his service? Are the chiefs able to act in an agnostic, non-partisan manner in a formal collective as the chief of staffs' committee, as it were, responsible for the holistic health of military capability? I'm not sure that we can be confident in any given generation that that has proven to be the case, where actually, when confronted with a set of unenviable choices, the chiefs have inevitably defaulted to their own service setting.'

Exploring alternatives to the existing structure of defence decision makers would take this book well beyond its current boundaries. However, given the discussion it generated during my research interviews, it remains a subject on my list for further investigation.

The conclusions from this section mirror those reached when analysing how the individual nature of the single services affects the translation of strategic direction into military capability. The service chiefs are the professional heads of their service, and their default will always be to do whatever is necessary to defend and promote them. That is only to be expected. However, in Defence's current organizational construct, the considerable influence they still maintain contributes to the problem that the needs of Defence can be, and often are, overlooked in favour of the aspirations of the single services. The resultant capability choices were not always optimised for the development of JF25, and, unless things change, future choices are unlikely to lead to the successful delivery of IR30 either.

Defence process and procedures

The delegated model remains the bedrock of current defence processes and procedures. While the Levene Reforms reached right across the MoD and the armed forces, the report recommendation that had the greatest influence on military capability planning and delivery was *Key Recommendation Six – Financial Management*. The most relevant sub-paragraph within that recommendation is detailed, in full, here:

> The Service Chiefs should take responsibility (and ultimately own the budget) for detailed capability planning and propose (through a Command Plan) how best to deliver the strategic direction set by the Defence Board across all lines of development. Once the Plan is agreed by Head Office, Chiefs should be given greater freedom to flex within their budgets, provided they continue to deliver the agreed objectives within their delegated resources. The Plan should be refreshed annually, including to enable cross TLB adjustments where necessary, but the department should aim to make major changes only at SDSRs. (MoD, 2011a, p 69)

During my research, the unanimous view of senior officials serving in single service or JFC appointments was that the processes and procedures introduced through the delegated model were an improvement on what had gone before. Typical of the positive comments was the following, from a defence decision maker: 'I think [the delegated model] has improved [the delivery of military capability] markedly, because someone like me now feels responsible, accountable and with authority for that bit of military capability which I own.' Another defence decision maker's observation was that the delegated model had aligned the responsibilities needed to deliver military capability. In his view, Defence should set the output requirement and then the single service should have the maximum ability to decide and develop the capabilities best to meet that standard. That maximum ability had been made possible by the delegated model, through the single services' control of money (including the power to flex between programmes), manpower, equipment and its associated support, and infrastructure. A similar sentiment was expressed by a former admiral who suggested that: 'Owning the whole capability management process has made us a better, sharper, more focused command.'

Away from the single services, however, opinions on the new processes and procedures were not universally positive. Wide-ranging concerns were expressed over issues such as poor implementation, differing interpretations of the new levels of responsibility, a lack of suitably qualified and experienced personnel, and an over-emphasis on environmental-specific capability over cross-cutting capability. More than one senior official believed that the delegated model had not been fully implemented, with a three-star civil servant suggesting the single services had 'cherry picked' those elements of the DRP's key recommendations that suited them. One former defence decision maker commented that 'Levene is the right answer, poorly executed'. Given the lack of detail included in the DRP, that is hardly surprising. For example, the section on capability planning and financial management is no more than six and a half pages of high-level detail. This lack of comprehensive direction has also given rise to some very different views over who is now responsible for what, as a three-star officer in a key MoD head office capability management appointment observed:

> 'The difficulty is people's view of the word 'delegation' is mixed. For some people, this means that they should decide everything. If you were a big corporate enterprise in the commercial sector, let's say Shell, head office still directs its operating divisions. So, the defence plan and the output map that is part of it are orders down to the TLBs.'

A major flaw identified in the introduction of the delegated model was the failure to recruit suitably qualified personnel, or provide the necessary training for defence's capability planners and financial managers to operate the revised processes and procedures. One RN three-star officer, who was an acquisition specialist, suggested that this was because Defence's staff training was focused on warfighting and not running a business. In his view, more emphasis was required on delivering an integrated programme of complex capabilities. This perspective was supported by a retired air marshal who believed:

> 'Just because you've been a programmer in the MoD does not turn you into a programme manager overnight, in terms of, you know, [the] hard graft of running a business. You can move numbers up and down spreadsheets – do it all day long. But can you genuinely deliver an outcome?'

A final concern aired by senior officials was the tendency for the delegated model to over-focus defence planners on environmental specific capability. One two-star RAF officer, with considerable capability management experience, believed that the disaggregation balance for traditional military capability was correct, but the delegated model had made it more difficult to manage cross-cutting capabilities. The single service concentration was, unsurprisingly, predominantly on ships, tanks and fast jets, at the expense of joint enablers, such as communications and logistics, which led one two-star army officer to observe that 'the delegation of money to the environments has made it more difficult to produce a joint force than before'.

An army three-star officer, with considerable capability planning experience, explained the procedures to manage the force structure had changed since the introduction of the delegated model. He confirmed that the new philosophy was focused on generating approximately 80 per cent of the capability requirement and then recognizing that the flexibility in the remainder of the programme existed to attend to future variations that would inevitably occur. Unfortunately, in the view of a defence decision maker responsible for delivering capability to the new procedures, that was easier said than done. He believed that all of Defence's energies were being used to maintain the extant programme, leaving no time or resource to react to the variations:

'[W]hat you're actually doing is fighting a programme where a vast amount of money is being spent on things which are held to be existential to a service, at the expense of smaller sums of money that you want to spend on the stuff you're actually using and are going to need in the future.'

This problem was expanded upon further by another four-star officer, who pointed out that Defence's biggest problem in adopting this new approach was its inability to identify and disinvest in capability it no longer required. His conclusion was simple: 'If we want a load of new things, we're absolutely going to have to stop doings some things too.' He considered that the recently introduced Defence Capability Assessment Register (DCAR) was a reasonable handrail for identifying and prioritizing new requirements, but had been less successful as a decision-support tool for disinvestment. To explain, he offered the following analogy:

'So, we need a new land EW [electronic warfare] capability, because our existing one is becoming obsolescent, or obsolete. So, we come to the table, we've identified in the DCAR that we need it, but it doesn't get funded, and it doesn't get funded because it's easier not to fund the new things than it is to stop funding the old things. Even though the new things may be more pressing than some of the old things … so instead of saying this is such an expensive capability, why don't we get out of it completely, and then we can distribute that largesse much more wisely, we've salami sliced.'

Another significant impediment to managing the force structure was, as one three-star officer described, the existence therein of 'exquisite irrelevance capability'. He applied this label to the growing number of increasingly expensive platforms being calibrated against the highest possible requirement, which resulted in prohibitive costs and a correspondingly reduced fleet size. Furthermore, he suggested that:

'They're rendered irrelevant for a number of reasons. They're not in the right space or the right place at the right time because you've not got many of these things. They are a very high technological risk therefore they do break sometimes … They may be calibrated against the wrong threat, i.e. the opposition is not playing cricket in the way that we thought they were going to play; they're playing a slightly different game. They're so expensive and valuable bits of commodities, you don't put them in harm's way anyway. As a consequence, you then find they've been rendered irrelevant.'

Several senior officials also discussed how the latest industry procurement techniques could be introduced into Defence's capability management toolbox to achieve the required flexible management of the force structure. Tailorable, adjustable and agile were the adjectives favoured by both delivery agent practitioners and single service capability deciders. Future acquisitions should exploit technology that could be incrementally improved by utilizing plug and play capability upgrades, or have their utility changed entirely through software drops. This approach, they argued, would allow Defence to preserve its existing policy of major platform procurement by safeguarding the relevance and utility of the platforms over a projected lifespan measured in decades. However, although some senior officials had seen this approach becoming more and more commonplace in comparable, high-tech industries, none were able to offer any evidence of it happening at any scale within Defence.

Another procedural barrier to the development of the optimal capabilities to populate future force structures was Defence's susceptibility to path dependence. This can be defined as the tendency of institutions or technologies to become committed to develop in certain ways as a result of their structural properties or their beliefs or values (Encyclopaedia Britannica, 2019). Timothy Edmunds (2010, p 386) claims that path dependence exists in UK defence planning because of competition over resources, the long-term nature of the procurement process, and established political, economic and institutional interests. This argument has been developed by Uttley et al (2019, p 815) who posit that even though the MoD is committed to futures work and horizon scanning, primarily through the work of its Development Concepts and Doctrine Centre, it is the UK's past and present that drive its vision of, and planning for, the future. The impact of this closed thinking was explored by several senior officials during discussions on contemporary defence procedures.

The clearest example given of defence planners' preoccupation with the recent past when considering how JF25 should be constructed related to the maintenance of force elements at readiness. A retired RAF three-star officer, who had commanded the JFC's Joint Force Development organization, argued that Defence continued to commit a disproportionate level of resource to maintain extremely high readiness forces. He was specifically referring to the Lead Commando Group and the Lead Airborne Task Force respectively, two battalion-sized forces permanently held at 48 hours' notice to move, even though the endorsed joint operational capability analysis suggested both an amphibious and airborne capability were not required to be permanently available for immediate deployment. He also asserted that similar arguments could be evidenced to support a reduction in command and control nodes, especially at brigade level or equivalent.

At the opposite end of the readiness scale, several senior officials considered that future force development should be influenced by greater clarity and an endorsed policy position with regard to warning times, to enable sensible decisions to be made on the maintenance of 'seed corn' capabilities[4] and their regeneration when required (HCDC, 2012). While not advocating a return to the ten-year rule of the early twentieth century, the argument was made that significant, cost-effective capability decisions could be made against an endorsed view on regeneration. A two-star army officer supported this approach, pointing out that if it takes ten years to build a warship, 15 years to develop a complex fast jet, but only five years to equip an army, then this should lead to different warning times and drive a different order of spending priorities. Such a policy would rely on a pragmatic view of risk, a willingness to maintain investment in seed corn capability, and a confidence in regeneration timelines. In the view of one three-star officer, it would also require that existing capability had to be as utilitarian as it could be for the contemporary problem set. As an example, he suggested:

'[T]he most beneficial platform … in the fleet at the moment is a Bay Class RFA [Royal Fleet Auxiliary]. They can use it as a C2 [command and control] node, a medical facility, a logistic disaster release facility, a helicopter platform. It can launch marines out the back as a mother ship; indeed, it can carry armoured tanks if I really needed it to. But

it's an RFA and if we put a gun on the front actually, it looks like a
warship so, I can hold a reasonable cocktail party as though it were
a warship. You get maximum utility out of it, but it is just an RFA.'

In the opinion of a four-star army officer, current force structure and path
dependency were inextricably linked. What's more, both were having a
considerable effect on the capability decision making shaping the future force.
In his view, the existing force structure drove employment protectionism
that stymied innovation and blocked change. For example, he suggested
the default option for replacing an obsolete capability was invariably the
acquisition of a more modern version of what was currently in the force
structure. This was because it generated the least amount of disruption across
the DLODs. The existing manpower could transition to the new version
of the equipment, which would be familiar to them and could probably
be maintained under existing repair and overhaul arrangements. Existing
training facilities were likely to require only minimal reconfiguration to
re-role the existing manpower, plus doctrine and organizational constructs
were unlikely to need significant amendment. Furthermore, this more-of-
the-same approach would probably be supported by the defence industrial
lobby, as it would, in all likelihood, maintain existing employment levels. It
would also be unlikely to lead to the disbandment of historical regiments or
squadrons, thus keeping both the retired senior officer cadre, and supporters
of the traditional military, happy. That said, he was firmly of the opinion that
replicating existing capability would seldom deliver the most cost-effective
solution, and the like-for-like approach would not provide the tailorable,
adjustable and agile capability needed by the future force structure. In
voicing this concern, he fully acknowledged that the principles of smart
acquisition had been designed to encourage a comprehensive examination
of all possible options to fulfil future requirements; however, he believed that
the path dependence behaviour of the single services was so deep rooted
that it regularly overrode smart acquisition process and procedure.

As senior officials discussed current processes and procedures within
Defence, the significance of MoD head office became more and more
obvious. Almost all considered its internal ways of working and its
touchpoints with the single services and delivery agents to be key elements
in the translation of strategic direction into military capability. Internally, the
interfaces between the staffs of the relevant floors[5] within the building were
regularly identified as vital to MoD head office's successful contribution to
the operation of the delegated model. However, in the opinion of a recently
retired general, the necessary system of aligning the programme from the
third floor, with operations from the fourth floor, to be led by the fifth floor
was simply not in place. In his view 'because of all sorts of personal institution
reasons, you have a third floor universe and a fourth floor universe dealing

with different bits of the fifth floor on different days'. The consequences of the internally siloed approach were highlighted by a three-star officer working in MoD head office, who explained how an arbitrary financial decision taken in isolation by a non-specialist programmer had effectively set the timeline to reduce the size of the army following the 2010 SDSR. He explained that 'you had a[n] … apparatchik who had no concept of the consequences of what they're doing, directing – in this case – the army to a trajectory of [manpower] reduction which the army would not have wished if it'd had any choice'.

The interaction between the staff in MoD head office and other elements of the department – in the main, the single services' headquarters but also, to a lesser extent, the delivery agents – was regularly cited by senior officials when considering the effectiveness of current processes and procedures. Probably the most consistently recognized failing was the lack of both expertise and capacity within MoD head office, with the result that it was regularly overmatched by its subordinate organizations. Another three-star officer went as far as to suggest that MoD head office had 'lost control over the TLBs'. The reason for the failing was, in the words of one defence decision maker, that 'most of the capability and resource to be able to do joined-up thinking was given back to the services'. Many senior officials supported the need to realign staff within MoD head office to make it more strategic and stronger. Thus, realizing one of the DRP's recommendations: 'The Head Office should … set strategic direction and provide a strong corporate and financial management framework for the Department' (MoD, 2011a, p 36). Ultimately, the consensus was that this issue was for MoD head office to solve, as summarized by an RAF two-star officer with considerable programming experience: 'the centre [MoD head office] has not matured its approach to properly enforce, deliver, manage, whatever verb you want to use, the delegated model.'

Another area of tension that regularly surfaced during discussions around the contribution of MoD head office to the delegated model concerned spans of responsibility. The view from outside MoD head office was both consistent and robust – the single services were now the decision makers for all capability management within their environmental portfolio. While this was not directly challenged by senior officials from within MoD head office, the extent of the responsibility that the single services believed they exercised was. It was argued that the central military capability staff were obliged to scrutinize and confirm that the requirements raised by the single services met the needs of policy within an affordable envelope. In short, it was a MoD head office responsibility to ensure defence policy was serviced within the available budget. The associated processes and procedures of the delegated model had created new relationships, which presented different problems to what had gone before, and, therefore, needed to be managed accordingly.

A final topic of conversation among senior officials regarding the delegated model was the need for further change to current processes and procedures. Everyone who expressed a view believed further change was required, with most suggesting that was only to be expected. One air marshal suggested that 'we've gone from a highly centralized model to a highly disaggregated model, and it shouldn't surprise us to find that the truth is probably somewhere in the middle'. A commonly held assessment was that better governance was needed, which required an adjustment to MoD head office's role in the process. Changes to the financial aspects of the delegated model were also recommended, but with contrary views expressed on the single services living within their financial control framework and not continually seeking additional resource, versus reintroducing some centrally held flexible resource to cope with the unexpected. There was also support for more robust financial management, with one four-star acquisition specialist advocating that the delegated model needed 'to be enumerated with a far more forensic precision'. Several interviewees agreed that delegation would not last forever and that the cyclical nature of organizational change would prompt a more centralized reset in due course. One enthusiastic supporter of the delegated model offered the following, pragmatic view:

> 'Delegation won't last forever. Banks do this thing where they basically empower their outstations and then ten years later, they recentralize again. Delegation will last for a bit. I'm sure in about five, seven or ten years' time, or maybe earlier, we will reimpose some form of centralist approach ... It's inevitable because that's the way businesses operate. Don't expect delegation to be a panacea forever. I just quite like it while it's here!'

Decision making in defence

A 1966 RAND Corporation project developed a theory of bureaucratic decision making that could be applied to government, civil and military establishments. Its most significant conclusion was that 'it is impossible to define the "perfectly efficient" behaviour for any bureau' (Downs, 1966, p vi). More recently, Richard Knighton (2009, p 22) studied how strategic decisions within the UK government are affected by psychological and cognitive biases. He argued that the complexity, ambiguity and uncertainty inherent in strategic decisions make them more susceptible to a series of psychological biases that can lead to seriously flawed decisions. He also contended that, although the effects of these biases could be mitigated to some extent, there were no simple formulae for success and concluded that 'strategic decision making is very definitely an art not a science'. This argument has support in the secondary literature on both decision making in general, and military decision making in particular (see, for example, Dixon, 1976; Gladwell, 2007; and Taleb, 2010).

In 2014, concerns regarding decision making in defence policy prompted the HCDC (2015a) to conduct an inquiry, which examined the relationships between ministers, officials and the military to understand the contemporary state of decision-making processes within the MoD and to assess whether changes needed to be made. The inquiry determined that, once high-quality, relevant information had been gathered, effective decision making in Defence was dependent on three further inter-related elements: who makes the decision; what is the process used to make the decision; and whether the option chosen is decided through a process of rational, logical consideration of the risks and alternatives available (2015a, pp 23–4).

The HCDC considered two separate case studies: the decision to deploy UK forces into Helmand Province in Afghanistan in 2006, and decisions surrounding the procurement of the Queen Elizabeth Class aircraft carriers. In both cases, the inquiry concluded that: 'the MoD seemed to have been poorly informed and misunderstood the nature of the problem; the structure of decision making was bewildering; and no-one admitted actually to taking the decision' (2015a, p 3). Although both case studies considered events that had taken place prior to the introduction of the delegated model, the HCDC concluded that significant problems, particularly relating to the evidence to support decision making and the ability of the decision makers to make good decisions, remained unaddressed even after the delegated model had been introduced. Against this backdrop, senior officials shared views on how decision making within defence affected the translation of strategic direction into military capability.

One four-star defence decision maker believed that, at a mechanistic level, Defence processes and procedures provided the wherewithal to support decision making. He suggested that 'fundamentally, if you want to go and see the things that the government said it was going to do in the SDSR, you will find them in the defence plan and you will find them in my command plan'. The inference here was that the associated decision making would be made by the owner of the command plan. The lack of detail included in SDSR reports provided a degree of flexibility that supported this view. As an RAF two-star officer explained, decisions were made during SDSRs to create a capability or support a task, but the subsequent report did not go into detail about the how they would be achieved. The consequence was, according to a three-star army officer, that most of the resultant optionality was Defence's choice. By way of example, he suggested:

'[I]f I said to you tomorrow, please go out there and make sure nobody crosses the road, you could do it in a number of ways. You could shout a lot, you could lay a barbed wire fence, you could do X or Y, but you have that choice.'

The same official saw it as a positive that Defence had been given a series of directions rather than an end state, and that some of the requirements were relatively subjective with no single point of success or failure.

The counter argument is that this approach has given the single services too much freedom to shape capability development that favours their own environment over the needs of the joint force. There was a general agreement among senior officials that the single services' influence over defence decision making had increased because of the delegated model. One MoD head office three-star officer talked about 'discretionary orders', which, in his view, was unequivocal direction from the centre that the single services had the strength either to amend subtly before implementing or simply ignore. Specific examples of this were given by an RAF three-star officer who explained that delivery teams in DE&S continued to support platforms in excess of the numbers directed in the 2015 SDSR because the relevant single service insisted on operating the fleet size at the pre-review level. In an organizational design where the chief executive officer, in this case the CDS, has no line management responsibility for his heads of division, the single services chiefs – a chain of command construct not even understood by the company chairman[6] – the opportunity for the heads of divisions and their teams to 'consent and evade' is undeniable (HCDC, 2015a, p 32). This situation is exacerbated by Defence's top committees' structure, which, just in the non-operational space, includes: a defence board (supported by investment approvals, audit and people subcommittees); three service boards;[7] an executive committee; a chiefs of staff committee; and a defence delivery group (MoD, 2020b, pp 19–20). The overlapping responsibilities and authorities of these committees do little to streamline decision making within defence.

An analysis of contemporary decision making in defence would not be complete without a consideration of the relevant lessons from the Iraq Inquiry – commonly referred to across government as the 'Chilcot Inquiry' (Chilcot et al, 2016). However, even though a Chilcot implementation directorate, under a two-star civil servant, had been established to progress the Defence-wide changes demanded by the inquiry, during my research only two interviewees raised the potential implications of the inquiry's findings on the translation of strategic direction into decision making). This was astonishing, not only because the work of everyone interviewed should have been affected in some way by the implementation of the inquiry's recommendations, but because the evidence in this section confirms that decision making in the round was clearly considered by many interviewees to be a significant influencing factor on the translation of strategic direction into military capability.

In headline terms, the Chilcot Inquiry suggested the UK government had a propensity for groupthink, which reflected insufficient challenge and a lack of diversity of thought, and suffered from multiple impediments to effective decision making. The MoD provided further clarification for the latter failing: 'structures and processes impeded the flow of information and evidence; strategy making was weak and inflexible; and insufficient attention was paid to the capability required for the operation [*Telic*] and to determining the resources required to ensure success' (MoD, 2017c, p 7). These conclusions were acknowledged by one interviewee who confirmed the inquiry's groupthink concern:

'I think the way we think, organizationally, is very much along those lines. You're taught, instructed, "staff-colleged" and everything to think a particular colour. If someone says to you "well the world has changed completely and what you need to worry about is the cyber threat from Russia and not delivering ordnance at Mach 1.1" ... It's very difficult to think that different thought because, "No, I'm springing back into shape. This is what I understand".'

Seven months after the Iraq Inquiry report was published, the House of Commons Public Administration and Constitutional Affairs Committee (HC PACAC) (2017) completed a review on lessons still to be learned. It recognized that the government was conducting a lessons-learned investigation across Whitehall and recommended that the findings be reported to parliament so that the HC PACAC and other relevant select committees could scrutinize and comment (2017, p 32). However, it did not identify any corrective actions being taken, or even considered, within the MoD. This supports the view of a major general who believed: 'We're starting to think Chilcot's learned and ignore it. I think in doing that, we're showing that actually we haven't learned the lessons from Chilcot.' If Defence is unable or unwilling to learn the lessons from what was probably the highest profile public inquiry of the last generation, which took seven years to complete at a cost of £13.1 million (The National Archives, 2017), it is difficult to see how it will ever correct the flaws in its decision-making process.

While recognizing that doing nothing, or choosing not to take an option, are still decisions, a key concern some senior officials had with defence decision making was simply not making a decision because it was difficult. One RAF two-star officer working in MoD head office confirmed:

'We failed, spectacularly, in the previous planning round in ABC [annual budget cycle] '17 to take any decisions that would have eased the situation we are in now. Some of that is politics. Some of that is we just were not willing to do it … you just need to be prepared to take some bloody decisions, which we find quite difficult.'

Another officer confirmed there were often political reasons why uncomfortable decisions were not made, suggesting that '[Gordon] Brown was a Rosyth MP, so the carriers were not going to disappear'. Some of the concerns expressed about defence's decision-making ability during SDSRs echoed the findings of the HCDC inquiry. For example, poor data quality was identified as a problem reaching all the way back to the 1998 SDR, and a lack of management information in general, as well as evidence to support cost estimates in particular, was seen as the dominant factor in some bad judgements made by senior officials in Defence in both the 2010 and 2015 SDSRs. In addition, the reliance on process and procedure over the ability of individuals to make good decisions was also raised as an issue. One RAF four-star officer questioned how much 'real brainpower and analysis' was being used to get to the right decisions for defence.

One issue that I was very keen to get opinions on was the existence or otherwise of the supposed men-in-grey-suits[8] within the MoD's decision-making process. A two-star civil servant confirmed their presence, but stressed they were not decision makers. In his view that was always the role of the secretary of state, the CDS and the permanent secretary. However, when prompted, he did recognize they had an influential role as holders-of-the-pen:

'They [the men in grey suits] were the holders of the pen, but the way these processes work is that you have to have people owning the pen to make the proposition that the decision makers sign up to – so, thesis, antithesis, synthesis and situation. If you just have a sea of everyone thinking thoughts, you never get to that point where someone is making a proposition which you can test. So, no, they didn't make the decisions, but they had to corral this process into putting forward propositions.'

All the senior officials interviewed who had experienced the MoD's contribution to the quinquennial review process at the highest level confirmed that the DSG remained its single decision-making body that filtered the Defence input up to the SDSR team in the Cabinet Office and thence to the NSC. In addition to the secretary of state, the CDS and the permanent secretary, the group also included the minister for defence procurement, the VCDS, the directors general for security and policy, and finance; and the deputy chief of the defence staff for military capability. Although the DSG was the forum within which the department agreed its inputs into the review, one of its members during the 2015 SDSR confirmed that, as part of the process, the higher-profile defence issues were also being concurrently staffed up to the prime minister and the chancellor of the exchequer through the Cabinet Office's SDSR team. The inevitable feedback from this approach, usually in the form of requests for more capability enhancements, led to the constant adjustment of the defence position with, more often than not, the need to unearth more efficiencies. As a result, the DSG's decision making was influenced just as much by political prompting from above as it was from single service arm-twisting from below.

How have the MoD and the single services affected military capability choices?

The long-term trend in changes to the higher management of defence has not been favourable to the single services. In a 2020 RUSI occasional paper that I co-authored with Trevor Taylor, we wrote:

> To some degree, almost all the change initiatives experienced by defence in recent times have had the effect of eroding the authority of the single services and a reasonable generalisation would be that, as a result, the single services resisted what they considered to be constraints on their independence from other defence institutions. (Taylor and Curtis, 2020, p 4)

The exception that proves the rule was the introduction of the delegated model. My research suggests that the post-20210 SDSR organizational changes to Defence increased the authority of the single services in general, and the service chiefs in particular. Unsurprisingly, within the cohort of senior officials interviewed, those serving within the single services were overwhelmingly supportive on the new ways of working; those elsewhere less so. When it is so easy for the single services to pursue their own capability agendas, the likelihood of Defence creating a balanced force structure, which recognizes and makes space for non-environmental capabilities such as joint logistics, is slim. With the integrated force aspirations of the 2021 IR placing even more emphasis on niche cross-environmental capabilities, as well as seeking more investment in emerging technologies to operate in the new domains of space and cyberspace, the strain on the delegated model is only likely to increase. All service chiefs would naturally want to hand their service to their successor in as good as, or better, shape than they inherited it. Centuries of history and tradition demand it. The delegated model has undoubtedly made it easier for them to put the needs of their service ahead of the needs of Defence. Moreover, some senior officials suggested the service chiefs are encouraged to prioritize their own service's needs because, even though it results in the sub-optimal management of defence, the culture and ethos that it engenders is considered critical to achieving success on operations.

How Defence goes about its day-to-day business, and especially the way it makes decisions, has a significant influence on why the UK has the military capability that it has. In all large bureaucratic organizations, care must be taken when mandating process and procedure. Too light a hand on the tiller can be just as debilitating as a plethora of rules and regulations that stifle innovation from top to bottom. A balance is clearly needed. Regrettably, the current processes and procedures around the delegated model do not provide that balance. Even though the DOM claims to be the 'authoritative statement of how the Department operates' (MoD, 2020b, p 1), the direction provided by its latest iteration – *How Defence Works Version 6* – lacks substance and is woefully incomplete. In an organization with as many chiefs as Defence has, opportunities to 'consent and evade' should be reduced wherever possible. The current version of the DOM does the opposite. Many of the senior officials interviewed during my research confirmed that there were serious failings with the promulgation of Defence's high-level ways of working, and recognized the need to change. Several of the senior officials who expressed concern are still serving, in some cases as defence decision makers. However, none of these concerns found their way into the 2021 IR. Even though the accompanying DCP included a chapter titled 'Transforming Our Ways of Working' (MoD, 2021b, pp 65–6), it saw no need to review and update the higher management of defence. It is no secret that militaries struggle with change (see, for example, Barno and Bensahel, 2020, pp 9–27); nevertheless, failing to confront a construct that is clearly sub-optimal does little to instil confidence in the processes and procedures behind Defence's capability decision making.

In announcing the IOpC in 2020, the then CDS, General Nick Carter, confirmed that 'some industrial age capabilities [would] increasingly have to meet their sunset to create the space for capabilities needed for sunrise' (GOV.UK, 2020a). However, that aspiration, while laudable, has always proved difficult for Defence to achieve. For example, even though the 2021 IR has resulted in several equipment types being withdrawn from service earlier than expected[9] (Brooke-Holland, 2021, p 3), most already have a like-for-like, or at least similar, replacement in the acquisition pipeline. For example, even though a reduction in the order from five to three was announced in the DCP (MoD, 2021b, p 57), the MoD had already signed a contract for the E-7 Wedgetail as a like-for like replacement for the RAF's existing fleet of E3-D Sentry airborne early warning and control aircraft two years earlier (RAF, 2019). Path dependency remains a major factor in military capability decision making. Moreover, while path dependency may, at first glance, appear to generate the least amount of disruption across the DLODs, this is not always the reality. The replacement for the army's combat vehicle reconnaissance (tracked) fleet with the similar, if considerably more modern, Ajax vehicle is the most obvious case in point (see Chuter,

2021). That said, there is some hope. The DCP did confirm that the RN will gradually replace its remaining 13 minehunters with remotely operated or autonomous systems (MoD, 2021b, p 28). If Defence is to make better capability choices to inform the future force structure outlined in the 2021 IR, MoD head office, the single services and the delivery agents must improve their collegiate working, avoid path dependency, and accept more altruistic, intelligent and integrated ways of working.

8

Why Does the UK Have the Military Capability That It Has?

In a perfect world, the four-step translation of strategic direction into military capability model should deliver a force structure able to implement extant defence policy. However, the analysis laid out in this book shows that this does not always happen. Not unexpectedly, there is no single reason why. The model is affected by untold factors, some of which are initiated by the government or defence decision makers themselves, others are determined by outside agencies. These include: politicians; elements of MoD head office, the single services and delivery agents; the defence industry; the media; the public; allies; and potential state and non-state adversaries. Except for the inputs of potential adversaries, most of the factors that these agencies introduce are likely to be in pursuit of valid and reasonable effects; nevertheless, they all add complexity to the model and make the task of providing fit-for-purpose armed forces considerably more challenging.

We know the translation of strategic direction into military capability is an open-ended activity. The introduction of uncontrollable and disruptive factors also make it complex and intractable. It has all the hallmarks of a wicked problem (see Rittel and Webber, 1973; and Head, 2008). No single action will resolve all the adverse effects of the events and influences that impact strategic direction into military capability activity; moreover, any attempt to mitigate the complexity that these factors introduce must be mindful of the following two points. In the first instance, an improvement in one aspect of the activity may well lead to a regression elsewhere. For example, several senior officials believed the freedoms within which the delegated model were implemented allowed the single services to introduce customized processes that best tackled the specific capability management demands within their environment. However, that resulted in considerable inefficiency within MoD head office and the delivery agents who then had to align with four bespoke operating models. Secondly, there will always be factors over which defence decision makers can never have control; for example, the actions of a potential adversary or a major natural hazard or environmental event.

Events and influences

While the events and influences that impact the translation of strategic direction into military capability do not lend themselves to neat pigeonholing, they can be drawn together into five loose groupings. These loose groupings formed the bases of the five analysis chapters and allow a more detailed redrawing of the four-step model shown in Figure 8.1.

All the relevant evidence generated during my research supports the supposition that developing national strategy is becoming ever more challenging. The changes to the roles of Defence during the Early Expeditionary period meant that strategic decision making became subject to external factors that had only previously impacted on ways and means. This unfixing of the UK's strategic ends introduced variables to the left-hand side of the 'ends equals ways plus means' equation, which has made formulating strategy considerably more complex. This situation still exists today, and the considered opinion of many senior officials aligns with both the government's view (see HM Government, 2021b, pp 24–32) and academia (see Black, 2019, p 37); complexity will endure for the foreseeable future.

How the government develops its national strategy clearly impacts the way it provides strategic direction to defence decision makers. For example, a risk management methodology is a perfectly acceptable way to develop national strategy; however, it is a reactionary posture, which is why it draws criticism that, when used, politicians become too focused on attending to events. Oliver Letwin's confirmation to the JCNSS (2012b, p 15) that the coalition government's default between 2010 and 2015 would be to 'do what we can that looks sensible at the time' reinforces this. A risk management approach to national strategy facilitates most politicians' preference for adaptability and flexibility in their decision making. That said, the authors of the 2021 IR appear to have rejected any notion of an underpinning methodology, making it difficult to align ways and means to the government's strategic aims, and impossible to identify its priorities. Defence decision makers may come to rue this lack of strategic direction as they grapple with some of the trickier capability choices needed to deliver the IF30.

The clear conclusion from my research is that military capability can never be fully aligned with strategic direction. The inability of current defence acquisition procedures to keep pace with the changing nature of potential threats was the most regularly cited reason for the enduring nature of the misalignment, although the acceptance at the political level of capability gaps and unrealistic ambition were also offered as excuses. Defence continues to pursue transformation activity to improve the agility of its procurement

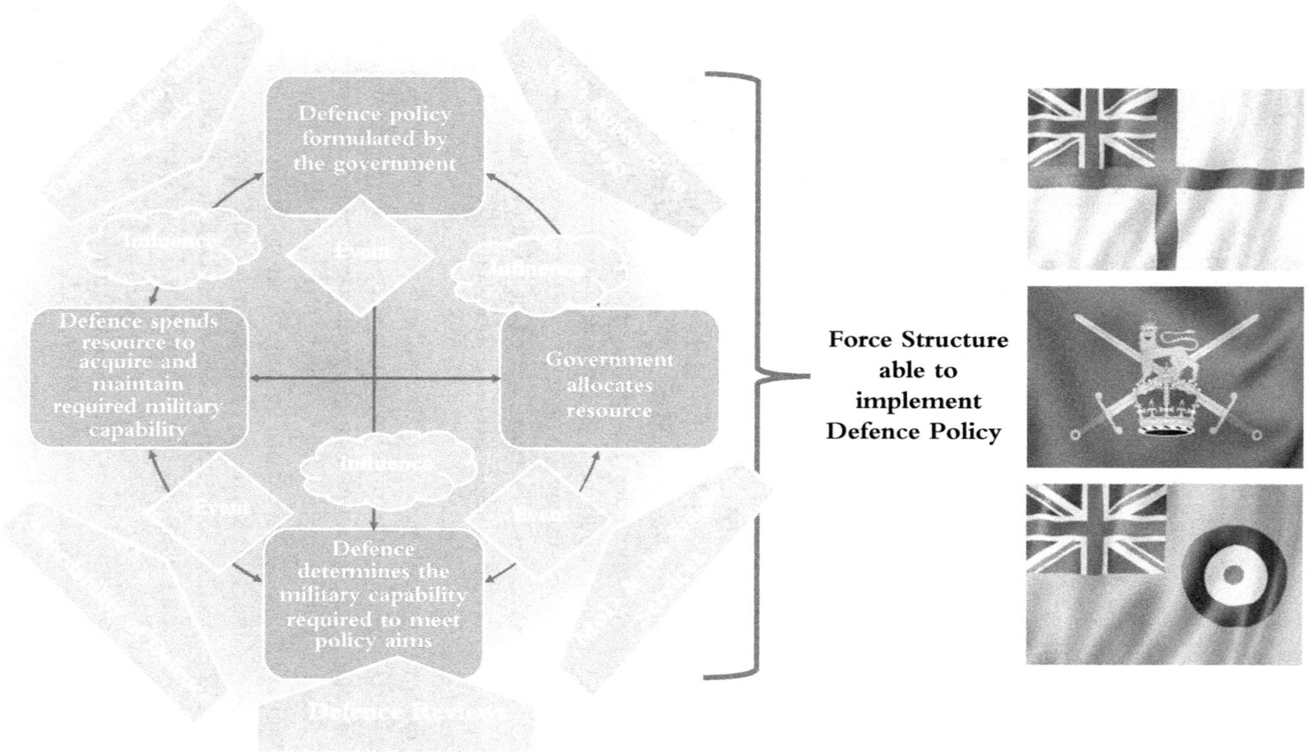

Figure 8.1: Translation of strategic direction into military capability model with events and influences overlay

and support contracts; however, it must be recognized that, for some of its highest-profile capabilities,[1] it is a junior partner in a collaborative programme and its ability to affect acquisition decisions and timelines is limited. There is certainly evidence to suggest that defence decision makers understand the imperative behind improving procurement processes, and either have, or are prepared to pay for, the knowledge and experience to identify the changes necessary to achieve the required effect. That said, even with the right answers, changing the course of the defence acquisition super tanker, and taking the defence industrial sector with it, will not be easy.

Finally, the impact of contemporaneous events on capability choices should not be overlooked. Analysis of both primary and secondary literature supports the conclusion that strategic shocks have had an impact on previous defence reviews and will do so again. The Suez Crisis and the end of the Cold War are both examples that were raised frequently during my research. In addition, the UK's exit from the EU may continue to have an effect on defence decision making, even though Michael Clarke and Helen Ramscar (2019, p 62) suggested that 'security, defence and foreign policy should be the least challenged areas of British policy as a result of the Brexit controversies'. As well as the obvious effects of a strategic shock, the relevance of lower-level events should not be ignored. The media storm around the lamentable state of military housing in the early 1990s, which influenced the Options for Change command paper, proves that an ostensibly tactical narrative can have a strategic effect. Moreover, as David Patrikarakos (2017, pp 255–67) argues, the impact of social media on military activity is continuing to increase. To that end, the seemingly most minor contemporaneous event could become a major influencing factor of a defence review in the future.

While not necessarily recognized as such, output targets have been included in all defence reviews over the last 75 years and are a key part of the government's strategic direction to defence decision makers. As the MoD has embraced more modern business practices, these output targets have become more sophisticated and, from the end of the Early Expeditionary period onwards, were also supported by a suite of defence planning assumptions. These assumptions provided additional direction on readiness; the notice period within which units must be available to deploy for a given operation; endurance, the likely duration of an operation; concurrency, the consideration of the number of operations, of a given scale of effort and duration, that the armed forces should be able to conduct at any time; and recuperation, the time needed after an operation to rehabilitate units, so they were capable of being deployed again.

The most comprehensive set of output targets were generated as part of the 1998 SDR. The review confirmed eight military missions, supported by 28 military tasks. This level of detail provided clear direction to defence decision makers as they oversaw the armed forces' pivot towards expeditionary operations. An entire supporting essay was given over to future military capabilities, which included a scale of effort framework for the UK's contribution to expeditionary operations (MoD, 1998b). This was the level of forces over and above those required for day-to-day tasks, and facilitated the detailed planning necessary to create the force structure to be maintained as part of the new joint rapid reaction forces concept (HCDC, 1998b).

The 1998 SDR was undoubtedly the high watermark for the articulation of defence output targets. Since then, the level of detail available in the public domain had reduced considerably, and, by the time the 2021 IR was published, was barely a trickle. Indeed, apart from identifying five extremely high-level defence tasks, the DCP did not include any detail on what the IF30 will be expected, or resourced, to do. Of course, this information does exist, almost certainly within the latest edition of the MoD's internal and classified document, *Defence Strategic Direction*. Therefore, from the perspective of defence decision makers, the lack of detail in the public domain is probably immaterial. Nevertheless, generic details of the size and type of operations, frequency, concurrency and recuperation give defence analysts a framework against which to assess the development and suitability of the armed forces. This is especially relevant as Defence transitions to a new, integrated force, when significant quantities of sunset capabilities will be withdrawn, and sunrise capabilities introduced. As I argued in a 2021 essay for a King's College London study into the 2021 IR, without these guidelines in the public domain it is impossible to tell what the government expects to get for the money it is committing to the defence budget or, more importantly, whether more is being demanded of the armed forces then they are funded to do.

Overall, the clear articulation of defence roles, missions and tasks are a positive addition to the government's strategic direction to defence decision makers. Not only do they provide a high-level aiming point to assist capability choices, but they also give detail on what should not be planned for or resourced. Of course, no defence decision maker should ever be naïve enough to think the armed forces will never be engaged on operations beyond the scope of their mandated roles; nevertheless, some direction is always better than none. This is especially relevant in the UK's current strategic environment, where the discourse on national priorities is all but non-existent.

A defence review should be an examination, by the UK government, of its defence and security commitments and associated resources to ascertain whether they are still appropriate and, if necessary, initiate corrective action. Before 2010, defence reviews occurred when the government decided that its policy required either some revision, which could not be undertaken through the statement on the defence estimates process, or its policy needed to be changed. In reality, this usually meant immediately after a general election. The introduction of the quinquennial review cycle was supposed to bring some structure to the process and do away with Paul Cornish's and Andrew Dorman's four-phase, policy development process. The ability to plan and prepare for the 2015 SDSR in advance was certainly seen by senior officials as a positive. Nevertheless, the decision in 2019 by Boris Johnson to undertake an expanded, integrated review has potentially undermined the whole quinquennial review process. At the time of writing, it is far from clear whether there will be another review in 2025 and, if so, what form it will take. Given the short-term focus of politicians today, it is unlikely the subject has even been discussed at Cabinet level or by the NSC. This situation simply reinforces the view that defence reviews are owned by politicians and primarily undertaken to meet a political agenda. Unfortunately, too few senior officials within the MoD seem to appreciate this, which has caused significant friction in the build up to, and during, recent reviews.

In the view of defence decision makers, the default political approach to defence reviews is not collegiate, and the MoD's internal practices have developed accordingly. Evidence of this is the admission that a key consideration in its pre-planning for the 2015 SDSR was how to prepare arguments to counter an unfavourable budget allocation. That said, the misalignment of the military and politicians is also a contributing factor and, with the politicians' viewpoint always likely to prevail, defence decision makers will understandably adopt a more cautious approach to a review until the political direction of travel has been revealed. Reviews will always be about what the government seeks, which will always be politically motivated, but may not always satisfy the strategic direction expectations of defence decision makers. Nevertheless, prior to any review, Defence will be obliged to invest time and effort in considering the future operating environment, threats and risks, and strategic trends. It must always be prepared fully to contribute to a review, even if its analysis does not survive contact with the reality of the government's decision making.

Regardless of how much of a united front is presented during a review, behind the scenes it is a bruising and often unpleasant business. At the intra-department level, the MoD is battling for the largest possible share of a finite financial allocation. Below this, the single services are fighting what they see as a zero-sum game to safeguard their existing and aspirational capability programmes. In these contests, there are always winners and losers, even though the winners seldom achieve all they are striving for. Ultimately, whether it is a defence, a strategic defence and security, or an integrated review, the outcome really matters. It is the most significant strategic direction that defence decision makers will receive. It sets the direction of travel for Defence for the next five years, maybe more. An unfavourable review can be extremely debilitating for a particular service or the MoD as a whole. Recovery is a long-term operation that all defence decision makers have experienced; furthermore, it is often achieved only through a series of unpalatable capability cuts. Given this, the service chiefs' allegiance to their respective service above their commitment to Defence as a whole may be understandable. So too, perhaps, is their near absolute focus on resources and outputs.

The affordability of defence has been a dominant theme since Duncan Sandys' review in 1957. Indeed, the central tenet of most academic analysis on post-Second World War UK defence policy is that economic constraints on defence expenditure have been the most significant reason for the armed forces' ever-shrinking force structure. Ultimately, the size of the nation's defence budget is a matter of political judgement; moreover, given the general acceptance that providing security for the nation and its citizens is the government's most important responsibility, it is a matter of prime ministerial judgement. The more security-minded commentator might argue that prime ministers have traditionally played fast and loose with the defence budget. More recently, however, it could be suggested that the tide has turned. Even though austerity remained to the fore in 2015, David Cameron insisted on meeting NATO's 2 per cent of GDP target, which resulted in a real-term increase in defence spending. Five years later, Boris Johnson's multi-billion-pound, four-year cash increase also prioritized Defence at a time when government spending was facing considerable pressure because of the COVID-19 pandemic. Nevertheless, the default feeling among defence decision makers remains that governments do not, in general, adequately resource the military capability necessary to achieve their own strategic direction.

In January 2021, the NAO (2021, p 4) reported that the defence equipment plan for 2020–30 had a funding shortfall of £8.3 billion in its first five years. It was the fourth year in a row the MoD's plans had been found to be unaffordable. The NAO (2021, p 12) also concluded that the MoD's ambition far exceeded available resources, and blamed its short-term approach to financial management for increasing cost pressures and restricting the development of military capabilities. Worryingly, of the 32 senior officials interviewed during my research, only one expressed concern about Defence's financial regulatory construct. More worryingly, the disquiet was expressed by the interviewee with the least experience of working in the public sector. He was aghast at the lack of accountability within the MoD, as well as the lack of clarity of the numbers used to build detailed financial plans. Furthermore, he struggled to comprehend, as well as work with, certain processes exclusive to the department, for example constructing ten-year budget forecasts that contained mandated cash reductions – or wedges – with no idea how to realize them.

When influencing factors such as the Greenwoodery funding gap and hard-to-reach efficiency commitments are considered, it is clear the long-term affordability of defence remains a challenge. Despite a concerted effort by recent secretaries of state, most notably Philip Hammond (GOV. UK, 2012), to balance the defence budget, financial pressure on capability programmes remains ever-present. The MoD's inability to deliver on its heroically assumed efficiency targets certainly has not helped. Moreover, the current rule allowing the reinvestment of efficiencies, introduced at the 2015 SDSR, has proved a double-edged sword. In the rush to introduce more capability enhancements, the temptation for the single services to over-estimate upcoming efficiencies has made it all too easy to re-excavate the black hole in Defence's finances. This problem is regularly highlighted by the NAO (see NAO, 2018a, p 7; and NAO, 2018b, p 8). Notwithstanding this, the common view among the senior officials that I interviewed is that Defence's ongoing affordability problems are firmly of a political making. As they see it, defence decision makers are strictly in the space of managing an inadequate allocation of resource, in order to deliver the force structure required to underwrite the global ambitions of the government. Ultimately, it matters not who is responsible. Defence must find a sustainable, long-term balance between its available budget and the cost of its equipment programme. Until it does, most, if not all, of its future capability choices will eventually be compromised.

In his address to the 2021 Strategic Command conference, General Patrick Sanders suggested that Defence was still 'largely and recognisably a tri-service organisation' and that 'coordination across the services is still more of an afterthought than a reflex' (GOV.UK, 2021c). This situation was perpetuated by the Levene reforms and clearly affects the way military capability choices are made today. The single services can, and regularly do, put their own environmental agendas ahead of the wider needs of a future, integrated force structure. Looking back on his time as defence secretary, Denis Healey (1989, p 263) wrote: 'I sometimes felt that I had learnt nothing about politics until I met the Chiefs of Staff. Each felt his prime duty was to protect the interests and traditions of his service.' While the authority of the service chiefs has clearly lessened since the high point of the early 1950s, in the current era of the delegated model, Healey's observation seems ever more apposite.

Even though several senior officials claimed that single service advocacy was no longer a concern, and all significant capability choices were now holistic, finding supporting evidence has not been easy. Path dependency remains an issue, and there are many reasons why the RN, British Army and RAF remain predominantly focused on ships, tanks and fast jets. Aligning responsibility, accountability and authority for capability management is a good business model for Defence. However, because of the self-serving nature of its existing stovepipe organizations, much stronger checks and balances are needed to ensure the wider capability needs of the IF30 are realized. The only way for the major components of Defence to become more collegiate, altruistic and integrated is a root and branch reform of the MoD's ways of working. Until that happens, those with the responsibility, accountability and authority are likely to keep on making capability choices that are not always for the good of Defence.

Final thoughts

The interacting activities that translate strategic direction into military capability will always be disrupted by events and influences. Some of these disruptions will be minor and easily accommodated, others will necessitate substantial change to defence policy or force structure. It is impossible to state definitively which event or influence will have the most significant effect on capability choices; however, the following example underlines just how impactful a single factor can be.

On 16 October 1964, the day the Labour Party won the general election, China detonated its first nuclear device. Before the election, Labour shadow ministers had favoured opting out of the nuclear deterrence altogether; however, at a crucial early policy meeting at Chequers only a month after the event, the Labour Cabinet agreed to maintain the UK's nuclear deterrent status quo. Both Malcolm Chalmers (1985, p 79) and William Jackson (1990, p 96) linked the event to the decision. Since then, the nation has always maintained an independent nuclear deterrent, through the V-force until 1969 and thereafter through the continuous at sea deterrent (CASD), provided by the Polaris submarine force until 1994 and Trident to the present day. Identifying the effect that being a nuclear power has had on the UK's relationship with the US, its NATO partners and the rest of the world is a thesis in itself; however, the effect on the defence budget is easier to quantify. The total acquisition expenditure on the Trident programme was £12.5 billion[2] with estimated annual in-service costs of £2.2 billion, or 6 per cent of the defence budget. Moreover, the estimated cost of the design and manufacture of four replacement Dreadnought boats is £31 billion and the government has also set aside an additional £10 billion contingency reserve for the programme (Mills and Dempsey, 2019, p 9). Had the Labour government cancelled the Polaris programme in 1964, it is doubtful that subsequent governments would have had the financial freedom or the political appetite to reinvest in an independent nuclear deterrent. To that end, it could be argued that this one event in 1964 has had a profound effect on the UK armed forces, both in its obligation to maintain CASD and the reduced level of conventional military capability it has been able to field as a result.

Over the last 75 years, the armed forces have struggled to maintain a force structure capable of doing all that is asked of it. This is because consistently making good military capability choices is tough. Simply translating strategic direction from the government of the day is difficult enough. Weathering the storms created by external events, as well as recognizing and accommodating the myriad influences, both blatant and surreptitious, is even tougher. It is hardly surprising, therefore, that defence decision makers do not always get it right.

Notes

Chapter 1

[1] It is arguable the three-star appointments within UK Strategic Command that also have a MoD head office direct responsibility as functional owners could also be included in this list. They are: Chief of Defence Intelligence; Chief of Defence Logistics and Support; and Director General Defence Medical Services.

[2] The TSR-2 was a tactical strike and reconnaissance aircraft developed for the RAF in the late 1950s and early 1960s by the British Aircraft Corporation. The project was cancelled by the government in 1965.

[3] Departmental Expenditure Limit is the budget that is allocated to and spent by government departments. A department's DEL is determined as part of the government's spending review.

[4] The acquisition (or CADMID) cycle exists to assist the reduction of risk during the concept and assessment stages of a project so that, when it is presented for approval, there is a high level of confidence that targets for time, whole-life cost, annual cost of ownership and performance will be achieved. It has six stages: concept, assessment, demonstration, manufacture, in-service and disposal.

[5] For example, the decision to procure two new aircraft carriers was announced in the 1998 SDR. The first of these – HMS Queen Elizabeth – was not commissioned until 2017.

[6] Defined as the capacity to act independently and to make free choices.

[7] Details of all defence reviews considered are included in Chapter 2.

[8] The quantitative bibliometric survey employed by Dorman and Uttley identified the total population of articles on British defence and security policy published in academic peer reviewed journals between 1950 and 2014. Their database relied on seven online data sources: Ebsco, Proquest, Military Policy Research, Taylor & Francis, SAGE Journals, Wiley Journals and Oxford Journals were used to identify articles published in English between 1950 and 2014. These databases were selected because they are interdisciplinary and cover all major publication types. The databases were searched for articles containing the key words 'UK, United Kingdom, Great Britain, defence, defence policy, security, national security, defence strategy, security strategy, Strategic Defence and Security Review, SDSR, defence management' in the title, abstract or full text. The selection of these key words followed the assumption that it 'essentially permitted authors to self-select their work for review' on the grounds that authors who would want their work to be considered part of the British defence and security policy literature would foreground at least one of these terms in their text.

Chapter 2

[1] Recognizing that contributions from this group are invariably first cleared by their political masters.

2   The harmonized set of DLODs is training, equipment, personnel, information, concepts and doctrine, organization, infrastructure and logistics (often referred to by the acronym TEPID OIL).

3   The latest version of the MoD's operating model – *How Defence Works Version* 6 – published in September 2020 did not include a definition of military capability.

4   At the time of writing, the most senior ex-military MP in parliament is Bob Stewart, who left the British Army as a colonel Late The Cheshire Regiment in 1996.

5   Lieutenant commander (RN), major (British Army), squadron leader (RAF).

6   Even though the definition of military capability is the combination of equipment, trained personnel and support that gives the armed forces the capacity to achieve the tasks they are given, all DLOD costs must be considered. Therefore, for example, elements of infrastructure, inventory and arm's length bodies are also included.

7   Recognizing that a significant element of capital expenditure and inventory costs are on equipment.

8   The acquisition (or CADMID) cycle also includes disposal stage; however, with a few notable exceptions (for example nuclear-powered submarines), most costs lie within procurement and support.

9   Generally known as *The Downey Report*.

10 Cost-plus contracts guaranteed payment of the industry's costs plus a (limited) profit.

11 Executive agencies were semi-autonomous organizations within the MoD with their own budget and an element of freedom to reform organizational structures and process. Agency personnel remained in the military or civil service and budgets were subject to the rules of public accountability.

12 An SRO is a recognized appointment across government. The Infrastructure and Projects Authority confirms that an SRO is accountable (defined as ultimately answerable for an activity or decision) for ensuring a programme or project meets its objectives, delivers the projected outcomes and realizes the required benefits.

13 A TLB is the highest level of budgetary control within the MoD. TLB holders have personally to answer for the performance of their organizations as defined by their command plan. The service chiefs and UKStratCom commander are all TLB holders.

14 The Enabling Acquisition Change report was also the conduit for the creation of the DE&S through the merger of the DLO and DPA in 2007.

15 Stage 1 – capability definition; stage 2 – capability goal setting; stage 3 – baseline review and audit; stage 4 – shortfall and opportunity analysis; stage 5 – capability investigation; stage 6 – endorse the capability management plan.

16 © Crown copyright 2011, re-useable under the terms of the Open Government Licence, Available from: https://www.nationalarchives.gov.uk/doc/open-government-licence/version/3/ [Accessed 11 March 2022].

Chapter 3

1   This document outlines the broad philosophy and principles underpinning how the armed forces are employed. It is the basis from which all other subordinate national doctrine is devised.

2   Michael Howards exact quote, taken from a 1974 *RUSI Journal* article titled 'Military Science in an Age of Peace' is: 'when everybody starts wrong, the advantage goes to the side which can most quickly adjust itself to the new and unfamiliar environment and learn from its mistakes.'

3   Which he defines as 'a specific danger which can be precisely identified and measured on the basis of the capabilities an enemy has to realise a hostile intent'.

4   Articulated as 'the objective'.

5   For example: 'Wherever possible, we will tackle security challenges early' and 'Overseas, we will favour a multilateral approach'.

6   Defence Equipment and Support (DE&S); Defence Digital (formally Information Systems and Services, or ISS); and the Submarine Delivery Agency (SDA).

Chapter 4

1   An enduring operation was defined as one that lasts for more than six months and normally required units to carry out a tour of duty and then be replaced by other similar units.

2   A non-enduring operation was defined as on that lasts less than six months, and typically required a force to be deployed and then withdrawn without replacement.

3   The term 'complex operation' was not defined in the 2010 SDSR nor the supporting factsheets; instead, it was included in the operational definitions section of the 2013 edition of Defence Strategic Direction, which is classified Confidential UK Eyes Only. The complete definition attracts this security classification as it includes deployment timelines, and therefore cannot be reproduced in full here. However, an in-part and unclassified definition refers to a joint operation that is undertaken across more than one environment and therefore requires a contribution by at least two, and invariably all components, that is, maritime, land, air, logistics and special forces.

4   The term 'simple operation' is also not defined. Again, an unclassified and in-part definition refers to an operation that is predominantly focused on a single environment and can generally be undertaken by a single component.

5   This figure is taken from my own personal records. I served as the chief of staff of the Joint Task Force Headquarters for the duration of Operation *Deference* – the non-combatant evacuation operation of entitled personnel from Libya in 2011.

6   'The National Security Strategy of the United Kingdom is to use all of our national capabilities to build Britain's prosperity, extend our nations influence in the world and strengthen our security'.

7   'Ensuring a secure and resilient UK'; and 'Shaping a stable world'.

8   The 2010 NSS tier one risks were: international terrorism affecting the UK and its interests; hostile attacks on UK cyber space; a major accident or natural hazard that requires a national response; and an international military crisis between states, drawing in the UK and its allies.

9   In the view of General Houghton, this was defined as the critical mass of the combined armed forces – the combination of all the armed forces of the country – in meeting what is expected of them in terms of military tasks.

10   Joint Concept Note 1/20 defines multi-domain integration as the posturing of military capabilities in concert with other instruments of national power, allies and partners; configured to sense, understand and orchestrate effects at the optimal tempo, across the operational domains and levels of warfare.

11   The five operational domains are maritime, land, air, space and cyberspace.

12   © Crown copyright 2010, re-useable under the terms of the Open Government Licence, Available from: https://www.nationalarchives.gov.uk/doc/open-government-licence/version/3/ [Accessed 11 March 2022].

13   © Crown copyright 2015, re-useable under the terms of the Open Government Licence, Available from: https://www.nationalarchives.gov.uk/doc/open-government-licence/version/3/ [Accessed 11 March 2022].

14 © Crown copyright 2021, re-useable under the terms of the Open Government Licence, Available from: https://www.nationalarchives.gov.uk/doc/open-government-licence/version/3/ [Accessed 11 March 2022].

Chapter 5

1 For example: Healey's reviews from 1966 to 1968; the 1975 Mason review; and the 1998 SDR.

2 The NSCR work strands were national security doctrine; defence; counterterrorism; cyber; serious, organized, and economic crime; ports and borders; national resilience; global Britain; national security strategic communications; economic security, prosperity and trade; development; and cross-government funds.

3 De Gaulle had vetoed Harold Macmillan's first application in 1963.

4 In NATO, and UK operational-level planning doctrine, the concept of 'main effort' provides a focus for the activity that the Joint Force Commander considers crucial to success (MoD, 2013b).

5 The DSG supported the secretary of state, permanent secretary and CDS in formulating advice on defence strategy. Its members included VCDS, the deputy chief of the defence staff for military capability, and the directors general for strategy and International, and finance.

6 Under a supported/supporting relationship in the execution of military operations, one organization will aid, protect, complement, or sustain another force.

Chapter 6

1 For example, *The Long Retreat*; *The Long Recessional*; and *The Collapse of British Power*.

2 For example, *Defence in Transition: Options for Change*; *Soldiers of Fortune: Britain's new Military Role*; *British Defence Planning in a Changing World*; and *British Defence Choices beyond 'Options for Change'*.

3 The 1957 defence review only included figures for one FY – 1957–58. It forecast a saving of about £280 million, or 16.5 per cent, against a £1.7 billion defence estimate made in the previous year.

4 The 1966 defence review included a financial target of £2 billion, at 1964 prices, to be reached in FY 1969–70.

5 The average change in pay and prices of goods and services making up the defence budget with quality and quantity held constant.

6 The rising real unit costs between successive generations of new equipment.

7 The creation of a Joint Security Fund was a new fund announced in the 2015 SDSR for the armed forces and the security and intelligence agencies, which was set to grow to £1.5 billion by FY 2019–20.

8 Brigaded under acquisition, information, people, and support.

Chapter 7

1 Where a capability is employed in more than one environment and/or by more than one single service, it is assigned a 'lead command', by MoD head office that is responsible for all acquisition of that capability. The lead command should consider the requirements and aspirations of the other users during capability planning.

2 A widespread nickname for the RN used by all ranks.

3 The successor to the Trident class of submarines on which the continuous at sea deterrent is deployed.

4   The seed corn initiative was a series of targeted measures taken to ensure that the MoD could regenerate a military capability that it had disinvested in if necessary. An example was embedding RAF airmen in maritime patrol crews of friendly nations following the decision at the 2010 SDSR to cancel the Nimrod MRA4 programme.

5   The finance and capability management staff occupy the third floor of MoD Main Building in Whitehall, the military strategic operations staff work on the fourth floor, and ministers, CDS, the permanent secretary and second permanent secretary, and the single service chiefs are located on the fifth floor.

6   During the HCDC's inquiry into decision making in defence policy, former CDS Lord Richards pointed out that even the prime minister did not understand that the CDS did not command the service chiefs.

7   One each for the RN, the British Army, and the RAF.

8   Powerful and influential members of the organization operating in the background or behind the scenes.

9   For example, Warrior infantry fighting vehicles; Type 23 frigates, mine counter-measure vessels; tranche 1 Typhoon combat aircraft, E-3D Sentry airborne early warning and control aircraft; and Puma helicopters.

Chapter 8

1   For example, F-35B Lightning II, RC-135W Rivet Joint, P-8A Poseidon.

2   This equates to approximately £18 billion at 2017 prices.

Bibliography

Aberbach, J. D. and Rockman, B. A. (2002) 'Conducting and coding elite interviews', *Political Science & Politics*, 35(4): 673–6.

Allen, M. (2020) 'Prospects for an ethical foundation for a foreign policy in the context of democratic regression and authoritarian resurgence', in A. Hug (ed) *Finding Britain's Role in a Changing World: The Principles for Global Britain,* London: The Foreign Policy Centre.

Anelay, J. (2021) 'The UK's Integrated Review overpromises and under-delivers', Chatham House, [online] 2 April, Available from: https://www.chathamhouse.org/2021/04/uks-integrated-review-overpromises-and-under-delivers [Accessed 30 April 2021].

Anton, S. (2013) 'Conceptual insights of strategic shock and strategic surprise', *Strategic Impact*, 1: 58–67.

Ashcroft, M. A. and Oakshott, I. (2018) *White Flag? An Examination of the UK's Defence Capability,* London: Biteback Publishing.

Asteris, M. (1994) 'UK defence spending – trends and implications', *The RUSI Journal*, 139(5): 38–71.

Bangert, D., Davies, N. and Watson, R. (2017) 'Managing defence acquisition cost growth', *The RUSI Journal*, 162(1): 60–7.

Barnett, C. (1991) 'Total strategy and the collapse of british power', *The RUSI Journal*, 136(4): 1–6.

Barnett, C. (1993) 'Ten year rule to "Options for Change": the case for a return to strategy', *The RUSI Journal,* 138(4): 60–6.

Barno, D. W. and Bensahel, N. (2020) *Adaptation under Fire: How Militaries Change in Wartime,* New York, NY: Oxford University Press.

Barry, B., Childs, N. and Barrie, D. (2021) 'Can the UK deliver on its bold ambitions for a global military presence?', IISS, [online] 18 March, Available from: https://www.iiss.org/blogs/analysis/2021/03/uk-global-military-presence-integrated-review [Accessed 30 April 2021].

Bartlett, C. J. (1972) *The Long Retreat: A Short History of British Defence Policy, 1945–70,* London: Macmillan Press.

Baylis, J. (ed) (1977) *British Defence Policy in a Changing World*, London: Croom Helm.

Baylis, J. (ed) (1983) *Alternative Approaches to British Defence Policy*, London: Macmillan Press.

Baylis, J. (1986a) 'The evolution of british defence policy, 1945–86', in M. Edmonds (ed) *The Defence Equation: British Military Systems – Policy, Planning, and Performance,* London: Brassey's Defence Publishers.

Baylis, J. (1986b) 'Greenwoodery and british defence policy', *International Affairs*, 62(3): 443–57.

Baylis, J. (1989) *British Defence Policy: Striking the Right Balance*, New York, NY: St. Martin's Press.

Baylis, J. and Macmillan, A. (1993) 'The British Global Strategy Paper of 1952', *Journal of Strategic Studies*, 16(2): 200–26.

BBC (2015) 'UK defence spending "concerns" US Army chief Raymond Odierno', News, [online] 2 March, Available from: https://www.bbc.co.uk/news/uk-31688929 [Accessed 12 April 2021].

BBC (2016) 'EU referendum: David Cameron confirms UK vote date', News, [online] 20 February, Available from: https://www.bbc.co.uk/news/av/uk-politics-eu-referendum-35620941/eu-referendum-david-cameron-confirms-uk-vote-date [Accessed 1 November 2021].

BBC (2018) 'Marine cuts would "undermine UK security"', News, [online] 4 February, Available from: https://www.bbc.co.uk/news/uk-42933845 [Accessed 5 September 2019].

BBC (2021) 'Covid: pandemic "exposes" UK security planning gaps', News, [online] 1 December, Available from: https://www.bbc.com/news/uk-55358379 [Accessed 16 November 2021].

Beale, J. (2020) 'British Army could axe ageing tanks as part of modernisation plans', BBC News, [online] 25 August, Available from: https://www.bbc.co.uk/news/uk-53909087 [Accessed 12 April 2021].

Bell, M. (2000) 'Leaving Portsoken – defence procurement in the 1980s and 1990s', *The RUSI Journal*, 145(4): 30–6.

Bell, S. (2007) 'The UK's risk management approach to national security', *The RUSI Journal* 152(3): 18–22.

Bellamy, C. (1992) 'Soldiers of fortune: Britain's new military role', *International Affairs* 68(3): 443–56.

Bellany, I. (1994) *Reviewing Britain's Defence*, Aldeshot: Dartmouth Publishing Company.

Black, J. (2006) *The Dotted Red Line: Britain's Defence Policy in the Modern World,* London: The Social Affairs Unit.

Black, J. (2019) 'Rethinking strategy', *The RUSI Journal*, 164(3): 32–7.

Blackburn, G. (2015) 'UK defence policy 1957–2015: the illusion of choice', *Defence Studies*, 15(2): 85–104.

Blagden, D. (2009) 'Strategic thinking for the age of austerity', *The RUSI Journal*, 154(6): 60–6.

Blagden, D. (2015) 'Global multipolarity, European security and implications for UK grand strategy: back to the future, once again', *International Affairs*, 91(2): 333–50.

Blitz, R. and Lewis, L. (2016) 'Pound tumbles to 30-year low as Britain votes Brexit', *Financial Times*, [online] 24 June, Available from: https://www.ft.com/content/8d8a100e-38c2-11e6-a780-b48ed7b6126f [Accessed 1 November 2021].

Bloomberg (2019) 'GBPUSD: Cur X-Rate', [online]. 24 June, Available from: https://www.bloomberg.com/quote/GBPUSD:CUR [Accessed 24 June 2019].

Bolton, D. (1991) 'Defence in transition: options for change', *The RUSI Journal*, 136(3): 1–3.

Bond, D. (2017) 'Uncertain future of UK assault ships raises fears over naval capability', *Financial Times*, [online] 4 December, Available from: https://www.ft.com/content/1125f706-d4f9-11e7-8c9a-d9c0a5c8d5c9 [Accessed 1 November 2021].

Borger, J. (2016) 'What will Brexit do to Britain's place in the world', *The Guardian,* [online] 25 June, Available from: https://www.theguardian.com/politics/2016/jun/25/what-will-brexit-do-to-britain-place-in-the-world [Accessed 3 November 2021].

Boyce, M. (2002) 'UK strategic choices following the Strategic Defence Review & 11th September', *The RUSI Journal*, 147(1): 1–7.

Bradford, J. P. (2010) 'The aircraft carrier debate & Australia moving 500 miles westwards: plus-ca-change', Defence Industrial Base, [online]. 26 October, Available from: http://defenseindustrialbase.blogspot.com/2010/10/aircraft-carrier-debate-australia.html [Accessed 20 August 2019].

Brands, H. (2012) *The Promise and Pitfalls of Grand Strategy*, Carlisle, PA: Strategic Studies Institute, U.S. Army War College.

Braybrooke, D. and Lindblom, C. E. (1964) 'A strategy of decision; policy evaluation as a social process', *Political Science Quarterly*, 79(4): 584–8.

British Army (2016) *Army Operating Model, version 1.6*, Andover: Army HQ.

Broadbent, E. (1988) *The Military and Government: from Macmillan to Heseltine*, New York, NY: St. Martin's Press.

Brooke-Holland, L. (2017) *The Defence Capability Review: Equipment, House of Commons Library Briefing Paper Number 08112,* London: The Stationery Office.

Brooke-Holland, L. (2018) *The Modernising Defence Programme, House of Commons Library Briefing Paper Number 08469,* London: The Stationery Office.

Brooke-Holland, L. (2020) *The Integrated Review: A Look Ahead to the Government's Review, House of Commons Library Briefing Paper Number 09052,* London: The Stationery Office.

Brooke-Holland, L. (2021) *Defence Command Paper 2021: Equipment Cuts, House of Commons Library Briefing Paper Number 9188*, London: The Stationery Office.

Brown, D. (2010) *The Development of British Defence Policy: Blair, Brown and Beyond*, Farnham: Ashgate.

Brown, G., Cameron, D. and Clegg, N. (2010) 'UK general election: defence perspectives', *The RUSI Journal*, 155(2): 6–12.

Bryman, A. (2012) *Social Research Methods*, Oxford: Oxford University Press.

Byrd, P. (ed) (1991) *British Defence Policy: Thatcher and Beyond*, Hemel Hempstead: Philip Allan.

Carter, N. (2013) 'The divisional level of command', *British Army Review*, 157: 7–16.

Carver, M. (1992) *Tightrope Walking: British Defence Policy since 1945*, London: Hutchinson.

Cary, M. and Foxley-Norris, C. (1976) 'Britain's armed forces after the defence cuts', *The RUSI Journal*, 121(1): 1–6.

Caudle, S. L. and De Spiegeleire, S. (2010) 'A new generation of national security strategies: early findings from the Netherlands and the United Kingdom', *Journal of Homeland Security and Emergency Management*, 7(1): 1–22.

Cavanagh, M. (2011) 'Missed opportunity: how failures of leadership derailed the SDSR', *The RUSI Journal*, 156(5): 6–13.

Chalmers, M. (1985) *Paying for Defence: Military Spending and British Decline*, London: Pluto Press.

Chalmers, M. (2010) *Unbalancing the Force? Prospects for UK Defence after the SDSR, RUSI Future Defence Review Working Paper No. 9,* London: RUSI.

Chalmers, M. (2011) 'Keeping our powder dry? UK defence policy beyond Afghanistan', *The RUSI Journal*, 156(1): 20–8.

Chalmers, M. (2014) *The Financial Context for the 2015 SDSR: The End of UK Exceptionalism? RUSI Briefing Paper.* London: RUSI.

Chalmers, M. (2015a) *A Force for Order: Strategic Underpinnings of the Next NSS and SDSR, RUSI Briefing Paper,* London: RUSI.

Chalmers, M. (2015b) *Mind the Gap: the MoD's Emerging Budgetary Challenge, RUSI Briefing Paper,* London: RUSI.

Chalmers, M. (2016a) 'The 2015 SDSR in context: from boom to bust – and back again?', *The RUSI Journal*, 161(1): 4–12.

Chalmers, M. (2016b) *Spending Matters: Defence and Security Budgets after the 2015 Spending Review, RUSI Briefing Paper,* London: RUSI.

Chalmers, M. (2016c) *Would a New SDSR Be Needed after a Brexit Vote? RUSI Briefing Paper,* London: RUSI.

Chalmers, M. (2018) *Decision Time – The National Security Capability Review 2017–2018 and Defence, RUSI Whitehall Report 1-18,* London: Royal United Services Institute.

Chalmers, M. (2021) *A New Direction for the Ministry of Defence's Budget? Implications of the November Spending Review, RUSI Policy Brief,* London: RUSI.

Chalmers, M. and Jessett, W. (2020) *Defence and the Integrated Review: A Testing Time, RUSI Whitehall Report 2-20,* London: RUSI.

Channel 4 (2010) 'Accepting war in Afghanistan is critial', News, [online] 3 February, Available from: http://www.channel4.com/news/articles/uk/aposaccepting%2Bwar%2Bin%2Bafghanistan%2Bis%2Bcriticalapos/3524 657.html [Accessed 9 February 2018].

Chapman, B. (2016) 'Geopolitics of the 2015 British Defense White Paper and its historical predecessors', *Geopolitics, History, and International Relations,* 8(2): 42–63.

Charmaz, K. (2014) *Constructing Grounded Theory,* London: Sage Publications.

Chichester, M. and Wilkinson, J. (1982) *The Uncertain Ally: British Defence Policy, 1960–1990,* Aldershot: Gower.

Chiefs of Staff (1950) *Defence Policy and Global Strategy, CAB 131/9,* London: Ministry of Defence.

Chiefs of Staff (1952) *Defence Policy and Global Strategy, CAB 131/12,* London: Ministry of Defence.

Chilcot, J., Freedman, L., Lyne, R. and Prashar, U. (2016) *The Report of the Iraq Inquiry – Executive Summary, HC 264,* London: The Stationery Office.

Chin, W. (2013) *Britain and the War on Terror: Policy, Strategy and Operations,* Farnham: Ashgate.

Chuter, A. (2018) 'Britain eyes a more lethal force in newly revealed defense modernisation review', *Defense News,* [online] 18 December, Available from: https://www.defensenews.com/global/europe/2018/12/18/brit ain-eyes-a-more-lethal-force-in-newly-revealed-defense-modernization-review/ [Accessed 3 November 2021].

Chuter, A. (2020a) 'UK defense plans could take major hit from coronavirus fallout', *Defense News,* [online] 23 April, Available from: https://www.defe nsenews.com/global/europe/2020/04/23/uk-defense-plans-could-take-major-hit-from-coronavirus-fallout/ [Accessed 12 April 2021].

Chuter, A. (2020b) 'UK hits pause in defense review due to coronavirus', *Defence News,* [online] 15 April, Available from: https://www.defensen ews.com/global/europe/2020/04/15/uk-hits-pause-on-defense-review-due-to-coronavirus/ [Accessed 30 April 2021].

Chuter, A. (2021) 'Shaken and stirred: British Army's Ajax troubles cast a long shadow', *Defense News,* [online] 3 November, Available from: https://www.defensenews.com/digital-show-dailies/feindef/2021/11/03/shaken-and-stirred-british-armys-ajax-troubles-cast-a-long-shadow/ [Accessed 30 November 2021].

Clarke, M. (2007) 'Strategy and fortune: British security policy in transition', *The RUSI Journal,* 152(5): 6–12.

Clarke, M. (2008) 'The overdue defence review: old questions, new answers', *The RUSI Journal*, 153(6): 4–10.

Clarke, M. (2010) 'Preliminary RUSI Briefing: The National Security Strategy 2010', RUSI, [online] 18 October, Available from: https://rusi.org/commentary/preliminary-rusi-briefing-national-security-strategy-2010 [Accessed 3 November 2021].

Clarke, M. and Ramscar, H. (2019) *Tipping Point: Britain, Brexit and Security in the 2020s*, London: I. B. Tauris.

Clarke, M. and Sabin, P. A. G. (eds) (1993) *British Defence Choices for the Twenty-First Century*, London: Brassey's.

Codner, M. (1998) 'The Strategic Defence Review: how much? how far? how joint is enough? *The RUSI Journal*, 143(4): 5–10.

Codner, M. and Clarke, M. (2011) *A Question of Security: The British Defence Review in an Age of Austerity*, London: I. B. Tauris.

Coker, C. (1986) *A Nation in Retreat? Britain's Defence Commitment*, London: Brassey's.

Coker, C. (1992) 'Britain's defence options', *The World Today*, 48(4): 72–5.

Coker, C. (1993) 'Options for change: an academic critique', in RUSI (ed) *Brassey's Defence Yearbook 1993*, London: Brassey's.

The Conservative and Unionist Party (2010a) *Invitation to Join the Government of Britain: The Conservative Manifesto 2010,* London: The Conservative and Unionist Party.

The Conservative and Unionist Party (2010b) *A Resilient Nation – National Security – The Conservative Approach,* London: The Conservative and Unionist Party.

The Conservative and Unionist Party (2019) *Get Brexit Done – Unleash Britain's Potential – The Conservative and Unionist Party Manifesto 2019,* London: The Conservative and Unionist Party.

Cornish, P. (2010) *Strategy in Austerity: The Security and Defence of the United Kingdom*, London: Chatham House.

Cornish, P. (2018) 'The National Security Capabilities Review and the lure of the 'strategic holiday', Research Gate, [online] 1 February, Available from: https://www.researchgate.net/publication/323167769_The_National_Security_Capabilities_Review_and_the_Lure_of_the_'Strategic_Holiday [Accessed 2 March 2022].

Cornish, P. (2021) *Incoherent, Under Strength, Over Stretched: The UK National Strategy and Defence Review 2021*, London: City Forum.

Cornish, P. and Dorman, A. M. (2009a) 'Blair's wars and Brown's budgets: from Strategic Defence Review to strategic decay in less than a decade', *International Affairs*, 85(2): 247–61.

Cornish, P. and Dorman, A. M. (2009b) 'National defence in the age of austerity', *International Affairs*, 85(4): 733–53.

Cornish, P. and Dorman, A. M. (2010) 'Breaking the mould: the United Kingdom Strategic Defence Review 2010', *International Affairs*, 86(2): 395–410.

Cornish, P. and Dorman, A. M. (2011) 'Dr Fox and the philosopher's stone: the alchemy of national defence in the age of austerity', *International Affairs*, 87(2): 335–53.

Cornish, P. and Dorman, A. M. (2012) 'Smart muddling through: rethinking UK national strategy beyond Afghanistan', *International Affairs*, 88(2): 213–22.

Cornish, P. and Dorman, A. M. (2013) 'Fifty shades of purple? A risk-sharing approach to the 2015 Strategic Defence and Security Review', *International Affairs*, 89(5): 1183–202.

Cornish, P. and Dorman, A. M. (2015) 'Complex security and strategic latency: the UK Strategic Defence and Security Review 2015', *International Affairs*, 91(2): 351–70.

Croft, S., Dorman, A. M., Rees, W. and Uttley, M. (2001) *Britain and Defence 1945–2000: A Policy Re-evaluation,* Harlow: Pearson Education Limited.

Crum-Ewing, H. (1998) 'After the UK Strategic Defence Review: the need for an ongoing reasoned critique of positions, policies and operations', *Defence & Security Analysis*, 14(3): 323–34.

Dannatt, R. (2016) *Boots on the Ground: Britain and Her Army since 1945,* London: Profile Books.

Darby, P. (1973) *British Defence Policy East of Suez, 1947–1968,* London: Oxford University Press.

De Waal, J. (2014) 'Is the UK's expeditionary posture both necessary and sustainable?', *The RUSI Journal*, 159(6): 20–6.

De Waal, J. (2015) 'This SDSR hides problems for the future', Chatham House, [online] 2 December, Available from: https://www.chathamho use.org/expert/comment/sdsr-hides-problems-future [Accessed 3 November 2021].

Deloitte LLP (2017) *Transform Support, Deliver Capability – The Defence Support Network Report,* London: MoD, Deloitte LLP.

Dempsey, N. (2021) *UK Defence Personnel Statistics, House of Commons Library Briefing Paper Number 7930,* London: The Stationery Office.

Devanny, J. and Gearson, J. (eds) (2021a) *The Integrated Review in Context: A Strategy Fit for the 2020s?* London: King's College London.

Devanny, J. and Gearson, J. (eds) (2021b) *The Integrated Review in Context: Defence and Security in Focus,* London: King's College London.

Devanny, J. and Harris, J. (2014) *The National Security Council: National Security at the Centre of Government,* London: Institute for Government and King's College London.

Dillon, G. M. (1977) 'Recurring dilemmas and decision-making for defence', in J. Baylis (ed) *British Defence Policy in a Changing World,* London: Croom Helm.

Dillon, G. M. (ed) (1988) *Defence Policy Making: A Comparative Analysis*, Leicester: Leicester University Press.

Dixon, N. F. (1976) *On the Psychology of Military Incompetence*, London: Pimlico.

Dockrill, M. (1989) *British Defence since 1945*, Oxford: Blackwell.

Dodd, T. (1993) *Defence Reviews: Past, Present? and Future? House of Commons Research Paper 93/91,* London: The Stationery Office.

Dodd, T. (1994) *Frontline First: The Defence Costs Study, House of Commons Research Paper 94/101,* London: The Stationery Office.

Dodd, T. (1997) *The Strategic Defence Review, House of Commons Research Paper 97/106,* London: The Stationery Office.

Dorman, A. M. (2001a) 'Crises and reviews in British defence policy', in S. Croft et al (eds) *Britain and Defence 1945–2000: A Policy Re-evaluation*, Harlow: Pearson Education Limited.

Dorman, A. M. (2001b) 'John Nott and the Royal Navy: the 1981 Defence Review revisited', *Contemporary British History*, 15(2): 98–120.

Dorman, A. M. (2001c) 'Reconciling Britain to Europe in the next millennium: the evolution of british defense policy in the post-Cold War era', *Defense Analysis*, 17(2): 187–202.

Dorman, A. M. (2001d) Viewpoint – the Nott Review: dispelling the myths?', *Defence Studies*, 1(3): 113–21.

Dorman, A. M. (2002) *Defence under Thatcher*, Basingstoke: Palgrave.

Dorman, A. M. (2009) *Blair's Successful War: British Military Intervention in Sierra Leone*, Farnham: Ashgate.

Dorman, A. M. (2010) 'Providing for defence in an age of austerity: future war, defence cuts and the 2010 SDSR', *The Political Quarterly*, 81(3): 376–84.

Dorman, A. M. (2011) 'Making 2+2=5: the 2010 Strategic Defence and Security Review', *Defense & Security Analysis,* 27(1): 77–87.

Dorman, A. M., Smith, M. L. R. and Uttley, M. (2002) *The Changing Face of Military Power: Joint Warfare in the Expeditionary Era*, Basingstoke: Palgrave.

Dorman, A. M. and Uttley, M. (2015) 'International affairs and the British defence and security policy debate: the bibliometric context', *International Affairs*, Virtual Issue.

Dorman, A. M., Uttley, M. and Wilkinson, B. (2016) The curious incident of Mr Cameron and the United Kingdom defence budget: a new legacy?', *The Political Quarterly*, 87(1): 46–53.

Dover, R. and Phythian, M. (2011) 'Lost over Libya: the 2010 Strategic Defence and Security Review – an obituary', *Defence Studies*, 11(3): 420–44.

Dowdy, J. (2003) *Streamlining End to End Air and Land Logistics*, London: McKinsey & Company.

Downer, A. (2021) 'The Integrated Review as strategy', in J. Devanny and J. Gearson (eds) *The Integrated Review in Context: A Strategy Fit for the 2020s?* London: King's College London.

Downs, A. (1966) *Bureaucratic Structure and Decisionmaking*, Santa Monica, CA: Rand Corporation.

Dunbabin, J. (1975) 'British rearmament in the 1930s: a chronology and review', *The Historical Journal*, 18(3): 587–609.

Dunn, D. H. (1992) 'UK defence planning and the new parliament', *The RUSI Journal*, 137(3): 57–60.

Dunn, M., Eggington, B., Pye, N., Taylor, T. and Watters, B. (2011) 'From defence reform to defence transformation', *The RUSI Journal*, 156(5): 14–19.

Edmonds, M. (1986) *The Defence Equation: British Military Systems – Policy, Planning, and Performance*, London: Brassey's.

Edmunds, T. (2010) 'The defence dilemma in Britain', *International Affairs*, 86(2): 377–94.

Edmunds, T. (2014) Complexity, strategy and the national interest', *International Affairs*, 90(3): 525–39.

Edmunds, T. and Forster, A. (2007) *Out of Step: The Case for Change in the British Armed Forces*, London: Demos.

The Electoral Commission (2019) 'Results and turnout at the EU referendum', electoralcommission.org.uk., [online] 25 September, Available from: https://www.electoralcommission.org.uk/who-we-are-and-what-we-do/elections-and-referendums/past-elections-and-refe rendums/eu-referendum/results-and-turnout-eu-referendum [Accessed 1 November 2021].

Elliott, C. L. (2015) *High Command: British Military Leadership in the Iraq and Afghanistan Wars*, London: Hurst.

Ellis, A. (2020) 'Letter to the Chair of the Joint Committee on National Security Strategy and Chairs of the Defence, Foreign Affairs and International Development Committee', 8 July.

Encyclopedia Britannica (2019) 'Path dependence', [online] Available from: https://www.britannica.com/topic/path-dependence [Accessed 1 October 2019].

English Oxford Living Dictionaries (2018) 'Definition of Strategy in English', [online], Available from: https://en.oxforddictionaries.com/definition/ strategy [Accessed 12 January 2018].

Evans, A. (2014) 'Organizing for British national strategy', *International Affairs*, 90(3): 509–24.

Farmer, B. (2015) 'MoD "insults defence experts with sham 200 word consultation"', *The Telegraph*, 15 August.

Farmer, B. (2018) 'Royal Marine cuts "military illiterate" say MPs', *The Telegraph*, [online] 4 February, Available from: https://www.telegraph. co.uk/news/2018/02/04/royal-marines-cuts-militarily-illiterate-say-mps/ [Accessed 5 September 2019].

Fisher, L. (2020) 'Boris Johnson's foreign policy, defence and security review in turmoil, say insiders', *The Times*, 22 February.

Freedman, L. (1987) 'Why a military review is not a defeat', *The Independant*, 25 June.

Freedman, L. (1999) *The Politics of British Defence, 1979–98*, New York, NY: St. Martin's Press.

Freedman, L. (2013) *Strategy: A History*, Oxford: Oxford University Press.

Freier, N., Robert, H. and John, S. (2020) *Restore 'Shock' in Strategic Planning*, Carlisle, PA: Strategic Studies Institute, US Army War College.

Fry, R. (2014) 'Smart power and the strategic deficit', *The RUSI Journal*, 159(6): 28–32.

Garden, T. (1999) 'Last post for the chiefs?', *The RUSI Journal*, 144(1): 47–51.

Gaskarth, J. (2014) 'Strategizing Britain's role in the world', *International Affairs*, 90(3): 559–81.

Gaskarth, J. (2015) 'Strategy in a complex world', *The RUSI Journal*, 160(6): 4–11.

Gifkin, J., Ralph, J., Jarvis, S. (2018) 'Diplomats reveal concerns over UK's waning influence on UN Security Council', *The Conversation*, [online] 26 September, Available from: https://theconversation.com/diplomats-rev eal-concerns-over-uks-waning-influence-on-un-security-council-103043 [Accessed 3 November 2021].

Giles, C, and Fray, K. (2018) 'The UK economy since the Brexit vote – in 6 charts', *Financial Times*, [online] 11 October, Available from: https:// www.ft.com/content/cf51e840-7147-11e7-93ff-99f383b09ff9 [Accessed 1 November 2021].

Gladwell, M. (2007) *Blink: The Power of Thinking without Thinking*, London: Penguin Books.

Glaser, B. G. (1978) *Advances in the Methodology of Grounded Theory: Theoretical Sensitivity*, Mill Valley, CA: Sociology Press.

Glaser, B. G. (1992) *Basics of Grounded Theory Analysis: Emergence vs Forcing*, Mill Valley, CA: Sociology Press.

Glaser, B. G. and Strauss, A. L. (1967) *The Discovery of Grounded Theory: Strategies for Qualitative Research*, Chicago, IL: Aldine Publishing.

GOV.UK (2010a) 'Bernard Gray appointed Chief of Defence Materiel', MoD, [online] 16 December, Available from: https://www.GOV.UK/ government/news/bernard-gray-appointed-chief-of-defence-materiel [Accessed 6 April 2021].

GOV.UK. (2010b) 'The National Security Strategy – a strong Britain in an age of uncertainty', Cabinet Office, [online] 18 October, Available from: https://www.gov.uk/government/publications/the-national-security-strategy-a-strong-britain-in-an-age-of-uncertainty [Accessed 28 April 2021].

GOV.UK (2010c) 'Statement on Strategic Defence and Security Review', Prime Minister's Office, 10 Downing Street, [online] 19 October, Available from: https://www.gov.uk/government/speeches/statement-on-strategic-defence-and-security-review [Accessed 6 April 2021].

GOV.UK (2012) 'Defence Secretary balances MOD budget', MoD, [online] 14 May, Available from: https://www.gov.uk/government/news/defence-secretary-balances-mod-budget [Accessed 7 December 2021].

GOV.UK (2016) 'Secretary of State's speech to the RUSI Land Warfare Conference', MoD, [online] 29 June, Available from: https://www.gov.uk/government/speeches/secretary-of-states-speech-to-the-rusi-land-warfare-conference [Accessed 3 November 2021].

GOV.UK (2017a) 'Confidence and supply agreement between the Conservative and Unionist Party and the Democratic Unionist Party', Cabinet Office, [online] updated 23 January 2020, Available from: https://www.gov.uk/government/publications/conservative-and-dup-agreement-and-uk-government-financial-support-for-northern-ireland/agreement-between-the-conservative-and-unionist-party-and-the-democratic-unionist-party-on-support-for-the-government-in-parliament [Accessed 2 March 2022]

GOV.UK (2017b) 'Strategic Defence and Security Review implementation', Cabinet Office, [online] 20 July, Available from: https://www.gov.uk/government/news/strategic-defence-and-security-review-implementation [Accessed 6 April 2021].

GOV.UK (2018a) 'PM speech at Munich Security Conference: 17 February 2018', Prime Minister's Office, 10 Downing Street, [online] 17 February, Available from: https://www.gov.uk/government/speeches/pm-speech-at-munich-security-conference-17-february-2018 [Accessed 6 April 2021].

GOV.UK (2018b) 'Global Britain: delivering on our international ambition', Foreign & Commonwealth Office, [online] 13 June, Available from: https://www.gov.uk/government/collections/global-britain-delivering-on-our-international-ambition [Accessed 6 April 2021].

GOV.UK (2019a) 'Ministry of Defence Research Ethics Committee', MoD, [online] Available from: https://www.gov.uk/government/groups/ministry-of-defence-research-ethics-committees [Accessed 2 April 2021].

GOV.UK (2019b) 'Global Britain is leading the world as a force for good: article by Dominic Raab', Foreign & Commonwealth Office, [online] 23 September Available from: https://www.gov.uk/government/speeches/global-britain-is-leading-the-world-as-a-force-for-good-article-by-dominic-raab [Accessed 11 November 2021].

GOV.UK (2020a) 'Chief of the Defence Staff, General Sir Nick Carter launches the Integrated Operating Concept, MoD, [online] 30 September, Available from: https://www.gov.uk/government/speeches/chief-of-the-defence-staff-general-sir-nick-carter-launches-the-integrated-operating-concept [Accessed 1 October 2020].

GOV.UK (2020b) 'Integrated Review: call for evidence', Cabinet Office, [online] 13 August, Available from: https://www.gov.uk/government/publications/integrated-review-call-for-evidence [Accessed 30 April 2021].

GOV.UK (2020c) 'PM outlines new review to define britain's place in the world', Prime Minister's Office, 10 Downing Street, [online] 26 February, Available from: https://www.gov.uk/government/news/pm-outlines-new-review-to-define-britains-place-in-the-world [Accessed 6 April 2021].

GOV.UK (2020d) 'PM speech in Greenwich: 3 February 2020', Prime Minister's Office, 10 Downing Street, [online] 3 February, Available from: https://www.gov.uk/government/speeches/pm-speech-in-greenwich-3-february-2020 [Accessed 11 December 2021].

GOV.UK (2020e) 'UK armed forces equipment and formations 2020', MoD, [online] 10 September, Available from: https://www.gov.uk/government/statistics/uk-armed-forces-equipment-and-formations-2020 [Accessed 15 April 2021].

GOV.UK (2021a) 'Carrier Strike Group sets sail for first operational deployment', MoD, [online] 20 May, Available from: https://www.gov.uk/government/news/carrier-strike-group-sets-sail-for-first-operational-deployment [Accessed 7 November 2021].

GOV.UK (2021b) 'Chief of the General Staff RUSI Land Warfare Conference 2021', MoD, [online] 2 June, Available from: https://www.gov.uk/government/speeches/chief-of-the-general-staff-rusi-land-warfare-conference-2021, [Accessed 20 November 2021].

GOV.UK (2021c) Commander of Strategic Command RUSI Conference Speech', MoD, [online] 26 May, Available from: https://www.gov.uk/government/speeches/commander-of-strategic-command-rusi-conference-speech [Accessed 20 November 2021].

GOV.UK (2021d) Ministry of Defence Outcome Delivery Plan 2021 to 2022', MoD, [online] 15 July, Available from: https://www.gov.uk/government/publications/ministry-of-defence-outcome-delivery-plan/ministry-of-defence-outcome-delivery-plan-2021-to-2022 [Accessed 21 November 2021].

Gray, B. (2009) *Review of Acquisition for the Secretary of State for Defence: An Independent Report by Bernard Gray,* London: The Stationery Office.

Gray, C. S. (2008) 'Britain's national security: compulsion and discretion', *The RUSI Journal,* 153(6): 12–18.

Gray, C. S. (2010) 'Strategic thoughts for defence planners', *Survival,* 52(3): 159–78.

Gray, C. S. (2013) *Perspectives on Strategy,* Oxford: Oxford University Press.

Gray, C. S. (2014) *Strategy and Defence Planning: Meeting the Challenge of Uncertainty,* Oxford: Oxford University Press.

Greenwood, D. (1968) 'Economic constraints and the defence effort', *The RUSI Journal,* 113(652): 328–30.

Greenwood, D. (1975) 'The 1974 Defence Review in perspective', *Survival*, 17(5): 223–9.

Greenwood, D. (1976) 'Constraints and choices in the transformation of Britain's defence effort since 1945', *British Journal of International Studies*, 2(1): 5–26.

Greenwood, D. (1991) 'Expenditure and management', in P. Byrd (ed) *British Defence Policy: Thatcher and Beyond,* Hemel Hempstead: Philip Allan.

Guest Contributor (2019) 'The MDP Report – progress, but important questions remain', *UK Defence Journal*, [online] 7 January, Available from: https://ukdefencejournal.org.uk/the-mdp-report-progress-but-important-questions-remain/ [Accessed 3 November 2021].

Hampshire, E. (2015) 'NSS/SDSR 2015: the 2015 SDSR in context: a very unusual defence review?', Defence Studies Department, King's College London, [online] 24 November, Available from: https://defenceindepth.co/2015/11/24/nsssdsr-2015-the-2015-sdsr-in-context-a-very-unusual-defence-review/ [Accessed 3 November 2021].

Hansard (1955) 'Defence', [HC] volume 537, columns 1893–2012, [online] Available from: http://hansard.millbanksystems.com/commons/1955/mar/01/defence.

Hansard (1981) 'Defence estimates 1980–81', [HC] volume 997, column 153, [online] Available from: https://hansard.parliament.uk/Commons/1981-01-20/debates/6825ac74-68ef-40a8-9059-233032ccc3da/DefenceEstimates1980%E2%80%9381?highlight=defence%20planning#contribution-9a944bdc-2611-4f20-9c61-2d2f3f97f02f.

Hansard (1990) 'Defence (Options for Change)', [HC] volume 177, column 468, [online] Available from: https://hansard.parliament.uk/commons/1990-07-25/debates/95a0b854-43f0-4535-b675-942c0607fff6d/Defence(OptionsForChange)

Hansard (2010) 'Strategic Defence and Security Review', [HC] volume 516, columns 797–825, [online] Available from: https://hansard.parliament.uk/commons/2010-10-19/debates/10101928000003/StrategicDefenceAndSecurityReview.

Hansard (2011a) 'Defence reform', [HC] volume 350, column 634, [online] Available from: https://hansard.parliament.uk/Commons/2011-06-27/debates/1106279000003/DefenceReform?highlight=defence%20reform#contribution-1106279000316.

Hansard (2011b) 'Levene Review', [HC] volume 533, column 4, [online] Available from: https://hansard.parliament.uk/Commons/2011-10-10/debates/11101016000012/LeveneReview?highlight=defence%20reform#contribution-11101016000038.

Hansard (2014) 'Defence equipment and support', [HC] volume 850, column 146, [online] Available from: https://hansard.parliament.uk/Commons/2014-05-14/debates/14051447000007/DefenceEquipmentAndSupport?highlight=defence%20equipment%20support#contribution-14051447000022.

Hansard (2015a) 'Queen's Speech', [HL] volume 762, column 7, [online] Available from: https://hansard.parliament.uk/Lords/2015-05-27/debates/15052714000178/Queen%E2%80%99SSpeech.

Hansard (2015b) 'Financial Statement', [HC] volume 598, columns 321–334, [online] Available from: https://hansard.parliament.uk/Commons/2015-07-08/debates/15070837000001/FinancialStatement?highlight=budget#contribution-15070837000184.

Hansard (2018a) 'Modernising defence programme', [HC] volume 635, columns 424–425, [online] Available from: https://hansard.parliament.uk/commons/2018-01-25/debates/002ED98B-7B42-424B-8213-7EC5650664BC/ModernisingDefenceProgramme.

Hansard (2018b) 'Modernising defence programme', [HC] volume 651, columns 657–659, [online] Available from: https://hansard.parliament.uk/commons/2018-12-18/debates/6A3A04AB-1427-465A-9C69-573B84CF78CC/ModernisingDefenceProgramme.

Hansard (2018c) 'Modernising defence programme', [HC] volume 651, column 663, [online] Available from: https://hansard.parliament.uk/commons/2018-12-18/debates/6A3A04AB-1427-465A-9C69-573B84CF78CC/ModernisingDefenceProgramme#contribution-368F0544-9F5B-48C9-8CD1-EA27ED29E3AE.

Hansard (2019) 'Queen's Speech', [HL] volume 801, columns 8–9, [online] Available from: https://hansard.parliament.uk/Lords/2019-12-19/debates/C9EB1C3B-3551-473B-8C30-864B8B020409/Queen%E2%80%99SSpeech.

Hansard (2020a) 'Britain in the world', [HC] volume 669, columns 767–773, [online] Available from: https://hansard.parliament.uk/Commons/2020-01-13/debates/3C015023-C583-4D04-91DC-77AFC1994182/BritainInTheWorld.

Hansard (2020b) 'Integrated Review', [HC] volume 684, column 487, [online] Available from: https://hansard.parliament.uk/commons/2020-11-19/debates/CA347B2B-EE02-40DF-B5CE-1E8FAA07139E/IntegratedReview.

Hansard (2020c) 'Spending Review 2020 and OBR Forecast', [HC] volume 684, columns 827–832, [online] Available from: https://hansard.parliament.uk/Commons/2020-11-25/debates/6437F778-628F-48A1-ADF3-C06BA1C09EBA/SpendingReview2020AndOBRForecast.

Harrois, T. (2015) 'Little Britain? The debate on Britain's foreign and defence policy', *French Journal of British Studies*, 20(3): 1–14.

Hartley, K. (2010) 'The economics of the Defence Review', *The RUSI Journal*, 155(6): 4–8.

Hartley, K. (2011) *The Economics of Defence Policy: A New Perspective*, Abingdon: Routledge.

Hartley, K. (2016) 'UK defence inflation and cost escalation', *Defence and Peace Economics*, 27(2): 184–207.

HC Committee of Public Accounts (2017) *The Defence Equipment Plan: Fifty-sixth Report of Session 2016–17, HC 957,* London: The Stationery Office

HC Public Administration and Constitutional Affairs Committee (2017) *Lessons Still to Be Learned from the Chilcot Inquiry: Tenth Report of Session 2016–17, HC 656,* London: The Stationery Office.

HC Public Administration Committee (2010) *Who Does UK National Strategy? First Report of Session 2010–11, HC 435,* London: The Stationery Office.

HCDC (1998a) 'The Strategic Defence Review: Eighth Report of Session 1997–98, HC 138-I', parliament.uk, [online], 10 September, Available from: https://publications.parliament.uk/pa/cm199798/cmselect/cmdfence/138/13805.htm#a10 [Accessed 19 November 2021].

HCDC (1998b) 'Strategy and force structure', parliament.uk, [online] 10 September, Available from: https://publications.parliament.uk/pa/cm199798/cmselect/cmdfence/138/13815.htm [Accessed 8 December 2021].

HCDC (2001) 'The MOD's annual reporting cycle 2000-01', parliament.uk, [online], 24 July, Available from: https://publications.parliament.uk/pa/cm200102/cmselect/cmdfence/214/21404.htm [Accessed 6 April 2021].

HCDC (2006) *Delivering Front Line Capability to the RAF, HC 557,* London: The Stationery Office.

HCDC (2011a) *The Strategic Defence and Security Review and the National Security Strategy: Sixth Report of Session 2010–12, HC 761,* London: The Stationery Office.

HCDC (2011b) *The Strategic Defence and Security Review and the National Security Strategy: Government Response to the Committee's Sixth Report of Session 2010–12, HC 1639,* London: The Stationery Office.

HCDC (2012) 'Future maritime surveillance and regeneration', parliament.uk, [online], 19 September, Available from: https://publications.parliament.uk/pa/cm201213/cmselect/cmdfence/110/11007.htm [Accessed 10 January 2018].

HCDC (2014) *Towards the Next Defence and Security Review: Part One: Seventh Report of Session 2013–14 Volume I, HC 197,* London: The Stationery Office.

HCDC (2015a) *Decision-Making in Defence Policy: Eleventh Report of Session 2014–15, HC 682,* London: The Stationery Office.

HCDC (2015b) *Oral Evidence, Strategic Defence and Security Review, HC 626,* London: The Stationery Office.

HCDC (2015c) *Towards the Next Strategic Defence and Security Review: Part 3: Twelfth Report of Session 2014–15, HC 1127,* London: The Stationery Office.

HCDC (2017) *SDSR 2015 and the Army: Eighth Report of Session 2016–17, HC 108,* London: House of Commons Library.

HCDC (2018a) *Beyond 2 per cent – a Preliminary Report on the Modernising Defence Programme: Seventh Report of Session 2017–19, HC 818,* London: The Stationery Office.

HCDC (2018b) *Sunset for the Royal Marines? The Royal Marines and UK Amphibious Capability: Third Report of Session 2017–19 HC 622,* London: The Stationery Office.

HCDC (2020a) *In Search of Strategy – The 2020 Integrated Review, HC 165,* London: The Stationery Office.

HCDC (2020b) *Oral Evidence: Work of the Chief of Defence Staff, HC 594,* London: The Stationery Office.

HCDC (2021) *Oral Evidence: Work of the Chief of Defence Staff, HC 842,* London: The Stationery Office.

Head, B. W. (2008) 'Wicked problems in public policy', *Public Policy,* 3(2): 101–18.

Healey, D. (1989) *The Time of My Life: My Autobiography,* London: Penguin.

Healey, D. and Cross, K. (1969) 'British defence policy', *The RUSI Journal,* 114(656): 15–22.

Helco, H. and Wildavsky, A. B. (1974) *The Private Government of Public Money: Community and Policy inside British Politics,* London: Macmillan.

Hennessy, P. (2010) *The Secret State: Preparing for the Worst, 1945–2010,* London: Penguin Books.

HM Government (1946) *Central Organisation for Defence, Cmd 6923,* London: His Majesty's Stationery Office.

HM Government (1958) *Central Organisation for Defence, Cmnd 476,* London: Her Majesty's Stationery Office.

HM Government (2008a) *The National Security Strategy of the United Kingdom – Security in an Interdependent World, Cm 7291,* London: The Stationery Office.

HM Government (2008b) *National Risk Register 2008,* London: COI Communications on behalf of the Controller of The Stationery Office.

HM Government (2009) *The National Security Strategy of the United Kingdom: Update 2009 – Security for the Next Generation, Cm 7590,* London: The Stationery Office.

HM Government (2010a) *The Strategic Defence and Security Review 2010 – Securing Britain in an Age of Uncertainty, Cm 7948,* London: The Stationery Office.

HM Government (2010b) *National Risk Register of Civil Emergencies,* London: The Stationery Office.

HM Government (2010c) *The National Security Strategy 2010 – A Strong Britain in an Age of Uncertainty, Cm 7953,* London: The Stationery Office.

HM Government (2010d) *The Coalition: Our Programme for Government,* London: The Stationery Office.

HM Government (2015) *National Security Strategy and Strategic Defence and Security Review 2015 – A Secure and Prosperous United Kingdom, Cm 9161,* London: The Stationery Office.

HM Government (2016) *National Security Strategy and Strategic Defence and Security Review 2015: First Annual Report 2016,* London: The Stationery Office.

HM Government (2018) *National Security Capability Review,* London: The Stationery Office.

HM Government (2021a) *Conflict, Stability and Security Fund: Annual Report 2019/20,* London: The Stationery Office.

HM Government (2021b) *Global Britain in a Competitive Age: The Integrated Review of Security, Defence, Development and Foreign Policy, CP 403,* London: The Stationery Office.

HM Government (2021c) *National Space Strategy,* London: The Stationery Office.

HM Treasury (2020a) *Consolidated Budgeting Guidance: 2020–21, PU2956,* London: The Stationery Office.

HM Treasury (2020b) *Spending Review 2020, Cm 330,* London: The Stationery Office.

Hobkirk, M. (1987) 'Reform across the Sea: a comparison of defence policy making in the UK and the USA', *The RUSI Journal,* 132(3): 55–60.

Hopkinson, W. (2000) *The Making of British Defence Policy,* London: The Stationery Office.

Houghton, N., Brazier, J. and Lamb, G. (2011) *Future Reserves 2020: The Independent Commission to Review the United Kingdom's Reserve Forces,* London: The Stationery Office.

ICBH (1988) *The Move to the Sandys White Paper of 1957,* London: ICBH.

ICBH (2001) *The Nott Review Seminar,* London: ICBH.

Institute of Directors (2018) 'Factsheets: what is the role of the board?', Institute of Directors, [online] 21 November, Available from: https://www.iod.com/services/information-and-advice/resources-and-factsheets/details/What-is-the-role-of-the-board [Accessed 10 October 2019].

Institute of Risk Management (2010) *A Structured Approach to Enterprise Risk Management (ERM) and the Requirements of ISO 31000,* London: Institute of Risk Management.

International Churchill Society (2017) 'The Sinews of Peace ("Iron Curtain Speech")', International Churchill Society, [online] Available from: https://winstonchurchill.org/resources/speeches/1946-1963-elder-statesman/the-sinews-of-peace/ [Accessed 6 April 2021].

International Organisation for Standardisation (2018) *ISO 31000:2018 – Risk Management Guidelines*, Geneva: International Organisation for Standardisation.

Jackson, W. G. F. (1990) *Britain's Defence Dilemma: An Inside View: Rethinking British Defence Policy in the Post-Imperial Era*, London: B.T. Batsford Ltd.

Jackson, W. G. F. and Bramall, E. (1992) *The Chiefs: The Story of the United Kingdom Chiefs of Staff*, London: Brassey's.

James, W. (2020) 'Grandiose strategy? Refining the study and practice of grand strategy', *The RUSI Journal*, 165(3) 74–83.

Jamieson, A. (2015) 'British election: David Cameron wins surprise victory for Conservatives', NBC News, [online] 8 May, Available from: https://www.nbcnews.com/news/world/british-election-conservatives-look-be-winners-surprise-election-n355786 [Accessed 29 April 2021].

JCNSS (2012a) *First Review of the National Security Strategy 2010: First Report of Session 2010–12, HL Paper 265, HC 1384*, London: The Stationery Office.

JCNSS (2012b) *First Review of the National Security Strategy 2010: First Report of Session 2010–12, HL Paper 265, HC 1384*, London: The Stationery Office.

JCNSS (2015) *The Next National Security Strategy: First Report of Session 2014–15, HL Paper 114, HC 749*, London: The Stationery Office.

JCNSS (2016a) *National Security Strategy and Strategic Defence and Security Review 2015: First Report of Session 2016–17, HL Paper 18, HC 153*, London: The Stationery Office.

JCNSS (2016b) *Oral Evidence, Work of the National Security Adviser, HC 644*, London: The Stationery Office.

JCNSS (2018) *National Security Capability Review – A Changing Security Environment: First Report of Session 2017–19, HL Paper 104, HC 756*, London: The Stationery Office.

Jenkin, B. and Grank, G. (2010) *The Tipping Point: British National Strategy and the UK's Future World Role*, London: Henry Jackson Society.

Jessett, W., McKane, T. and Watkins, P. (2020) *Five Tests for the Integrated Review*, London: RUSI.

Jessett, W. (2021) 'The UK's Integrated Review: how does it stack up?', RUSI Commentary, [online] 24 March, Available from: https://rusi.org/explore-our-research/publications/commentary/uks-integrated-review-how-does-it-stack [Accessed 30 April 2021].

Johnson, B. (2016) *Global Britain: UK Foreign Policy in the Era of Brexit*, London: The Royal Institute of International Affairs.

Kampfner, J. (2003) *Blair's Wars*, London: Free Press.

Kay, J. A. (2010) *Obliquity: Why Our Goals Are Best Achieved Indirectly*, London: Profile Books.

Kellner, P. (2021) 'The hollowness of global Britain', Carnegie Europe, [online] 31 August, Available from: https://carnegieeurope.eu/strategic europe/85237 [Accessed 11 November 2021].

Kennedy, P. M. (1988) *The Rise and Fall of the Great Powers: Economic Change and Military Conflict from 1500 to 2000,* London: Unwin Hyman.

Keohane, D. (1993) *Labour Party Defence Policy since 1945*, Leicester: Leicester University Press.

Keohane, D. (2016) *Is Britain Back? The 2015 UK Defense Review,* Zurich: Center for Security Studies.

Kincaid, B. (1999) *Dancing with the Dinosaur: How to Do Business with MoD in the Smart Procurement World,* Newcastle-upon-Tyne: UK Defence Forum.

King, A. (2019) *Command: The Twenty-First-Century General,* Cambridge: Cambridge University Press.

Kirkpatrick, D. (2003) *A UK Perspective on Defence Equipment Acquisition,* Singapore: Institute of Defence and Strategic Studies.

Kirkpatrick, D. (2010) *Making Ends Meet: Challenges for the 2010 Strategic Defence and Security Review for the United Kingdom,* London: Centre Forum.

Kiszely, J. (2019) 'The political-military dynamic in the conduct of strategy', *Journal of Strategic Studies*, 42(2): 235–58.

Knighton, R. (2009) *How Are Strategic Decisions Affected by the Psychological and Cognitive Biases, and How Can These Effects Be Avoided?* London: Royal College of Defence Studies.

The Labour Party (1974) *Let's Work Together – Labour's Way Out of the Crisis: The Labour Party Manifesto for the Februry 1974 General Election,* London: The Labour Party.

The Labour Party (1997) *New Labour because Britain Deserves Better – The Labour Party 1997 General Election Manifesto,* London: The Labour Party.

The Labour Party (2010) *A Future Fair for All – The Labour Party Manifesto 2010,* London: The Labour Party.

The Labour Party (2017) *For the Many, Not the Few – The Labour Party Manifesto 2017*, Cramlington: The Labour Party.

The Labour Party (2019) *It's Time for Real Change – The Labour Party Manifesto 2019,* London: The Labour Party.

Lang, A. (2016) *Brexit and the UN Security Council, House of Commons Library Briefing Paper Number 7597,* London: The Stationery Office.

Layton, P. (2012) 'The idea of grand strategy', *The RUSI Journal*, 157(4): 56–61.

Layton, P. (2015) 'The 2015 National Security Strategy and Strategic Defence and Security Review choices: grand strategy, risk management or opportunism?' *Defence Studies*, 15(1): 28–45.

Levene, P. (2015) *Defence Reform – Fourth Annual Report,* London: MoD.

The Liberal Democrat Party (2010) *Change That Works for You: Liberal Democrat General Election Manifesto 2010,* London: The Liberal Democrat Party.

The Liberal Democrat Party (2019) *Stop Brexit – Build a Brighter Future – Liberal Democrat Manifesto 2019,* London: The Liberal Democrat Party.

Lider, J. (1985) *British Military Thought after World War II*, Aldershot: Gower Publishing Company.

Louth, J. (2016) 'SDSR 2015: doubts about affordability and dependency', *RUSI Newsbrief*, 36(1): 1–2.

Louth, J. and Taylor, T. (2019) *British Defence in the 21st Century*, London: Routledge.

Lunn, J. and Scarnell, E. (2015) *The 2015 UK National Security Strategy, House of Commons Library Briefing Paper Number 7431*, London: The Stationery Office.

Luttwak, E. (2009) *The Grand Strategy of the Byzantine Empire*, Cambridge, MA: Belknap Press.

Maddox, D. (2019) 'Boris reveals defence review with "big expansion" plan for Britain's warship building', *Sunday Express*, 1 December.

Makin-Isherwood, L. (2018) 'Defence Secretary criticised over "underwhelming" military funding update', The Forces Network, [online] 18 December, Available from: https://www.forces.net/news/modernising-defence-programme-findings-expected-today [Accessed 3 November 2021].

Markowski, S. and Hall, P. (1998) 'Challenges of defence procurement', *Defence and Peace Economics*, 9(1–2): 3–37.

Mason, R. (1975) 'Britain's security interests', *Survival*, 17(5): 217–23.

Mason, R. (1999) *Paying the Price*, London: Robert Hale.

Mason, R. A. (1982) *The Royal Air Force: Today and Tomorrow*, London: Ian Allan.

McConville, T. and Holmes, R. (eds) (2003) *Defence Management in Uncertain Times*, London: F. Cass.

McCourt, D. M. (2014) 'Has Britain found its role?', *Survival*, 56(2): 159–78.

McDowell, L. (1988) 'Elites in the City of London: some methodological considerations', *Environment and Planning A*, 30(12): 2133–46.

McGuire, S. (2021) 'Boris Johnson likes to tout "Global Britain". But he may be its biggest enemy', *The Washington Post*, [online] 25 October, Available from: https://www.washingtonpost.com/opinions/2021/10/25/boris-johnson-likes-tout-global-britain-he-may-be-its-biggest-enemy/ [Accessed 11 November 2021].

McInnes, C. (1998) 'Labour's Strategic Defence Review', *International Affairs*, 74(4): 823–45.

McIntosh, M. (1990) *Managing Britain's Defence*, Basingstoke: Macmillan.

Menon, A. (2015) 'Little England: the United Kingdom's retreat from global leadership', Foreign Affairs, 94(6): 93–100.

Milevski, L. (2016) *The Evolution of Modern Grand Strategic Thought*, Oxford: Oxford University Press.

Mills, C., Brooke-Holland, L. and Walker, N. (2020) *A Brief Guide to Previous British Defence Reviews, House of Commons Library Briefing Paper Number 07313*, London: The Stationery Office.

Mills, C. and Dempsey, N. (2019) *The Cost of the UK's Strategic Nuclear Deterrent, House of Commons Library Briefing Paper Number 8166*, London: The Stationery Office.

Mills, J., Bonner, A. and Francis, K. (2006) 'Adopting a constructivist approach to grounded theory: implications for research design', *International Journal of Nursing Practice*, 12(1): 8–13.

Ministry of Technology (1969) *Report of the Steering Group on Development Cost Estimating: Volume 1 – Report*, London: Her Majesty's Stationery Office.

MoD (1949) *Statement on Defence 1949, Cmd 7631*, London: His Majesty's Stationery Office.

MoD (1957) *Defence – Outline of Future Policy, Cmnd 124*, London: Her Majesty's Stationery Office.

MoD (1958) *Report on Defence Britain's Contribution to Peace and Security, Cmnd 363*, London: Her Majesty's Stationery Office.

MoD (1959) *Progress of the Five-Year Defence Plan, Cmnd 662*, London: Her Majesty's Stationery Office.

MoD (1963) *Central Organisation for Defence, Cmnd 2097*, London: Her Majesty's Stationery Office.

MoD (1966) *Statement on the Defence Estimates 1966. Part 1. The Defence Review, Cmnd 2901*, London: Her Majesty's Stationery Office.

MoD (1967) *Supplementary Statement on Defence Policy 1967, Cmnd 3357*, London: Her Majesty's Stationery Office.

MoD (1968) *Supplementary Statement on Defence Policy 1968, Cmnd 3701*, London: Her Majesty's Stationery Office.

MoD (1975) *Statement on the Defence Estimates 1975, Cmmd 5976*, London: Her Majesty's Stationery Office.

MoD (1981) *The United Kingdon Defence Programme: The Way Forward, Cmnd 8288*, London: Her Majesty's Stationery Office.

MoD (1984) *The Central Organisation for Defence, Cmnd 9315*, London: Her Majesty's Stationery Office.

MoD (1991) *Statement on the Defence Estimates 1991– Britain's Defence for the 90s, Cm 1559*, London: Her Majesty's Stationery Office.

MoD (1992) *Statement on the Defence Estimates 1992, Cm 1981*, London: Her Majesty's Stationery Office.

MoD (1994) *Front Line First: The Defence Costs Study*, London: Her Majesty's Stationery Office.

MoD (1996) *Statement on the Defence Estimates 1996, Cm 3223*, London: The Stationery Office.

MoD (1998a) *The Strategic Defence Review 1998, Cm 3999*, London: The Stationery Office.

MoD (1998b) *Supporting Essay Six-- Future Military Capabilities, The Strategic Defence Review 1998*, London: The Stationery Office.

MoD (1999) *The Defence White Paper 1999, Cm 4446*, London: The Stationery Office.

MoD (2002) *The Aquisition Handbook – Edition 4*, Bristol: DPA.

MoD (2003) *Delivering Security in a Changing World – Supporting Essays, Cm 6041-II*, London: The Stationery Office.

MoD (2004) *Delivering Security in a Changing World – Future Capabilities, Cm 6269*, London: The Stationery Office.

MoD (2005a) *Defence Industrial Strategy, Cm 6697*, London: The Stationery Office.

MoD (2005b) *Defence Lines of Development, 2005DIN03-012*, Shrivenham: JCDC.

MoD (2006a) *Defence Technology Strategy for the Demands of the 21st Century*, London: DGMC PR Graphics.

MoD (2006b) *Enabling Acquisition Change: An Examination of the Ministry of Defence's Ability to Undertake Through Life Capability Management*, London: MoD.

MoD (2007) *Capability Management Handbook (Interim Edition)*, Shrivenham: Defence Adademy of the United Kingdom.

MoD (2008a) *Defence Plan 2008–2012, Cm 7385*, London: The Stationery Office.

MoD (2008b) *Ministry of Defence Annual Report and Accounts 2007–2008, Volume I: Annual Performance Report, HC 850-I*, London: The Stationery Office.

MoD (2010a) *Adaptability and Partnership: Issues for the Strategic Defence Review, Cm 7794*, London: The Stationery Office.

MoD (2010b) *Defence Support Review Phase 1 Report (Refresh)*, London: Deloitte MCS Limited.

MoD (2010c) *Strategic Trends Programme – Global Strategic Trends – Out to 2040, 4th Edition*, Shrivenham: DCDC.

MoD (2011a) *Defence Reform: An Independent Report into the Structure and Management of the Ministry of Defence*, London: The Stationery Office.

MoD (2011b) *Intergenerational Equipment Cost Escalation. Economic Working Paper Series 1*, Bristol: DASA-DESA.

MoD (2011c) *The Strategy for Defence*, London: DMC Secretariat Graphics.

MoD (2012a) *Ministry of Defence Annual Report and Accounts 2011–12, HC 62*, London: The Stationery Office.

MoD (2012b) *National Security Through Technology: Technology, Equipment, and Support for UK Defence and Security, Cm 8278*, London: The Stationery Office.

MoD (2012c) *The New Operating Model: How Defence Works, Version 3.0*, London: Defence Design Authority.

MoD (2013a) *Better Defence Acquisition – Improving How We Procure and Support Defence Equipment, Cm 8626,* London: The Stationery Office.

MoD (2013b) *Allied Joint Publication-5, Joint Doctrine Publication 5-00 – Allied Joint Doctrine for Operational-level Planning,* Shrivenham: DCDC.

MoD (2014a) *Joint Doctrine Publication 0-01 (Fifth Edition) – UK Defence Doctrine,* Shrivenham: DCDC.

MoD (2014b) *Joint Doctrine Publication 01 – UK Joint Operations Doctrine,* Shrivenham: DCDC.

MoD (2014c) *Strategic Trends Programme Global Strategic Trends – Out to 2045, 5th Edition,* Shrivenham: DCDC.

MoD (2015a) *Finance and Military Capability Operating Model,* London: MoD.

MoD (2015b) *How Defence Works, Version 4.2,* London: Defence Design Authority.

MoD (2015c) *Strategic Defence and Security Review 2015: Defence Key Facts,* London: MoD DCC Graphics.

MoD (2016) *The Defence Equipment Plan 2016,* London: The Stationery Office.

MoD (2017a) *Acquisition System Operating Model,* London: MoD.

MoD (2017b) *The Defence Equipment Plan 2017,* London: The Stationery Office.

MoD (2017c) *The Good Operation: A Handbook for Those Involved in Operational Policy and Its Implementation,* London: The Stationery Office.

MoD (2017d) *Industry for Defence and a Prosperous Britain: Refreshing Defence Industrial Policy,* London: The Stationery Office.

MoD (2017e) *Joint Service Publication 892: Risk Management,* London: MoD.

MoD (2017f) *Ministry of Defence Annual Report and Accounts 2016–17, HC 21,* London: Williams Lea Group on behalf of the Controller of The Stationery Office.

MoD (2018a) *Acquisition System Handbook, Version 5.0,* London: MoD.

MoD (2018b) *Global Strategic Trends – The Future Starts Today, 6th Edition,* Shrivenham: DCDC.

MoD (2018c) *Ministry of Defence Annual Report and Accounts 2017–18, HC 1272,* London: APS Group on behalf of the Controller of The Stationery Office.

MoD (2018d) *Mobilising, Modernising and Transforming Defence – A Report on the Modernising Defence Programme,* London: The Stationery Office.

MoD (2019) *Ministry of Defence Annual Report and Accounts 2018–19, HC 2347,* London: APS Group on behalf of the Controller of The Stationery Office.

MoD (2020a) *The Defence Equipment Plan 2019,* London: The Stationery Office.

MoD (2020b) *How Defence Works, Version 6.0,* London: The Stationery Office.

MoD (2020c) *Introducing the Integrated Operating Concept,* London: MoD.

MoD (2020d) *Ministry of Defence Annual Report and Accounts 2019–20, HC 811*, London: APS Group on behalf of the Controller of The Stationery Office.

MoD (2021a) *Defence and Security Industrial Strategy – A Strategic Approach to the UK's Defence and Security Industrial Sectors, Cm 410*, London: The Stationery Office.

MoD (2021b) *Defence in a Competitive Age, CP 411,* London: The Stationery Office.

MoD (2021c) *Joint Doctrine Publication 0-01, UK Defence Doctrine (UKDD) 6th Edition – Draft,* Shrivenham: DCDC.

MoD and FCO (2017) *UK's International Defence Engagement Strategy,* London: MoD.

Molinelli, G. (2016) 'UK SDSR 2015: review and analysis', *Military Technology*, Special Issue, 82–88.

Moore, D. M. and Antill, P. D. (2001) 'Integrated project teams: the way forward for UK defence procurement', *European Journal of Purchasing & Supply Management*, 7(3): 179–85.

Morris, H. (2017) 'What's the point of scrambling a fighter jet – and would one ever shoot down a passenger plane?' *The Telegraph*, [online] 6 October, Available from: https://www.telegraph.co.uk/travel/travel-truths/scrambl ing-fighter-jets-shoot-down-planes/ [Accessed 17 November 2021].

Morris, J. (2011) 'How great is Britain? Power, responsibility and Britain's future global role', *The British Journal of Politics and International Relations,* 13(3): 326–47.

Mottram, R. (1991) 'Options for Change: process and prospect', *The RUSI Journal*, 136(1): 22–6.

NAO (2003) *Ministry of Defence Through Life Management, HC 698*, London: The Stationery Office.

NAO (2014) *The Major Projects Report 2013, HC 817-I,* London: The Stationery Office.

NAO (2015) *Reforming Defence Acquisition, HC 946*, London: The Stationery Office.

NAO (2017) *The Equipment Plan 2016 to 2026, HC 914*, London: The Stationery Office.

NAO (2018a) *The Equipment Plan 2017 to 2027, HC 717*, London: The Stationery Office.

NAO (2018b) *The Equipment Plan 2018 to 2028, HC 1621*, London: The Stationery Office.

NAO (2019) *Departmental Overview 2019: Ministry of Defence*, London: NAO.

NAO (2021) *The Equipment Plan 2020 to 2030, HC 1037*, London: The Stationery Office.

The National Archives (2003a) *Doctrine of the International Community,* The National Archives, [online] 29 January, Available from: http://web archive.nationalarchives.gov.uk/+/http://www.number10.gov.uk/ Page1297 [Accessed 6 April 2021].

The National Archives (2003b) 'The EEC and Britain's late entry', The National Archives, [online] Available from: https://www.nationalarchives. gov.uk/cabinetpapers/themes/eec-britains-late-entry.htm [Accessed 20 November 2021].

The National Archives (2017) 'The Iraq Inquiry', The National Archives, [online] 23 November, Available from: https://webarchive.nationalarchi ves.gov.uk/20171123123237/http://www.iraqinquiry.org.uk/ [Accessed 7 October 2019].

National Museum of the Royal Navy (2014) 'A brief history of the Royal Navy', [online] Available from: http://www.nmrn-portsmouth.org.uk/ sites/default/files/styles/homepage_collections_slidshows/public/modu les/image/A%20brief%20history%20of%20the%20RN.pdf [Accessed 31 March 2021].

NATO (2010) *AJP-01(D) – Allied Joint Doctrine*, Mons: NATO Standardisation Agency.

NATO (2014) 'Wales Summit Declaration', NATO, [online] 5 September, Available from: https://www.nato.int/cps/en/natohq/official_texts_112 964.htm [Accessed 12 April 2021].

Navias, M. S. (1989) 'The Sandys White Paper of 1957 and the move to the British new look: an analysis of nuclear weapons, conventional forces and strategic planning 1955–57', Doctorate of Philosophy, King's College London.

Newton, P., Colley, P. and Sharpe, A. (2010) 'Reclaiming the art of British strategic thinking', *The RUSI Journal*, 155(1): 44–50.

O'Hanlon, M. E. (2009) *The Science of War: Defense Budgeting, Military Technology, Logistics, and Combat Outcomes,* Princeton, NJ: Princeton University Press.

Ovendale, R. (1994) *British Defence Policy since 1945*, Manchester: Manchester University Press.

Owen, D. (1972) *The Politics of Defence*, New York, NY: Taplinger.

Page, L. (2007) *Lions, Donkeys and Dinosaurs: Waste and Blundering in the Military*, London: Random House.

Parker, G. and Pickard, J. (2015) 'A new mission: soldiers as MPs', *Financial Times*, [online], 31 July, Available from https://www.ft.com/content/ 353a6ace-356d-11e5-b05b-b01debd57852 [Accessed 4 September 2019].

Parker, G. and Warrell, H. (2020) 'Boris Johnson calls off meeting on Defence Review after policy split', *Financial Times*, 20 January.

Patrikarakos, D. (2017) *War in 140 Characters: How Social Media Is Reshaping Conflict in the Twenty-First Century*, New York, NY: Basic Books.

Peden, G. C. (2007) *Arms, Economics and British Strategy: From Dreadnoughts to Hydrogen Bombs*, Cambridge: Cambridge University Press.

Perkins, K. (1992) 'Smaller – but better? Military capabilities versus resources', *The RUSI Journal*, 137(6): 65–74.

Phillips, M. (2012) 'Policy-making in defence and security: lessons from the Strategic Defence and Security Review', *The RUSI Journal*, 157(1): 28–35.

Porter, P. (2010) 'Why Britain doesn't do grand strategy', *The RUSI Journal*, 155(4): 6–12.

Press Association (2017) 'Royal Navy could lose its two amphibious assault ships in cuts', *The Guardian*, [online] 5 October, Available from: https://www.theguardian.com/uk-news/2017/oct/05/royal-navy-could-lose-its-two-amphibious-assault-ships-in-cuts [Accessed 6 April 2021].

PwC LLP (2017) *Forces for Change 2017: The Public's View of Defence*, London: PwC LLP.

Quinlan, M. (1992) 'British defence planning in a changing world', *The World Today*, 48(8/9): 160–2.

RAF (2015a) *Air Finance and Military Capability Operating Model*, High Wycombe: HQ Air.

RAF (2015b) *Capability and Acquisition Development Programme – Graduation Report*, High Wycombe: HQ Air.

RAF (2019) 'Wedgetail to be RAF's new early warning radar aircraft', RAF, [online] 22 March, Available from: https://www.raf.mod.uk/news/articles/wedgetail-to-be-rafs-new-early-warning-radar-aircraft/ [Accessed 30 November 2021].

Rasmussen, M. V. (2006) *The Risk Society at War: Terror, Technology and Strategy in the Twenty-First Century*, Cambridge: Cambridge University Press.

Rees, W. (1989) 'The 1957 Sandys White Paper: new priorities in British defence policy?', *Journal of Strategic Studies*, 12(2): 215–29.

Reeve, R. (2015) *Cutting the Cloth: Ambition, Austerity and the Case for Rethinking UK Military Spending*, London: Oxford Research Group.

Richards, D. (2014) *Taking Command*, London: Headline Publishing Group.

Richards, J. (2012) *A Guide to National Security: Threats, Responses and Strategies*, Oxford: Oxford University Press.

Ricketts, P. (2021a) *Hard Choices: Britain and the New Geometry of Global Power*, London: Atlantic Books.

Ricketts, P. (2021b) 'The Integrated Review in context: the importance of hard choices', in J. Devanny and J Gearson (eds) *The Integrated Review in Context: A Strategy Fit for the 2020s?* London: King's College London.

Rittel, H. W. and Webber, M. M. (1973) 'Dilemmas in a general theory of planning', *Policy Sciences*, 4(2): 155–69.

RN (2015) *Navy Command Headquarters Capability Management Handbook*, Portsmouth: NCHQ.

RN (2019a) 'First Sea Lord', RN, [online] Available from: https://www.royalnavy.mod.uk/our-people/senior-naval-staff/first-sea-lord [Accessed 17 October 2019].

RN (2019b) 'Queen Elizabeth Class', RN, [online] Available from: https://www.royalnavy.mod.uk/the-equipment/ships/aircraft-carriers/queen-elizabeth-class [Accessed 7 November 2021].

Roberts, P. (2020) 'The UK's Integrated Review has restarted: are key questions and assumptions still valid?' RUSI Commentary, [online] 3 July, Available from: https://www.rusi.org/explore-our-research/publications/commentary/uks-integrated-review-has-restarted-are-key-questions-and-assumptions-still-valid [Accessed 30 April 2021].

Robertson, G. (1997) 'The Strategic Defence Review', *The RUSI Journal*, 142(5): 1–5.

RUSI (2017) 'Annual Chief of the Defence Staff Lecture 2017', RUSI, [online] 14 December, Available from: https://www.rusi.org/events/members-events/annual-chief-of-the-defence-staff-lecture-2017 [Accessed 6 April 2021].

RUSI (2018) 'Stephen Lovegrove on managing the UK Ministry of Defence', RUSI, [online] 5 March, Available from: https://www.rusi.org/events/members-events/stephen-lovegrove-on-managing-the-uk-ministry-of-defence-- [Accessed 6 April 2021].

Sabin, P. A. G. (1993) 'British defence choices beyond "Options for Change"', *International Affairs*, 69(2): 267–87.

Sapolsky, H. M., Gholz, E. and Talmadge, C. (2017) *US Defense Politics: The Origins of Security Policy*, New York, NY: Routledge.

Savill, M. (2011) 'UK security strategy: clarity or compromise?' *Defence Studies*, 11(3): 359–95.

Sawyer, J. S. (1972) 'Man-made carbon dioxide and the "greenhouse" effect', *Nature*, 239(5366): 23.

Sawyers, J. (2021) 'The Integrated Review: innovative thinking but still some blind spots', in J. Devanny and J. Gearson (eds) *The Integrated Review in Context: A Strategy Fit for the 2020s?* London: King's College London.

Self, R. C. (2010) *British Foreign and Defence Policy since 1945: Challenges and Dilemmas in a Changing World*, Basingstoke: Palgrave Macmillan.

Shapiro, J. and Witney, N. (2021) 'The delusions of global Britain: London will have to get used to life as a middle power', *Foreign Affairs*, [online] 23 March, Available from: https://www.foreignaffairs.com/articles/europe/2021-03-23/delusions-global-britain [Accessed 11 November 2021].

Shipman, T. and Tipley, T. (2020) 'Army "to be cut by 20,000" if No 10 plan is approved', *The Times*, 5 July.

SIPRI (2021) 'Military Expenditure Database', SIPRI, [online] Available from: https://www.sipri.org/databases/milex [Accessed 31 March 2021].

Slessor, J. (1957) 'British defence policy' *Foreign Affairs*, 35(4): 551–63.

Smith, K. (1998) 'What should smart procurement be?', *The RUSI Journal*, 143(2): 37–40.

Smith, P. (ed) (1996) *Government and the Armed Forces in Britain 1856–1990*, London: Hambledon Press.

Smith, R. (1990) 'Defence spending in the United Kingdom', in K, Hartley and T. Sandler (eds) *The Economics of Defence Spending*, London: Routledge.

Spellar, J. (1998) 'Smart procurement: an objective of the Strategic Defence Review', *The RUSI Journal*, 143(2): 33–6.

Stanton, J. (2015) 'Government slammed for "insulting" defence review allowing leading experts just a few hundred words to express their views', *Daily Mail*, 16 August.

Strachan, H. (2005) 'The lost meaning of strategy', *Survival*, 47(3) 33–54.

Strachan, H. (2006) 'Making strategy: civil–military relations after Iraq', *Survival*, 48(3): 59–82.

Strachan, H. (2008) 'Strategy as a balancing act: the UK's dilemma', *The RUSI Journal*, 153(3): 6–10.

Strachan, H. (2011) 'Strategy and contingency', *International Affairs*, 87(6): 1281–96.

Strachan, H. (2013a) 'British national strategy: who does it?', *Parameters*, 43(2): 43.

Strachan, H. (2013b) *The Direction of War: Contemporary Strategy in Historical Perspective*, Cambridge: Cambridge University Press.

Strachan, H., Armour, T., Healy, P. and Smith, M. (2010) *Report of the Task Force on the Military Covenant* London: MoD.

Strauss, A. L. (1987) *Qualitative Analysis for Social Scientists*, Cambridge: Cambridge University Press.

Strauss, A. L. and Corbin, J. M. (1990) *Basics of Qualitative Research: Grounded Theory Procedures and Techniques*, Newbury Park, CA: Sage Publications.

Street, T. (2016) *SDSR 2015: Continuity, Control and Crisis in UK Defence Policy*, London: Oxford Research Group.

Street, T. and Reeve, R. (2016) *Brexit: Whither UK Defence and Foreign Policy?* London: Oxford Research Group.

Sutherland, C. (2012) 'Operation deference: the multinational NEO evacuation coordination cell concept', *The RUSI Journal*, 157(3): 15–20.

Taleb, N. N. (2010) *The Black Swan: The Impact of the Highly Improbable*, New York, NY, Random House.

Taylor, C. (2003) *UK Defence Procurement Policy*, London: The Stationery Office.

Taylor, C. (2010a) *A Brief Guide to Previous British Defence Reviews*, London: The Stationery Office.

Taylor, C. (2011) *Defence Reform*, London: The Stationery Office.

Taylor, C., Lunn, J., Horne, A., Downing, E., Smith, L., Thompson, G., Gore, D., Gower, M. and Almandras, S. (2011) *UK Defence and Security Policy: A New Approach, House of Commons Library Research Paper 11/10,* London: The Stationery Office.

Taylor, T. (2010b) 'What's new? UK defence policy before and after the SDSR', *The RUSI Journal,* 155(6): 10–14.

Taylor, T. (2016a) 'Brexit and UK defence: put the equipment plan on hold?', RUSI, [online], 6 July, Available from: https://rusi.org/com mentary/brexit-and-uk-defence-put-equipment-plan-hold [Accessed 1 November 2021].

Taylor, T. (2016b) 'The Ministry of Defence's post-Brexit spending power: assumptions, numbers, calculations and implications', RUSI, [online] 12 August, Available from: https://rusi.org/explore-our-research/ publications/commentary/ministry-defences-post-brexit-spending-power-assumptions-numbers-calculations-and-implications [Accessed 3 November 2021].

Taylor, T. (2019) 'The significant parts of the modernising defence programme', RUSI, [online] 7 January, Available from: https://www. rusi.org/commentary/significant-parts-modernising-defence-programme [Accessed 3 November 2021].

Taylor, T. and Curtis, A. (2020) *Management of Defence after the Levene Reforms: What Comes Next?* London: RUSI.

The Telegraph (2010) 'General election 2010: education, employment and economy key poll issues', *The Telegraph,* [online] 16 March, Available from: https://www.telegraph.co.uk/news/election-2010/7449225/Gene ral-election-2010-education-employment-and-economy-key-poll-issues. html [Accessed 28 April 2021].

The Telegraph (2011) 'Obituary: Admiral of the Fleet Sir Henry Leach', [online]. London: Telegraph Media Group Limited. Available from: https://www. telegraph.co.uk/news/obituaries/military-obituaries/naval-obituaries/ 8474861/Admiral-of-the-Fleet-Sir-Henry-Leach.html [Accessed 10 October 2019].

Thomson, C. P. and Blagden, D. (2018) 'A very British national security state: formal and informal institutions in the design of uk security policy', *The British Journal of Politics and International Relations,* 20(3): 573–93.

The Times (2011) 'Obituary for Admiral of the Fleet Sir Henry Leach', *The Times,* [online] 26 April, Available from: https://www.thetimes.co.uk/ article/admiral-of-the-fleet-sir-henry-leach-59s0gntbmtk [Accessed 10 October 2019].

T.W. (2015) 'Britain's election surprise', *The Economist,* [online] 8 May, Available from: https://www.economist.com/the-economist-explains/ 2015/05/08/britains-election-surprise [Accessed 29 April 2021].

UK Parliament (2018) 'National Security Capability Review and Strategic Defence and Security Review Annual Report', UK Parliament, [online] 28 March, Available from: https://www.parliament.uk/business/publications/written-questions-answers-statements/written-statement/Commons/2018-03-28/HCWS604/ [Accessed 6 April 2021].

United Nations (1945) *Charter of the United Nations and Statute of the International Court of Justice*, San Francisco, CA: United Nations.

Urban, M. (2017) 'Royal Navy could lose "fight on beaches" ships in planned cuts', BBC News [online] 5 October, Available from: https://www.bbc.co.uk/news/uk-41511790 [Accessed 6 April 2021].

Uttley, M., Wilkinson, B. and Van Rij, A. (2019) 'A power for the future? Global Britain and the future character of conflict', *International Affairs*, 95(4): 801–16.

Walker, N. and Mills, C. (2015) *A Brief Guide to Previous British Defence Reviews, House of Commons Library Briefing Paper Number 07313*, London: The Stationery Office.

Ward, V. (2015) 'MoD forced to ask US for help in tracking "Russian submarine"', *Daily Telegraph*, 9 January.

Warrell, H. (2020) 'Britain's military still faces hard choices despite spending boost', *Financial Times*, 19 November.

Warrell, H. and Parker, G. (2019) 'Funding crisis rasies concerns on armed forces readiness', *Financial Times*, 18 December.

White, R. (2012) *Vulcan 607*, London: Random House.

Woodward, S. and Robinson, P. (1992) *One Hundred Days: The Memoirs of the Falklands Battle Group Commander*, Annapolis, MD: Naval Institute Press.

Wyatt, C. (2010) 'Struggle at the top over decision to scrap UK Harriers', BBC News, [online] 15 December, Available from: https://www.bbc.com/news/uk-11997084 [Accessed 2 December 2021].

Young, S. (2016) 'The United Kingdom's 2015 Strategic Defence and Security Review – Economic, Procurement and Brexit Implications', 11th Defence and Security Economics Workshop, Ottawa, Canada.

Younger, G. (1976) 'British defence policy – a critical analysis', *The RUSI Journal*, 121(1): 15–19.

Yue, Y. and Henshaw, M. (2009) 'An holistic view of UK military capability development', *Defense & Security Analysis*, 25(1): 53–67.

Index

Printed in the USA
CPSIA information can be obtained
at www.ICGtesting.com
JSHW012158070524
62711JS00004B/41